AF786398

EUL VERLAG

Macroeconomic news effects in commodity futures and German stock and bond futures markets

Price effects, liquidity effects, and cross-market information flow

Inauguraldissertation

zur

Erlangungung des Doktorgrades

der

Wirtschafts- und Sozialwissenschaftlichen Fakultät

der

Universität zu Köln

vorgelegt

von

Diplom-Kaufmann He Huang

aus

Wuhan

Erstgutachter: Prof. Dr. Dieter Hess

Zweitgutachter: Prof. Dr. Alexander Kempf

Tag der Promotion: 3. Juli 2009

Reihe: Finanzierung, Kapitalmarkt und Banken · Band 67

Herausgegeben von Prof. Dr. Hermann Locarek-Junge, Dresden, Prof. Dr. Klaus Röder, Regensburg, und Prof. Dr. Mark Wahrenburg, Frankfurt

Dr. He Huang

Macroeconomic news effects in commodity futures and German stock and bond futures markets

EUL VERLAG

Bibliografische Information der Deutschen Nationalbibliothek

Die Deutsche Nationalbibliothek verzeichnet diese Publikation in der Deutschen Nationalbibliografie; detaillierte bibliografische Daten sind im Internet über <http://dnb.d-nb.de> abrufbar.

Dissertation, Universität zu Köln, 2009

ISBN 978-3-89936-892-5
1. Auflage Februar 2010

JOSEF EUL VERLAG GmbH
Brandsberg 6
53797 Lohmar
Tel.: 0 22 05 / 90 10 6-6
Fax: 0 22 05 / 90 10 6-88
http://www.eul-verlag.de
info@eul-verlag.de

Bei der Herstellung unserer Bücher möchten wir die Umwelt schonen. Dieses Buch ist daher auf säurefreiem, 100% chlorfrei gebleichtem, alterungsbeständigem Papier nach DIN 6738 gedruckt.

For My Parents

Dr. Huang, Li

and

Fu, Haiyun

Contents

List of Tables

List of Figures

1 Introduction

In most countries, government agencies and research institutes regularly release information about the current and expected future state of the economy. These announcements include, for example, the employment report, consumer price index, or other macroeconomic figures. Most figures are released at a scheduled time. The employment report in the United States, for instance, is typically released on the first friday each month at 8:30 am. The effects of these macroeconomic announcements on security prices have been receiving considerable attention in the financial press for a long time. Financial commentators oftentimes relate large price movements in financial assets to news about economic fundamentals. The academic literature has been dealing with macroeconomic news effects on financial markets for little more than the past two decades. The main focus of research has been the macroeconomic announcement effects on the domestic stock and bond market in the United States. On the one hand, this is understandable, as US data is readily availably and US financial markets are the world's largest. On the other hand, this is surprising given the enormous importance of other financial markets. For example, the United State's stock market only make up a third of the world's total stock market capitalization.[1] Also, alternative asset classes other than stocks and bonds are becoming increasingly popular.

[1]Source: World Federation of Exchanges, Annual Report and Statistics 2007.

This doctoral dissertation investigates the effects of US macroeconomic news on three financial markets that have received less attention in the literature so far. The markets of interest are the commodity futures market, the German stock index futures market, and the German bond futures market. I investigate not only price effects, but also liquidity effects as well as the channels of cross-border information flow. My research is centered around three main research questions:

1. How do commodity futures indices respond to macroeconomic news?

2. What are the price and liquidity effects of domestic and foreign US economic news in the German stock index futures market?

3. What are the channels of information transmission from the US to German bond markets around the release of US economic news?

A well-known concept in modern capital market theory is that only systematic (i.e. non-diversifiable) risk factors are priced and only these factors yield a risk premium.[2] The importance of economic news for asset pricing stems from the fact that the state of the economy is one of the prime candidates for such source of non-diversifiable risk. In addition, the state of the economy directly affects marketwide variables such as interest rates, corporate earnings, and demand for commodities. These variables are relevant for pricing all sorts of asset classes. Moreover, in todays increasingly globalized world the state of the economy in one country certainly also affects the state of the economy in another country. Because of the importance of macroeconomic news for asset pricing, it is important to understand the effects that these announcements have on financial markets. In particular, this thesis offers three main contributions towards understanding macroeconomic news effects on the analyzed financial markets:

[2]For example, the APT by Ross (1976) and the models of Merton (1973) and Cox, Ingersoll, and Ross (1985) are consistent with this view.

First, I investigate the impact of seventeen US macroeconomic announcements on two of the most important commodity futures indices, the CRB and the GSCI. This is the first empirical investigation of how commodity futures indices respond to surprises in macroeconomic announcements. Commodities have gained increasing popularity in recent years as an alternative investment. For example, the world's largest commodity futures exchange NYMEX has more than quadrupled its trading volume in the past ten years from 84 million in 1997 to 354 million in 2007.[3] I contribute to the understanding of this important alternative asset class by studying how daily CRB and GSCI returns are related to surprises in macroeconomic news in the period 1989 to 2005. I find that the commodity futures price response is state-dependent. During recessions, news about higher (lower) inflation and real activity lead to positive (negative) adjustments of commodity futures prices. In contrast, I find no significant reactions during economic expansions. These findings are of value for commodity investors as they help to explain the price movement in the commodity futures market on days with macroeconomic news. In addition, my analysis gives further evidence that the effects of macroeconomic news might depend on the state of the economy. This was previously found only for the effect on stock prices.

The second main contribution of this dissertation is that it offers a comprehensive depiction of the price and liquidity effects of economic news. The analysis is conducted on German stock index futures data and includes a large number domestic German and foreign US macroeconomic announcements. I find that both domestic and foreign economic news affect the German stock index futures on multiple dimensions, including: prices, trading volume, volatility, quoted spreads, inventory holding costs and the informational role of trading. There seems to be a strong correlation between price and liquidity effects, as those announcement types that induce large price movements also affect liquidity. Con-

[3] See http://www.nymex.com/md_annual_volume2.aspx.

trary to some prior evidence, there is no qualitative difference in how domestic and foreign economic news is processed. However, the impact of US news on prices and liquidity in the German stock market is considerably larger than the impact of domestic German news. This result highlights the outstanding worldwide importance of the US economy. Moreover, my findings are valuable for investors in the German stock market to better adjust trading strategies around important events such as macroeconomic news releases.

The final main contribution is a study on the channels of cross-border information transmission around US economic news releases. The analysis is conducted on German bond futures data. I study not only the direct effects of US economic news on German bond prices but also how information is transmitted to Germany via the US price response to the news. This is done by relating price movements in German bond futures to surprises in US macro announcements as well as to lagged US bond futures returns. I find that both surprises in the announcement itself and the US price response contribute to the German price response to the announcements. I also find that following the announcement, US bond price movements impose an abnormally high influence on subsequent German bond returns, even after the public news is fully processed. My study adds to the understanding of cross-border information flow. I demonstrate that there are two channels for transmitting US news to German bond markets: the direct response in Germany to the US news and the indirect German response to the US response to the news. Moreover, my investigation reveals that the level of cross-border transmission of price movements is not always the same, but follows predictable patterns. When the global component in US price movements is presumably high after a macroeconomic announcement, German bond prices follow US bond prices more strongly than at other times.

In summary, my dissertation adds to the understanding of how macroeconomic news is processed on the commodity futures market and on the German stock and bond market.

The analysis is carried out on data superior to that used in most prior studies: the investigated sample is longer and/or the data frequency is higher than in comparable prior studies. Research has so far focused mostly on the US stock and bond market's response to macroeconomic news. I find that commodity markets as well as international stock and bond markets are likewise affected by the release of US macroeconomic news. For an investor in any of these markets, my dissertation provides valuable information on how to adjust his trading strategies around the release of macroeconomic news. Moreover, my findings contribute to the understanding of cross-border information flow. First, I find that both domestic and foreign economic news induce significant price and liquidity effects. Second, I find that there are two important channels of information transmission for foreign news: the direct response to the news and the indirect response to the foreign response to the news.

This dissertation is structuctured into three main chapters which follow this introduction. The thesis is concluded by a short conclusion. Each of the main chapters deals with one of the three main research questions:

The second chapter studies the price response of two commodity futures indices to the announcement of US macroeconomic news. Macroeconomic news is known to be an important driver of asset prices. Several studies have documented the impact of macroeconomic announcements on bond markets (see, e.g., Fleming and Remolona (1999), and Balduzzi, Elton, and Green (2001)), stock markets (see, e.g, McQueen and Roley (1993), and Boyd, Hu, and Jagannathan (2005)), and foreign exchange markets (see, e.g., Andersen, Bollerslev, Diebold, and Vega (2003)). In contrast to this large body of evidence, the literature on the reaction of commodity prices to macroeconomic announcements is scarce. Previous studies only investigate the impact of macroeconomic news on individual commodity futures types (see, e.g., Barnhart (1989), Christie-David, Chaudry, and Koch (2000), and

Cai, Cheung, and Wong (2001)). This is surprising because investors are increasingly looking for alternative investments such as commodities (see, e.g., Gorton and Rouwenhorst (2006), and Kat and Oomen (2007)). Our study is the first to investigate the price reaction of two broad commodity futures indices to several US macroeconomic announcements. Additionally, we allow for an asymmetric commodity price response depending on the state of the economy.

Although commodity futures are widely accepted as a distinct asset class, it is well known that the correlation between different types of commodity futures is very low, much lower than for example the correlation between different stock sectors (see Erb and Harvey (2006)). Therefore, existing results regarding the price impact of macroeconomic announcements on individual commodity types are of minor importance for most commodity investors who hold a diversified portfolio of commodity futures. Our investigation sheds light on this issue by investigating the price response of two broad commodity futures indices to seventeen US macroeconomic news releases. Commodity futures indices represent commodity portfolio strategies that are replicated by many investors. Since there is no universally accepted commodity futures index, we choose two very distinct indices in order to account for two representative commodity investment strategies. First, we consider the Reuters CRB Commodity Index which assigns equal weights to its index constituents. Second, we consider the S&P GSCI Commodity Index which is weighted by world production quantities.

Based on a large sample of daily observations over the period from 1989 to 2005, we find that the impact of macroeconomic news on commodity prices is dependent on the state of the economy. As long as the business cycle is not considered, we find only moderate and mostly insignificant reactions of the CRB index and the GSCI to macroeconomic announcements. However, in a state-dependent model, surprises in several macroeconomic news are significantly positively related to both indices during recessions, but not during economic expansions. Moreover, we document that many price response coefficients are significantly larger during recessions than during expansions. Our findings are robust to several alternative business cycle definitions.

Our analysis offers two major contributions. First, we contribute to the literature on the link between macroeconomic conditions and commodity prices (see, e.g., Erb and Harvey (2006), Gorton and Rouwenhorst (2006), Kat and Oomen (2007)) by studying the price response of two representative commodity futures indices. By analyzing two diverse indices we document that during recessions, macroeconomic announcements are relevant to many commodity investors who hold a diversified portfolio of commodity futures. Second, we contribute to the literature on the state-dependent impact of macroeconomic news on asset prices (see, e.g, McQueen and Roley (1993), and Boyd, Hu, and Jagannathan (2005) for evidence on state-dependent effects on stock prices) by showing that the price impact of macroeconomic news on commodity futures is also dependent on the state of the economy. This gives further evidence that macroeconomic news might be interpreted differently in different states of the economy.

The third chapter deals with macroeconomic announcement effects on the German stock market. My analysis compares the impact of domestic German and foreign US macroeconomic news on the German stock index futures. The analysis pursues two goals. First, to give a complete depiction of the price and liquidity dynamics in the German stock market around a large number of important US and German economic news. This identifies important scheduled news events for German stock traders and reveals potential liquidity risks around the news releases. The second goal is to compare the effects of domestic and foreign economic news in the German stock market. This reveals whether German stock prices are affected more by domestic economic news or news about the world's leading economy.

The analysis is carried out with 21 types of foreign US economic news and 17 types of domestic German economic news. First, I assess the news impact on high frequency prices of the German stock index futures in order to reveal the magnitude, sign and speed of the price response of German stocks. Second, I compare trading patterns, including trading volume, return volatility and bid-ask spreads around the news releases with trading patterns on non-announcement days. Lastly, I investigate the news impact on the effective spread components — costs of inventory control and information asymmetry — in the German stock market. I find that the announcement of domestic and foreign economic news exerts large effects on the German stock index futures. There seems to be a strong correlation between price and liquidity effects, as those announcements that induce large price movements also affect liquidity. The price response is completed within the first five-minute interval whereas liquidity is affected for a much longer period. Trading volume, for instance remains elevated for up to 90 minutes past the announcement. Spreads widen for a few minutes before and up to 30 minutes after the announcement. The general pattern is similar in response to domestic and US economic news. However, there seems to be a larger number of relevant US announcements and US news exerts larger price and liquidity effects on the German stock market than domestic news does.

Previously, the price effects of macroeconomic news on German stock prices have been studied by Funke and Matsuda (2006) and Entorf and Steiner (2007). In contrast to Funke and Matsuda (2006), my analysis is conducted on a high frequency dataset which allows a more precise estimate of the effects. In contrast to Entorf and Steiner (2007), my study includes a large number of important US and German macroeconomic news, whereas Entorf and Steiner (2007) study the high frequency price response to only one single announcement. Also, my investigation is the first to deal with liquidity effects of macroeconomic news releases in the German stock market. Franke and Hess (2000), Hess and Malinowska (2008), and Malinowska (2008) conduct similar analyses for the German bond futures. However, their analyses pool all announcements together (Franke and Hess (2000)) or only incorporate a single macroeconomic announcment, the US employment report (the latter two studies). Compared to the pioneering studies on liquidity effects around macroeconomic news in the US bond market, namley Fleming and Remolona (1999), Balduzzi, Elton, and Green (2001), and Green (2004), my investigation additionally reveals that the strength of the price response is positively related to the strength of the liquidity effect.

A number of previous studies have investigated the effects of US announcements in international financial markets. This includes, among others, King and Wadhwani (1990), Becker, Finnerty, and Friedman (1995), Connolly and Wang (2003), Ahn, Cai, and Cheung (2002), Wongswan (2006), Albuquerque and Vega (2007), and Andersen, Bollerslev, Diebold, and Vega (2007). Some interesting differences between domestic and foreign news effects were found. First, King and Wadhwani (1990) and Albuquerque and Vega (2007) find that UK and Portuguese stock markets do not immediately respond to US macroeconomic news. The price reaction is delayed until one hour later, when the US stock market opens. Second, Albuquerque and Vega (2007) find that liquidity increases on days with a US macroeconomic announcement but decreases on days with domestic Portuguese news. However, there is also contrary evidence in the literature. Thus, my study provides further evidence that there are no qualitative differences regarding how domestic and foreign economic news is processed.

My results highlight the leading role that the US economy has on the world's financial markets. Although Germany is a large economy itself, US economic news affects German stock markets even more than domestic news does. From a German investor's point of view, US macroeconomic news releases might very well be the most important scheduled news event for the German stock market. However, trading in response to these announcements might be costly as liquidity is low. My study offers a comprehensive depiction of the price and liquidity dynamics around macroeconomic news in the German stock market. Taking these findings into account helps German stock traders to better adjust trading around important events such as US or domestic economic news releases.

The fourth chapter of the dissertation, like the third chapter, also deals with the effects of US macroeconomic news on international financial markets. However, in this chapter I study the channels of information transmission. My study investigates how US information is transmitted to German bond futures around the release of US economic news. US macroeconomic announcements are suitable for this analysis because they convey information that is highly important for both US and German bond prices. Most previous studies analyze the direct impact of surprises in US announcements on international asset prices. My analysis additionally focuses on a second transmission channel: Transmission of information revealed through US price movements. I find that information about US economic news is transmitted also through US price movements. German bond traders don't respond solely to the news itself but also condition their price response on the US price response. Afterwards, when the public news is already fully incorporated into prices, German traders still try to infer private US interpretations of the news by following US bond price movements more strongly than usual.

This study is most closely related to prior research that deals with the question whether US economic news is fundamentally relevant to foreign stock markets, or whether the foreign market response is due to contagion. In that context, contagion is usually defined as the finding that the foreign stock market co-moves with the US market *as usual* on US announcement days. Under the contagion hypothesis US economic news carries no information that is genuinely relevant to the foreign market. The foreign market only reacts to US news because it co-moves with the US market. The alternative hypothesis is that US economic news conveys information that is fundamentally relevant for the foreign market. Under the alternative hypothesis one would expect that co-movement between US and foreign markets increases on announcement days due to the large global relevance of US economic news. Empirical evidence in the literature is mixed. Karolyi and Stulz (1996) find that the correlation between Japanese and US stocks is not higher on US announcement days. However, Franke and Hess (2000) find that return correlation between US and German bonds is higher immediately following US macroeconomic announcements.

In order to guide the analysis, I apply the rational learning model of Chan (1993) to cross-border information transmission. This yields two main predictions: First, German bond traders condition their price response to US economic news on both the news itself and the US price response. Second, the cross-market dependencies vary if the relative share of globally relevant information in US price innovations varies. The empirical analysis is carried out on a high frequency dataset of US and German bond futures prices. I extend the Hasbrouck (1991) quote revision model by relating transaction returns in German bond futures not only to their own lagged returns and order flow, but also to lagged price movements in US bond futures. Studying high frequency data is necessary, because todays futures markets are highly efficient and information is processed near-instantaneously. For example, each price movement in the US bond futures market is fully incorporated into German bond futures prices within about 20 seconds.

I find that during the announcement of US economic news, German bond prices respond to both the announcement surprise itself and the US price response. Further, the dependency of German bond returns on lagged US returns varies over time. Surprises in public US macro announcements need less than one minute to be fully incorporated into US and German bond prices. During this period, I find that US bond price movements impose an abnormaly high influence on subsequent German bond returns. A unit increase in the US bond price leads to a cumulative increase of about 0.33 in German bond prices. During the subsequent 29 minutes, a unit US impulse leads to a German bond price movement of about 0.19, whereas the effect during the non-announcement sample is only 0.14. As a consequence, correlation between US and German bond futures is abnormally high following US macro announcements compared to non-announcement days. After about 60 minutes the level of price transmission returns to normal levels.

My study adds to the understanding of cross-border information flow by showing how information is transmitted to foreign markets via public news releases and price movements. The German bond price response to US economic news is driven by the news surprise and the US price response. Further, I show empirically that the level of cross-border price transmission is not always the same but follows predictable patterns. When the global component in US price innovations is presumably high German bond returns follow US bond price movements more strongly than otherwise. Moreover, my findings also contribute to the discussion whether US economic news is fundamentally relevant to international asset prices or whether the reaction is due to contagion. My results favor the economic fundamentals hypothesis and cast doubt on the contagion hypothesis. German and US bond futures do not simply co-move *as usual* following a US macroeconomic announcment. Rather, there is a significant *increase* in the transmission of price movements. I relate this increase to the fact that US price innovations in response to US macroeconomic announcements reveal interpretations about US economic news that complement the news itself.

2 How do commodity futures respond to macroeconomic news?

2.1 Motivation

This chapter studies the impact of US macroeconomic news on commodity prices.[1] Over the last few years, the optimistic growth prospects of large developing countries like Brazil, China and India, and the accompanying need for oil, industrial metals and construction supplies, have made commodities an increasingly attractive alternative investment. In comparison to other financial markets, there has been little research into commodity markets. Most notable are the studies by Erb and Harvey (2006) and Gorton and Rouwenhorst (2006) who study long-term return characteristics of commodity futures. The literature on the reaction of commodity prices to macroeconomic announcements is very scarce. Previous studies only investigate the impact of macroeconomic news on individual commodity futures types (see, e.g., Barnhart (1989), Christie-David, Chaudry, and Koch (2000), and Cai, Cheung, and Wong (2001)). Our investigation fills that gap by examining the price response of two commodity futures indices to several US macroeconomic announcements.

[1]The chapter is based on my research paper 'How do commodity futures respond to macroeconomic news?'. Since this paper is co-authored with Dieter Hess and Alexandra Niessen, I will use the plural form (we, our, etc.) when refering to our work.

Commodity futures are widely accepted as a distinct asset class. At the same time, it is well known that the correlation between different groups of commodity futures is very low, much lower than for example the correlation between different stock sectors (see Erb and Harvey (2006)). Therefore, existing results regarding the price impact of macroeconomic announcements on individual commodity types are of minor importance for most commodity investors who hold a diversified portfolio of different commodity futures. Moreover, most commodity investors prefer to invest into commodity futures indices. In 2007, total investments in commodities reached USD 178bn[2] out of which USD 120bn[3] was invested into commodity indices. Our study is the first to investigate the price reaction of two diverse commodity futures indices: the equal weighted Reuters CRB, and the S&P GSCI which is weighted by world production quantities. Thus, we reveal how typical investors in this increasingly important alternative market are affected by the announcement of macroecnonomic news.

Additionally, we allow for an asymmetric commodity price response depending on the state of the economy. Macroeconomic announcements convey two important pieces of information about future economic conditions: real activity and inflation. Gorton and Rouwenhorst (2006) show that both factors affect commodity futures returns. However, the sign of the overall relation between macroeconomic news and commodity prices is not evident. There are two opposing effects on commodity prices that might depend on the state of the economy.

On the one hand, higher than expected real activity might have a positive effect on commodity prices due to an increase in the demand for commodities as input goods for rising production levels.[4] Given that supply is rather fixed in the short run, rising demand

[2]Source: Bloomberg News 'Commodity investments up 50%, AIG reports', published August 13, 2007.
[3]Source: Reuters News 'Commodities investments hit $178 billion in 2007', published March 10, 2008.
[4]Our examples are based on the announcement of higher than expected real activity/inflation figures. Of course, the opposite relation also applies to the announcement of lower than expected figures.

will lead to higher prices. Likewise, the announcement of higher than expected inflation figures also has a positive effect on commodity prices. Commodity returns are positively correlated with inflation and they are better suited to hedge against inflation than stocks or bonds. For example, Gorton and Rouwenhorst (2006) report the following correlation coefficients of 1-year returns with inflation: -0.10 for stocks, -0.30 for bonds, and +0.29 for commodity futures. Thus, positive inflation news might cause investors to assign a larger portfolio weight to commodities, which creates additional demand and leads to higher prices.

On the other hand, higher than expected real activity or inflation also might have a negative effect on commodity prices due to increasing interest rates. According to the Taylor (1993) rule, the FED is committed to contain an overheating economy and rising inflation by increasing interest rates, and it is committed to promote growth by lowering interest rates. Rising interest rates, however, are negatively related to commodity prices through various channels (see, e.g., Frankel (2006)). First, high interest rates increase storage costs. As a consequence, commodities are rather brought to the market instead of being held in storage. Second, high interest rates make financial assets such as bonds more attractive relative to physical goods, and thus encourage investors to shift their portfolios out of commodities into bonds. The negative relation between interest rates and commodity prices is supported theoretically by Bond (1984) and Chambers (1985) and empirically by Frankel (2006).

To sum up, macroeconomic news may have a positive as well as a negative impact on commodity prices. We propose that the relative strength of these effects could be state dependent, i.e., the overall price reaction might depend on whether positive or negative effects prevail. We expect that during economic expansions positive and negative effects cancel out each other. In contrast, during recessions, when interest rate concerns are lower, we expect to find a positive relation between the commodity price response and surprises in macroeconomic announcements. These hypotheses are derived from the literature on the stock market response to macroeconomic news. McQueen and Roley (1993) show that a positive surprise in real activity news primarily signals cash flow growth during recessions, while it primarily signals an increase in discount rates during expansions. Similarly, Andersen, Bollerslev, Diebold, and Vega (2007) find that stronger anti-inflationary monetary policies during expansion periods strengthen the influence of the interest rate component. In terms of commodity prices, this would mean that during recessions the positive effects from increasing demand prevail, and during expansions the negative effects from rising interest rates prevail. Therefore our empirical model will allow for state dependent effects in order to test whether the macroeconomic news impact on commodity prices is dependent on the state of the economy.

We find that the impact of macroeconomic news on commodity prices is indeed dependent on the state of the economy. During recessions, news about higher (lower) inflation and real activity lead to positive (negative) adjustments of commodity futures prices. In contrast, we find no significant reactions during economic expansions. Moreover, we document that many price response coefficients are significantly larger during recessions than during expansions. These findings are robust to several alternative business cycle definitions. Our study offers two major contributions. First, we reveal the effects of US macroeconomic news on two representative commodity futures indices. This is an important finding, as most commodity investors are invested into indices. Thus, we document that investors in this increasingly important alternative market are affected by macroeconomic news. Second, we show that the price impact of macroeconomic news on commodity futures is dependent on the state of the economy. This was formerly known only from the stock market response. Therefore, our findings provide further evidence that macroeconomic releases are interpreted differently in different states of the economy.

Finally, our results provide important implications for hedging and diversification from an investor's point of view. During recessions, we find that the direction of the commodity futures price response to macroeconomic announcements is mostly opposite to that of stocks and bonds. Thus, a negative price reaction of bond and stock prices to macroeconomic news could be offset by a positive price reaction of commodity futures within a portfolio consisting of these three asset classes. The fact that the hedging value of commodities with regard to macroeconomic risks is predominantly found during recessions emphasizes that it is important to consider the business cycle for asset allocation decisions.

This chapter proceeds as follows. In section 2 we describe the data used in our empirical analysis. Section 3 provides the results of our empirical investigation and section 4 concludes this chapter.

2.2 Data

We investigate the impact of macroeconomic news on two distinct commodity futures indices: the Reuters/Jefferies-CRB Index (formerly: Reuters-CRB Futures Price Index), which is traded on the New York Board of Trade, and the S&P GSCI, which is traded on the Chicago Mercantile Exchange. The return data is obtained through Thomson Financial Datastream. Both indices measure the return from investing in nearby commodity futures and rolling them forward each month, always keeping an investment in close to maturity futures. A detailed list of the individual components of both indices is given in Table 2.1. The CRB index consists of 17 equally-weighted constituents, while the GSCI includes 24 commodity futures weighted by world production output. For both indices, we calculate daily log returns from the respective excess return index. Studying excess return indices abstracts from the price response of the T-Bill collateral and is better suited to investigate the commodity-specific price response.[5]

It is unclear which index best represents commodity futures as an asset class. Many prominent studies (see, e.g., Bodie and Rosansky (1980), and Gorton and Rouwenhorst (2006)) have focused on equally-weighted commodity futures portfolios. They argue that their performance reveals the average commodity futures performance and thus, they are a good measure for the aggregate market. Other studies such as Arnott, Hsu, and Moore (2005) point out that equally-weighted indices have return characteristics that are not representative for the aggregate market as they overweight small and illiquid index constituents. Erb and Harvey (2006) conclude that due to the lack of an objective, market-capitalization based weighting scheme for commodity futures each index represents an alternative commodity portfolio strategy. Thus, to ensure that our results hold for different commodity portfolio strategies, we investigate the CRB index as well as the GSCI, which represent two distinct portfolio strategies. The CRB index is the world's oldest commodity index. We choose this index in accordance with Gorton and Rouwenhorst (2006) to investigate the average commodity futures response to macroeconomic news. The GSCI is the most traded commodity index, accounting for USD 70bn of the total USD 120bn invested worldwide into commodity indices.[6] This index, while heavily skewed towards energy commodities, presumably best represents the average commodity investors' portfolios.

[5] A commodity total return index assumes that for each Dollar invested in a certain commodity futures contract one Dollar is also invested into a risk free asset until that futures contract matures. This risk free investment, usually T-Bills, is referred to as the collateral. By contrast, an excess return index does not assume a collateral position. Note that the excess return index does not exactly equal the total return index performance minus the risk free rate. See http://www2.goldmansachs.com/gsci/ for a detailed discussion about the differences.

[6] Figures according to Bloomberg News "Commodity investments up 50%, AIG reports", published August 13, 2007.

Table 2.1: Composition of the CRB index and the GSCI

Commodity Future	CRB index	GSCI
Aluminium	-	0.029
Cocoa	0.059	0.003
Coffee	0.059	0.006
Copper	0.059	0.023
Corn	0.059	0.031
Cotton	0.059	0.011
Crude Oil	0.059	0.284
Brent Crude Oil	-	0.131
Feeder Cattle	-	0.008
Gas Oil	-	0.045
Gold	0.059	0.019
Heating Oil	0.059	0.081
Lead	-	0.003
Hogs	0.059	0.021
Live Cattle	0.059	0.036
Natural Gas	0.059	0.095
Nickel	-	0.008
Orange Juice	0.059	-
Platinum	0.059	0.000
Silver	0.059	0.002
Soybeans	0.059	0.019
Soybean Oil	-	0.000
Sugar	0.059	0.014
Unleaded Gas	-	0.085
Wheat	0.059	0.029
Read Wheat	-	0.013
Zinc	-	0.005
Total	1.000	1.000
No. of Futures Contracts	17	24

This table contains the portfolio weights of the CRB index and the GSCI as of May 2004. Source: Erb and Harvey (2006).

To compare the price response of commodity futures to macroeconomic news with the price response of other asset classes, we additionally investigate the reaction of stock and bond returns to the same news releases. We use daily log returns for the S&P 500 and the Datastream 10-year constant maturity US Government Bond Benchmark (T-Bond) index in our analysis. Summary statistics for both commodity indices' daily log returns as well as their correlation with the S&P 500 and the T-Bond are presented in Table 2.2. We report results for the whole sample from 1989 to 2005 (Column 1), as well as for the sample divided into announcement days (i.e., days on which a macroeconomic announcement occurs) vs. non-announcement days (Column 2, 3), and expansion vs. recession periods according to the NBER classification (Column 4, 5). The first two rows in Panel A and B contain the annualized means and standard deviations of both indices.[7] Overall, the GSCI is more volatile and yields higher returns than the CRB index. These differences can be attributed to the fact that the GSCI mainly consists of energy and oil contracts, which are known to be more volatile and yield high returns (see Kat and Oomen (2007)).[8] In line with Gorton and Rouwenhorst (2006), we find that the correlation with stocks and bonds is consistently negative across all subsamples. This supports the view of commodity futures as a good hedge for a stock and bond portfolio.

To investigate the impact of macroeconomic news on commodity futures, stock returns, and bond returns, we use data on seventeen US macroeconomic announcements. Although commodities are demanded by investors worldwide, we restrict our analysis to US announcements for two reasons. First, both commodity indices are listed in the US and are presumably predominantly traded by US investors. Second, it is known that US macroe-

[7] We obtain annualized means by multiplying the daily value with 252, the approximate number of trading days in a year. Likewise, we obtain annualized standard deviations by multiplying with $\sqrt{252}$.

[8] For example, on January 17, 1991 the GSCI loses 18.5% on one day due to a 30% drop in crude oil prices on that day. The oil price shock was caused by the end of the first Gulf War. Our results (not reported) hold when we exclude this day from our analysis. This price shock does not affect our results, as there was only one announcement on that day, the insignificant housing starts announcement.

Table 2.2: Summary statistics of daily CRB/GSCI log returns

Panel A: CRB index	1989-2005	AD	NAD	Expansion	Recession
Ann. Mean (in %)	1.9001	5.7708	-1.3608	3.5028	-14.868
Ann. Std. Dev. (in %)	9.1390	9.3152	8.9834	9.0501	9.9644
Median (in %)	0.0140	0.0231	0.0001	0.0183	-0.0252
Min (in %)	-2.2831	-2.2831	-2.2363	-2.2363	-2.2831
Max (in %)	2.4645	2.3798	2.4645	2.4645	1.7594
Correlation with S&P 500	-0.0142	-0.0102	-0.0206	0.0000	-0.1216
Correlation with T-Bond	-0.0761	-0.0980	-0.0549	-0.0749	-0.0865
Panel B: GSCI	**1989-2005**	**AD**	**NAD**	**Expansion**	**Recession**
Ann. Mean (in %)	4.8636	2.0513	7.2576	6.2496	-9.3240
Ann. Std. Dev. (in %)	19.435	19.808	19.119	17.622	32.844
Median (in %)	0.0170	0.0001	0.0240	0.0118	0.0620
Min (in %)	-18.4549	-18.4549	-5.6908	-5.1451	-18.4549
Max (in %)	7.5349	4.7481	7.5349	6.5389	7.5349
Correlation with S&P 500	-0.0747	-0.0684	-0.0797	-0.0267	-0.2861
Correlation with T-Bond	-0.0513	-0.0667	-0.0348	-0.0244	-0.2112
Observations	4288	1959	2329	3912	376

This table contains summary statistics for CRB index daily log returns (Panel A) and GSCI daily log returns (Panel B). Annualized means and standard deviations, medians, minimum and maximum values as well as correlations with the S&P 500 and the 10-year T-Bond are given for the whole sample period from 1989 to 2005 (Column 1), the sample split into announcement days (AD, Column 2) and non-announcement days (NAD, Column 3) as well as expansions (Column 4) and recessions (Column 5). Recessions and expansions are defined according to the NBER business cycle classification.

conomic releases are of great importance for financial markets worldwide (see, e.g., Andersen, Bollerslev, Diebold, and Vega (2007)). The primary source of the announcement data is Money Market Services (MMS), which has been used as a data source in many similar previous studies such as Balduzzi, Elton, and Green (2001), Andersen, Bollerslev, Diebold, and Vega (2003, 2007) and Green (2004). However, analyst coverage by MMS ends in 06/2003. Since Bloomberg is a second well established provider of macroeconomic news data,[9] we use Bloomberg whenever MMS data is not available. This provides one of the most comprehensive and longest series of US economic announcement data used so far.

Assuming efficient markets, only unexpected news will impact commodity futures. Therefore, we have to isolate the surprise component of the announcements. As a proxy for market expectations regarding upcoming announcements, we use median analyst forecasts. Each Friday, MMS polls analysts' forecasts of several economic indicators to be released in the following week. Survey responses are received over a 3 to 4-hour period every Friday morning via fax or phone. The surprise component is computed as

$$S_{i,m} = \frac{A_{i,m} - F_{i,m}}{STD(A_i - F_i)}. \tag{2.1}$$

In each month m, for each announcement i (with $i = 1, ..., 17$ indicating the announcement type investigated), the surprise value is defined as the difference between the actually released value, $A_{i,m}$, and the median analyst forecast, $F_{i,m}$. In line with Balduzzi, Elton, and Green (2001), we standardize the surprise value of each announcement observation by the standard deviation across the time series of all observations of this announcement type. This yields the standardized surprise $S_{i,m}$ which is then used in our empirical analysis.

[9]Bloomberg has been used as a data source for economic news announcements in Fleming and Remolona (1997) and Bollerslev, Cai, and Song (2000), among others.

This procedure facilitates a comparison of the estimated coefficients across different announcement types. Summary statistics for all seventeen macroeconomic announcements are given in Table 2.3.

All announcements are released each month on a prescheduled day at a fixed time.[10] We divide them into three broad categories: real activity news, inflation news, and other news. The number in the abbreviation of some announcement types indicates that this announcement consists of more than one relevant headline figure. For example, the US employment report consists of headline figures regarding nonfarm payrolls (E1), unemployment rate (E2) and hourly earnings (E3). The '2' in PPI2, CPI2 and RS2 denotes that these are the core value for the respective announcement. CPI2, for instance, excludes very volatile products such as food and energy.

All announcement data are available for at least twelve and a half years, most of them for the entire investigation period from 1989 to 2005. We report minimum, maximum and mean values for the standardized surprise in the rightmost part of Table 2.3. The mean standardized surprise indicates whether an announcement was more often above or below analysts' expectations. For instance, a negative mean surprise of the US trade balance indicates that in our sample period the announced trade balance figure was on average lower than expected by analysts. However, mean values are mostly very close to zero, indicating that median analyst forecasts are not biased, i.e., analysts do not systematically forecast too high or too low. The unbiasedness of forecasts collected by MMS has also been repeatedly confirmed by Pearce and Roley (1985), McQueen and Roley (1993), and Balduzzi, Elton, and Green (2001). In unreported results, we also validate that there are no systematic differences between mean surprises in expansions and recessions.

[10] GDP is a quaterly figure, but there is an announcement each month. In the first month of each quarter, the Bureau of Economic Analysis releases an advance estimate for the last quarter. In the second month it releases a preliminary figure. The final figure is released in the third month. We do not differentiate between advance, preliminary and final figure to allow for more observations.

Table 2.3: US macroeconomic announcements

Abbr.	Announcment	Obs.	Source	Availability from	Availability until	Release Time	Stand. Surprise min	Stand. Surprise mean	Stand. Surprise max
Real Activity									
DGO	Durable Good Order	203	BC	01/89	12/05	8:30	-2.62	0.02	3.78
E1	Nonfarm Payrolls	204	BLS	01/89	12/05	8:30	-2.94	-0.17	3.67
HS	Housing Starts	199	BC	01/89	12/05	8:30	-3.17	0.13	2.96
IP	Industrial Production	204	FRB	01/89	12/05	9:15	-2.77	0.08	4.31
ISM	ISM Index	191	ISM	01/90	12/05	10:00	-2.37	-0.03	3.65
RS2	Retail Sales	197	BC	07/89	12/05	8:30	-3.05	-0.09	2.54
CC	Consumer Confidence	174	CB	07/91	12/05	10:00	-2.59	0.06	2.65
CS	Construction Spending	204	BC	01/89	12/05	10:00	-2.45	0.09	2.50
E2	Unemployment Rate	204	BLS	01/89	12/05	8:30	-2.79	-0.25	2.79
GDP	Gross Domestic Product	161	BEA	01/90	06/03	8:30	-2.20	0.24	3.11
PI	Personal Income	203	BEA	01/89	12/05	8:30	-3.71	0.18	5.77
BI	Business Inventories	204	BC	01/89	12/05	8:30	-3.95	0.16	2.64
Inflation									
CPI2	Consumer Price Index	197	BLS	07/89	12/05	8:30	-1.69	0.06	3.37
PPI2	Producer Price Index	197	BLS	07/89	12/05	8:30	-4.83	-0.15	3.22
E3	Hourly Earnings	192	BLS	10/89	12/05	8:30	-2.38	0.05	2.85
Other									
TRD	Trade Balance	204	BEA	01/89	12/05	10:00	-4.27	-0.13	3.55
LI	Leading Indicators	204	CB	01/89	12/05	10:00	-3.74	0.09	4.81

This table reports the availability of US macroeconomic announcement and corresponding survey data that we use in our study. We partition news announcements into three broad categories: real activity news, inflation news, and other news. The following abbreviations indicate the respective sources of each announcement: Bureau of Labor Statistics (BLS), Bureau of the Census (BC), Bureau of Economic Analysis (BEA), Institute for Supply Chain Management (ISM), Conference Board (CB). All release times are given in Eastern Standard Time (EST). The last three columns report summary statistics for the standardized surprise in the announcements, i.e., announced figure minus market expectation according to MMS surveys, standardized by the sample standard deviation.

Figure 2.1: Alternative business cycle definitions

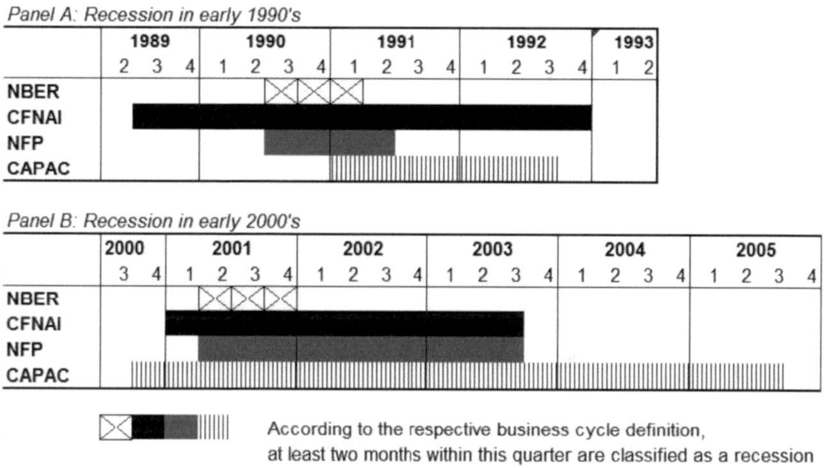

This figure shows recession periods in our sample according to the alternative business cycle definitions used in this study. Business cycles are defined according to the NBER classification, the CFNAI definition, the nonfarm payroll (NFP) definition and the capacity utilization definition (CAPAC).

To investigate the effect of macroeconomic news dependent on the state of the economy, it is necessary to find an appropriate definition of expansion and recession periods. The most widely used (see, e.g., Boyd, Hu, and Jagannathan (2005), or Gorton and Rouwenhorst (2006)) business cycle definition is released by the National Bureau of Economic Research (NBER). Business cycle turning points are observed and announced by the NBER Business Cycle Dating Committee. Its decisions are based on overall economic activity, usually visible in real GDP, real income, employment, industrial production, and wholesale-retail sales. In line with the literature, we define expansion and recession periods according to the NBER.[11] In addition, we test the robustness of our results on three alternative busi-

[11]The business cycle definition of the NBER is obtained from http://www.nber.org/cycles.html.

ness cycle definitions. We also divide our sample according to the Chicago FED National Activity Index (CFNAI), consecutive changes in nonfarm payroll figures (E1), and the capacity utilization (CAPAC).[12] Figure 2.1 reports the recession periods according to all four business cycle definitions.

In our sample period from 1989 to 2005, all four definitions yield two recession periods, one in the early 1990's and the second one in the early 2000's. However, the two recession periods according to CFNAI and capacity utilization are longer than the recession periods as defined by NBER and nonfarm payroll figures.

2.3 Results

2.3.1 Unconditional price impact of macroeconomic announcements on commodity futures

We first examine the impact of macroeconomic news on the CRB index and the GSCI without conditioning on the state of the economy. We also investigate the price response of the 10-year T-Bond and the S&P 500 to compare our results for commodity futures with those for other asset classes. Our initial estimation approach for each of the three asset classes follows the literature on the stock market impact of macroeconomic announcements (see, e.g., McQueen and Roley (1993), and Adams, McQueen, and Wood (2004)). We regress the daily log return on the surprise component in macroeconomic announcements on that day according to the following equation:

[12]The CAPAC classification distinguishes strong and weak states of the economy based on the median capacity utilization. In addition to recession months, "weak months" according to CAPAC also include those months that occur right before and after a recession. We use this alternative classification to test the robustness of our results.

$$R_t = c + \beta \cdot R_{t-1} + \sum_{i=1}^{17} \delta_i \cdot S_{i,t} + \epsilon_t, \tag{2.2}$$

where R_t represents the daily log return of either the CRB index, the GSCI, the T-Bond, and the S&P 500, respectively. Following Flannery and Protopapadakis (2002), we include the lagged return, R_{t-1}, to control for autocorrelation, because most commodity futures exhibit significant degrees of serial correlation in daily returns (see Kat and Oomen (2007)). $S_{i,t}$ is the standardized surprise of announcement type i. If i is not released on day t, then $S_{i,t}$ is zero. δ_i represents the price response coefficient to the surprise component of announcement i. All regressions are estimated with Newey-West heteroscedasticity and autocorrelation consistent error terms. Empirical results are given in Table 2.4.

The first and second columns contain the CRB index and GSCI price response coefficients to each of the seventeen macroeconomic news in our sample.[13] Without conditioning on the business cycle, both commodity futures indices do not significantly react to the release of macroeconomic announcements. The only exception is a positive reaction of both indices to a surprise in the consumer price index (CPI) and a positive response of the GSCI to the GDP announcement. For example, a one standard deviation positive surprise in the CPI announcement on average leads to a 0.07% price increase in the CRB index and a 0.18% increase in the GSCI. The autocorrelation coefficient for the CRB index is positive and highly significant while it is not significant for the GSCI. This might be caused by the higher weighting of smaller, illiquid futures in the CRB index which are more likely to be subject to autocorrelation due to non-synchronous trading (see Scholes and Williams (1977)).

[13]The sign of business inventory announcements and the unemployment rate has been reversed to make the coefficient signs comparable to the other real activity announcements, i.e., positive values equal higher economic activity.

Table 2.4: Unconditional price impact

	CRB index		GSCI		TBOND		S&P 500	
Intercept	0.0001		0.0002		0.0002	***	0.0004	**
AR(1)	0.0652	***	0.0041		0.0476	***	-0.0081	
DGO	0.0004		0.0003		-0.0008	*	-0.0006	
$E1$	0.0005		-0.0001		-0.0030	***	-0.0014	
HS	0.0001		0.0008		0.0001		-0.0007	
IP	0.0002		0.0011		-0.0008	***	0.0014	**
ISM	0.0005		0.0001		-0.0024	***	0.0001	
$RS2$	-0.0002		0.0000		-0.0009	**	-0.0006	
CC	-0.0001		0.0014		-0.0013	***	0.0005	
CS	0.0005		0.0007		0.0000		-0.0006	
$-E2$	0.0003		0.0000		-0.0003		0.0002	
GDP	0.0004		0.0014	*	0.0001		0.0016	***
PI	-0.0003		0.0003		0.0000		0.0004	
$-BI$	0.0003		0.0007		-0.0001		0.0004	
$CPI2$	0.0007	*	0.0018	**	-0.0012	***	-0.0036	***
$PPI2$	-0.0004		-0.0013		-0.0006	**	-0.0012	**
$E3$	-0.0002		-0.0004		-0.0015	***	-0.0019	
TRD	-0.0005		-0.0007		-0.0005	*	0.0011	
LI	-0.0003		0.0001		-0.0002		0.0007	
R^2	0.77%		0.37%		6.12%		1.18%	
D.-W. Stat.	1.99		1.99		1.99		2.00	
Observations	4,288		4,288		4,288		4,288	

This table contains regression results of the following equation: $R_t = c+\beta \cdot R_{t-1}+\sum_i \delta_i \cdot S_{i,t}+\epsilon_t$. R_t denotes the daily log return of the CRB index (Column 1), the GSCI (Column 2), the 10-year T-Bond (Column 3), or the S&P 500 (Column 4), respectively. The daily returns are related to an autoregressive parameter, $AR(1)$, and the standardized surprise component of several macroeconomic announcements, $S_{i,t}$. The signs for Business Inventories (BI) and Unemployment Rate (E2) have been reversed to make their interpretation comparable to the other announcements: higher than expected inflation or real activity equals a positive sign. Robust standard errors are estimated with Newey West heteroscedasiticy and autocorrelation consistent covariance. Significance levels are indicated as follows: *** 1% significance, ** 5% significance and * 10% significance.

Column 3 reports the price response of daily 10-year T-Bond returns to the release of macroeconomic announcements. In line with previous studies such as Fleming and Remolona (1999) and Balduzzi, Elton, and Green (2001), we find that T-Bond returns are significantly negatively related to several macroeconomic announcements. The sign of the price response coefficient is in line with standard economic theory: higher than expected inflation or real activity leads to expectations of increasing interest rates, and thus a decrease of bond prices. Column 4 contains results for the price reaction of daily S&P 500 returns. The sign of the price response coefficient depends on the released announcement. We observe a significantly negative relation between stock returns and surprises in the two price indices (CPI and PPI2), and we find a significantly positive relation between stock returns and surprises in industrial production and gross domestic product.

The explanatory power of the empirical model in terms of the R^2 for the commodity indices (0.77% for the CRB index and 0.37% for the GSCI) is lower than the R^2 values for stocks (1.2%) and bonds (6.2%). The latter values are comparable to previous studies on the response of daily stock and bond returns to macroeconomic news. Looking only at the unconditional results, one might conclude that macroeconomic announcements do not have a significant impact on commodity prices. However, it might also be the case that macroeconomic releases contain positive as well as negative information for commodities that cancel out each other in expansions, while positive effects prevail in recessions. In that case only an asymmetric model allowing for state dependent differences would reveal the macroeconomic news impact on commodity indices. Therefore we investigate the price response conditional on the state of the economy in the next subsection.

2.3.2 Asymmetric price impact conditional on the business cycle

We now split our sample according to the NBER business cycle definition into two subsamples: expansion and recession. We use the following specification for our empirical analysis:

$$R_t = c + \beta \cdot R_{t-1} + \sum_{i=1}^{17} \delta_i^{exp} \cdot D_t^{exp} \cdot S_{i,t} + \sum_{i=1}^{17} \delta_i^{rec} \cdot D_t^{rec} \cdot S_{i,t} + \epsilon_t, \tag{2.3}$$

where D_t^{exp} (D_t^{rec}) is a dummy variable that takes the value of one if the economy is in an expansion (a recession) according to the NBER classification, and zero otherwise. All other variables are defined as in Equation (2.2). We report the results in Table 2.5.

In contrast to the results in the unconditional model, Table 2.5 shows that the CRB index (Column 1) and the GSCI (Column 2) are significantly positively related to several macroeconomic announcement surprises during recessions, while there is no significant price response during expansions. During recessions, both commodity futures indices are positively related to surprises in CPI and GDP announcements. In addition, we find a positive relation between the returns of the CRB index and surprises in durable good orders (DGO), nonfarm payrolls (E1) and retail sales (RS), while the GSCI is positively related to consumer confidence (CC) announcements. Although the CRB index is based on equal weights and the GSCI constituents are weighted by worldwide production output, results are qualitatively similar for both indices. Therefore, we conclude that during recessions most commodity investors' portfolios will be affected by macroeconomic announcements.

Table 2.5: State dependent price impact

	CRB index		GSCI		TBOND		S&P 500	
Intercept	0.0001		0.0002		0.0003	***	0.0004	***
AR(1)	0.0639	***	-0.0043		0.0473	***	-0.0083	
DGO^{exp}	0.0002		0.0004		-0.0011	***	-0.0007	
$E1^{exp}$	0.0003		0.0000		-0.0033	***	-0.0018	*
HS^{exp}	-0.0001		-0.0001		0.0001		-0.0007	
IP^{exp}	0.0001		0.0012		-0.0010	***	0.0013	*
ISM^{exp}	0.0006		-0.0001		-0.0024	***	0.0005	
$RS2^{exp}$	-0.0005		-0.0002		-0.0008	**	-0.0007	
CC^{exp}	-0.0002		0.0012		-0.0012	***	-0.0001	
CS^{exp}	0.0005		0.0010		-0.0001		-0.0007	
$-E2^{exp}$	0.0003		0.0003		-0.0005		0.0000	
GDP^{exp}	0.0002		0.0003		0.0002		0.0018	***
PI^{exp}	0.0000		0.0003		-0.0003		0.0008	
$-BI^{exp}$	0.0002		0.0007		0.0000		0.0003	
$CPI2^{exp}$	0.0006		0.0006		-0.0011	***	-0.0032	***
$PPI2^{exp}$	-0.0002		-0.0008		-0.0006	**	-0.0016	**
$E3^{exp}$	-0.0002		-0.0007		-0.0016	***	-0.0017	**
TRD^{exp}	-0.0005		-0.0008		-0.0004		0.0009	
LI^{exp}	-0.0003		0.0002		-0.0002		0.0011	
DGO^{rec}	**0.0013**	**	0.0001		0.0006		0.0001	
$E1^{rec}$	**0.0015**	**	-0.0014		-0.0014		0.0024	
HS^{rec}	0.0030		0.0131		0.0002		0.0003	
IP^{rec}	0.0014		-0.0009		0.0006		0.0019	
ISM^{rec}	-0.0004		0.0011		-0.0034	***	-0.0036	
$RS2^{rec}$	**0.0021**	**	0.0007		0.0013		0.0005	
CC^{rec}	0.0010		0.0035	**	-0.0030	***	0.0062	**
CS^{rec}	-0.0004		-0.0018		0.0002		-0.0011	
$-E2^{rec}$	-0.0002		-0.0022		0.0011		0.0017	
GDP^{rec}	**0.0025**	***	**0.0104**	***	-0.0006		0.0000	
PI^{rec}	-0.0017		0.0004		0.0017	***	-0.0006	
$-BI^{rec}$	0.0028		0.0000		-0.0020		0.0006	
$CPI2^{rec}$	0.0014	**	**0.0073**	**	-0.0017	***	-0.0053	***
$PPI2^{rec}$	-0.0022		-0.0067		-0.0007		0.0028	
$E3^{rec}$	0.0002		0.0042		-0.0005		-0.0059	**
TRD^{rec}	-0.0002		0.0008		-0.0008		0.0026	
LI^{rec}	-0.0004		-0.0011		-0.0003		-0.0020	
R^2	1.28%		1.33%		6.75%		1.72%	
D.-W. Stat.	1.99		1.99		2.00		2.00	
Observations	4,288		4,288		4,288		4,288	

(description for Table 2.5)
This table contains regression results of the following equation: $R_t = c + \beta \cdot R_{t-1} + \sum_i \delta_i^{exp} \cdot D^{exp} \cdot S_{i,t} + \sum_i \delta_i^{rec} \cdot D^{rec} \cdot S_{i,t} + \epsilon_t$. R_t denotes the daily log return of the CRB index (Column 1), the GSCI (Column 2), the 10-year T-Bond (Column 3), or the S&P 500 (Column 4), respectively. The daily returns are related to an autoregressive parameter, $AR(1)$, and the standardized surprise component of several macroeconomic announcements, $S_{i,t}$. The response is conditional on the business cycle according to the NBER definition. The signs for Business Inventories (BI) and Unemployment Rate (E2) have been reversed to make their interpretation comparable to the other announcements: higher than expected inflation or real activity equals a positive sign. Robust standard errors are estimated with Newey West heteroscedasiticy and autocorrelation consistent covariance. Significance levels are indicated as follows: *** 1% significance, ** 5% significance and * 10% significance. Bold numbers indicate whether a coefficient is significantly larger (one-sided test) during economic recessions than during economic expansions on at least the 10% level or higher.

An explanation for these findings might be that the commodity price response to macroeconomic announcements is driven by two opposing factors that are interpreted differently, depending on the state of the economy. During expansions, unexpectedly high real activity announcements signal higher demand for commodities as input goods, and unexpectedly high inflation news signals higher demand for commodities as an inflation hedge. But at the same time, both types of economic news are connected with substantial fears of rising interest rates, which are negatively related to commodity prices due to rising storage costs and portfolio adjustments from commodities into bonds. As a consequence, both effects cancel out each other during expansions. In contrast, interest rates are much less of a concern during recessions and therefore the positive effects prevail.

In order to provide further evidence about the asymmetric price effect, we check whether the price response coefficients are larger during recessions than during expansions. Therefore, we conduct a one-sided Wald coefficient test for every price response coefficient. For example, we test the following hypothesis for the price response coefficients of durable goods orders (DGO) announcements: $\delta_{DGO}^{rec} > \delta_{DGO}^{exp}$. For the sake of brevity, we do not include the results of each coefficient test in our table. However, bold numbers in Table 2.5 indicate whether a coefficient is significantly larger during economic recessions than during economic expansions on at least the 10% level. Our findings suggest that six out of eight significant price response coefficients are significantly larger in recessions than in expansions.

With respect to the price response of stocks and bonds, we find that the reaction of the 10-year T-Bond (Column 3) is still consistently negative for both subsamples and for the majority of announcements. It is important to note that in comparison to high frequency event studies on the impact of macroeconomic news on bond prices (see, e.g., Balduzzi, Elton, and Green (2001) or the other chapter in this thesis), daily returns are noisier. This makes it more difficult to obtain statistically significant results. Thus, our findings regarding the significance of price response coefficients can be regarded as conservative. The stock price reaction (Column 4) is consistently negative for inflation news, while it mostly depends on the business cycle for real activity news. In line with Boyd, Hu, and Jagannathan (2005), we find a significantly negative impact of employment news on stock prices during expansions, while we find the opposite reaction to this news in recessions.[14] Comparing the overall results provides an interesting implication. Bonds and stocks seem to be mostly negatively related to the majority of announcements, while commodity futures are positively related to some of these announcements during recessions. Hence, commodity futures might be especially valuable to hedge against macroeconomic risks during recessions.

2.3.3 Robustness to alternative business cycle definitions

Since our main results hinge on the distinction between expansion and recession periods, it is critical to test the robustness of our findings by applying alternative business cycle

[14] In contrast to Boyd, Hu, and Jagannathan (2005), we include two employment figures in our analysis, nonfarm payrolls and unemployment rate. Given the significant reaction of nonfarm-payrolls, it is not surprising that we do not find a significant reaction of the unemployment rate.

definitions. Apart from the NBER classification, there is a large number of alternative definitions that has been used in previous studies to define the state of the economy. Therefore, we reexamine the state-dependent price impact using three alternative definitions of the business cycle states: the Chicago FED National Activity Index (CFNAI), consecutive changes in the same direction of the nonfarm payroll employment (E1), and the US capacity utilization compared to its long-term median value (CAPAC). For each alternative definition, we estimate the price response based on Equation (2.3) but include dummy variables indicating high or low economic activity based on the respective business cycle definition. The three alternative indices have very distinct features, which allows us to draw a more comprehensive conclusion regarding the state-dependent effects we have presented in the previous subsection.

Following Basistha and Kurov (2008), we use the CFNAI index as an alternative business cycle measure because it is commonly regarded as a "next generation" indicator.[15] Similar to the NBER business cycle definition, the CFNAI defines expansion and recession periods based on a broad assessment of the overall economic situation: it is the weighted average of 85 monthly indicators of economic activity.[16] However, both NBER and CFNAI have the disadvantage that they are not suitable to define business cycles in real time. That is, the information about the state of the economy is not available at the time of an announcement's release, but it is only available ex-post.[17] In order to apply an ex-ante available indicator, we follow Andersen, Bollerslev, Diebold, and Vega (2007) and define the start of a recession as a three month consecutive decline in nonfarm payroll employment, and the end of a recession as a three months consecutive rise in nonfarm payroll

[15] For a further discussion, see http://ksghome.harvard.edu/JStock/xri/.

[16] We obtain historical values of the CFNAI from the website of the Federal Reserve Bank of Chicago.

[17] As of 2007, the CFNAI is released with a one month delay. The last NBER trough in November 2001 was announced as late as July 17, 2003.

employment.[18] Our final indicator follows McQueen and Roley (1993), who use capacity utilization data to divide their sample into periods of high and low economic activity.[19] We use the 25-year median capacity utilization during the period from 1980 to 2005 as our break point. This alternative definition yields two almost equally large subsamples. This specification allows us to test if commoditiy futures respond to macroeconomic news only during recessions, or if they also respond during weaker states of the economy that are typically not considered recession periods. Results for the three alternative definitions are presented in Table 2.6.

Despite the differences in defining the state of the economy, the results are qualitatively similar and robust across all three alternative business cycle definitions and for both commodity futures indices. The CRB index and the GSCI hardly respond to macroeconomic news in expansions, while both indices are significantly positively related to several macroeconomic announcements in recessions. The only exception is a significantly negative GSCI response during expansion periods to surprises in the ISM purchasing manager index and in the retail sales announcement. However, this finding is consistent with the view that the interpretation of macroeconomic news depends on the state of the economy. It seems that during expansions positive ISM and retail sales news primarily signal rising interest rates, which leads to a decrease in GSCI prices. In contrast, during recessions positive ISM and retail sales news primarily signal rising economic activity and more demand for commodities, thus leading to an increase in the GSCI. The notion of a state-dependent effect is again supported by comparing the price response coefficients for recessions and expansions. Several price response coefficients are larger during recessions (again marked in bold).

---

[18]We obtain monthly data on seasonally adjusted total nonfarm employment from the Bureau of Labor Statistics.

[19]We obtain monthly data on US capacity utilization from the Federal Reserve Bank of St. Louis.

Table 2.6: State dependent price impact (alternative business cycle definition)

	CFNAI				NFP				CAPAC			
	CRB		GSCI		CRB		GSCI		CRB		GSCI	
Intercept	0.0001		0.0002		0.0001		0.0002		0.0001		0.0002	
$AR(1)$	0.0640	***	0.0023		0.0651	***	0.0001		0.0656	***	0.0037	
DGO^{exp}	0.0000		-0.0002		0.0001		0.0001		-0.0002		0.0000	
$E1^{exp}$	0.0005		0.0000		0.0005		0.0004		0.0005		-0.0005	
HS^{exp}	-0.0003		-0.0008		-0.0001		-0.0003		0.0001		0.0003	
IP^{exp}	0.0000		0.0013		0.0001		0.0010		0.0003		0.0012	
ISM^{exp}	-0.0002		-0.0018	*	-0.0001		-0.0019	**	-0.0005		-0.0018	**
$RS2^{exp}$	-0.0010		-0.0020	*	-0.0007		-0.0011		0.0005		-0.0002	
CC^{exp}	-0.0008		-0.0003		-0.0006		0.0003		-0.0006		-0.0004	
CS^{exp}	0.0005		0.0013		0.0006		0.0013		0.0002		0.0012	
$-E2^{exp}$	-0.0002		-0.0002		0.0000		-0.0008		0.0000		-0.0006	
GDP^{exp}	-0.0006		0.0008		0.0004		0.0004		0.0005		0.0014	
PI^{exp}	0.0000		-0.0009		-0.0001		-0.0006		0.0003		0.0003	
$-BI^{exp}$	-0.0001		0.0009		-0.0001		0.0007		-0.0004		0.0006	
$CPI2^{exp}$	0.0004		0.0009		0.0003		0.0004		0.0001		-0.0003	
$PPI2^{exp}$	-0.0002		-0.0011		-0.0002		-0.0010		-0.0004		-0.0010	
$E3^{exp}$	-0.0006		-0.0005		-0.0003		-0.0010		-0.0005		-0.0007	
TRD^{exp}	-0.0005		-0.0013		-0.0005		-0.0009		-0.0002		0.0007	
LI^{exp}	0.0000		0.0005		-0.0001		0.0005		-0.0002		-0.0001	
DGO^{rec}	**0.0008**	**	0.0008		**0.0012**	**	0.0010		**0.0011**	**	0.0008	
$E1^{rec}$	0.0004		-0.0003		0.0002		-0.0024		0.0007		0.0011	
HS^{rec}	0.0007		**0.0030**		0.0007		0.0046		0.0000		0.0011	
IP^{rec}	0.0003		0.0009		0.0005		0.0005		-0.0001		0.0009	
ISM^{rec}	**0.0015**	*	**0.0031**	*	**0.0025**	**	**0.0068**	***	**0.0015**	*	**0.0021**	
$RS2^{rec}$	**0.0006**		**0.0018**		0.0007		0.0018		-0.0007		0.0002	
CC^{rec}	**0.0007**		**0.0035**	***	0.0013		**0.0041**	**	0.0004		**0.0032**	***
CS^{rec}	0.0005		-0.0006		-0.0001		-0.0015		0.0012		-0.0001	
$-E2^{rec}$	**0.0010**	**	0.0004		0.0012		**0.0025**	*	0.0009		**0.0014**	
GDP^{rec}	-0.0008		**0.0026**	*	0.0007		**0.0045**	**	0.0001		0.0017	
PI^{rec}	-0.0005		0.0013		-0.0011		0.0010		-0.0010		0.0002	
$-BI^{rec}$	0.0009		0.0002		0.0011		-0.0002		**0.0010**		0.0006	
$CPI2^{rec}$	0.0008	**	0.0024	**	**0.0015**	**	**0.0051**	***	**0.0015**	**	**0.0047**	***
$PPI2^{rec}$	-0.0007		-0.0017		-0.0009		-0.0021		-0.0005		-0.0018	
$E3^{rec}$	**0.0005**		-0.0001		0.0005		0.0029		**0.0005**		0.0006	
TRD^{rec}	-0.0004		0.0003		-0.0005		-0.0005		-0.0007		-0.0017	
LI^{rec}	-0.0005		0.0000		-0.0006		-0.0005		-0.0004		0.0003	
R^2	1.25%		0.99%		1.32%		1.47%		1.32%		0.88%	
D.-W. Stat.	2.00		1.99		1.99		1.99		2.00		1.99	
Observations	4,288		4,288		4,288		4,288		4,288		4,288	

(description for Table 2.6)
This table contains regression results of the following equation: $R_t = c + \beta \cdot R_{t-1} + \sum_i \delta_i^{exp} \cdot D^{exp} \cdot S_{i,t} + \sum_i \delta_i^{rec} \cdot D^{rec} \cdot S_{i,t} + \epsilon_t$. R_t denotes the daily log return of the CRB index, or the GSCI, respectively. Business Cycles are defined according to the nonfarm payroll classification (Column 1), the CFNAI definition (Column 2) and the capacity utilization definition (Column 3). The daily returns are related to an autoregressive parameter, $AR(1)$, and the standardized surprise component of several macroeconomic announcements, $S_{i,t}$. The signs for Business Inventories (BI) and Unemployment Rate (E2) have been reversed to make their interpretation comparable to the other announcements: higher than expected inflation or real activity equals a positive sign. Bold numbers indicate whether a coefficient is significantly larger during economic recessions than during economic expansions on at least the 10% level or higher. Robust standard errors are estimated with Newey West heteroscedasiticy and autocorrelation consistent covariance. Significance levels are indicated as follows: *** 1% significance, ** 5% significance and * 10% significance. Bold numbers indicate whether a coefficient is significantly larger (one-sided test) during economic recessions than during economic expansions on at least the 10% level or higher.

2.4 Concluding remarks

Previous studies documented a link between macroeconomic news and individual commodity futures. However, correlation between different commodities is low and most investors are invested into commodity indices. This study is the first to investigate the impact of macroeconomic announcements on two broad and representative commodity futures indices. Specifically, we analyze how the equally-weighted CRB index and the production output-weighted GSCI respond to the release of seventeen US macroeconomic announcements. Thus, our analysis reveals how typical investors in this increasingly important alternative market are affected by the announcement of macroecnonomic news. Additionally, in order to account for a state-dependent response, we differentiate between expansion and recession periods based on several alternative business cycle definitions.

We document that both commodity futures indices significantly react to several macroeconomic announcements during recession periods. The reaction is most pronounced for the announcement of consumer prices, durable goods orders, the Institute for Supply Management (ISM) survey, and unemployment figures. Surprises in all of these announcements are positively related to commodity prices. In contrast, we find almost no significant price response of either commodity index during economic expansions. We attribute this asymmetric response to the state-dependent effect of real activity and inflation news. We support this view by showing that price response coefficients are larger during recessions than during expansions. The results are robust to several alternative business cycle definitions.

Our findings further provide important implications for asset management. In line with Dahlquist and Harvey (2001), the results suggest that it is important to consider the business cycle for asset allocation decisions. During recessions, the typical diversified commodity portfolio is positively related to surprises in several macroeconomic announcements, while there is no significant response during expansions. Stocks and bonds, on the other hand, are mostly negatively related to macroeconomic news during both expansions and recessions. Thus, commodity futures might be especially valuable to hedge against macroeconomic risks during weak states of the economy. Although an investor cannot anticipate the sign of the announcement surprise, and therefore does not know the direction of the commodity price movement in advance, adding commodities to a stock/bond portfolio might reduce its sensitivity to macroeconomic announcements during bad states of the economy. Accordingly, a successful risk diversification strategy based on commodities requires active portfolio management depending on the business cycle.

3 Price and liquidity effects of domestic and US economic news in the German stock market

3.1 Motivation

This chapter investigates the price and liquidity dynamics in the German stock index futures market around macroeconomic announcements. I include a large number of foreign US and domestic German economic news, including virtually all news types known to be relevant from earlier studies. The primary goal is to provide a comprehensive depiction of the price and liquidity effects in the German stock market around these important recurring events. Such analysis provides valuable information for German stock traders, as it is important to know which announcement types induce large price movements and how costly it is to trade in response to the news. The second goal is to compare the effects of domestic and foreign economic news in the German stock market. This reveals whether German stock prices are affected more by domestic economic news or news about the world's leading economy.

Germany is suited for such analysis because German stock markets, contrary to US stock markets,[1] are open when US economic news is released. In addition, almost all important German macroeconomic announcements also occur during trading hours. This allows an investigation of the immediate impact of the news announcements and it also allows to assess the duration of announcement effects. My analysis also benefits from data availability. The German stock index futures (FDAX) is highly liquid and high frequency data is readily available for a very long time period from 1991 to 2005. Data on German economic news announcements is also available for many years.

My investigation includes multiple dimensions of the price and liquidity impact of macroeconomic announcements. The analysis is carried out with 21 types of foreign US economic news and 17 types of domestic German economic news. First, I assess the news impact on high frequency prices of the German stock index futures. This reveals the magnitude, sign and speed of the price response of German stocks. Second, I compare trading patterns, including trading volume, return volatility and bid-ask spreads around the news releases with trading patterns on non-announcement days. Lastly, I investigate the news impact on effective spread components — costs of inventory control and information asymmetry — in the German stock market. The relationship between price and liquidity effects is analyzed via non-parametric rank order correlations.

I find that the announcement of domestic and foreign economic news exerts large effects on the German stock market. The price response is completed within the first five-minute interval whereas liquidity is affected for a much longer period. Trading volume, for instance remains elevated for up to 90 minutes past the announcement. Spreads widen for a few minutes before and up to 30 minutes after the announcement. The general pattern is

[1]The S&P index futures can be traded virtually around the clock, but trading is very thin outside regular trading hours which begin at 3:30 pm Central European Time (CET). All times in this dissertation are given as CET.

similar in response to domestic and US economic news. However, there seems to be a larger number of relevant US announcements and US news exerts larger price and liquidity effects on the German stock market than domestic news does. Further, I find a strong correlation between the price and liquidity effect of different announcement types. Thus, the larger the price impact of an economic news type, the more does it increase trading volume and decrease liquidity around the release.

Interestingly, although Germany is a large economy itself, US economic news affects German stock markets even more than domestic news does. There are more relevant US economic news announcements and most of these have a larger price and liquidity impact. This result highlights the leading role that the US economy has on the world's financial markets. Clearly, the state of the United States' economy also affects German stock prices. From a German investor's point of view, US macroeconomic news releases might very well be the most important scheduled news event for the German stock market. However, trading in response to these announcements might be costly as liquidity is low. Taking these findings into account helps German stock traders to better adjust trading around important events such as US or domestic economic news releases.

The remainder of this chapter is structured as follows. In section 2 I review the relevant literature, and section 3 presents the data used in this study. Section 4 investigates the price impact of US and German economic news on the German stock index futures. In section 5 I compare trading patterns on announcement days and non-announcement days. Section 6 studies the impact of economic news announcements on costs of inventory control and information asymmetry. Section 7 concludes this investigation.

3.2 Literature

This study pursues two goals: to depict the price and liquidity dynamics in the German stock market around a large number of recurring macroeconomic announcements, and to compare the effects of foreign US and domestic German economic news. Therefore it is related to prior research on macroeconomic announcement effects in German financial markets, international transmission of economic news in general, and studies on price and liquidity effects of macroeconomic news in US financial markets.

Previously, the price effects of macroeconomic news on German stock prices have been studied by Funke and Matsuda (2006) and Entorf and Steiner (2007). Entorf and Steiner (2007) study the high frequency price and volatility response of the German stock index DAX to the ZEW announcement, which is an important German business confidence indicator. Funke and Matsuda (2006) investigate how daily DAX returns are related to surprises in a large number of German and US economic news. My analysis, similar to Funke and Matsuda (2006), extends on Entorf and Steiner (2007) by including a much larger number of macroeconomic announcements. Unlike Funke and Matsuda (2006), however, my analysis is conducted on a high frequency dataset which allows a more precise estimate of the effects. Most importantly, my study additionally includes liquidity effects of the announcements, and reveals that effects on prices and liquidity are related.

In contrast to the German stock market, a lot of research is available on macroeconomic announcement effects on German bond markets. Many studies deal with the price and volatility effects of domestic and/or US economic news, including: Becker, Finnerty, and Kopecky (1995), Ahn, Cai, and Cheung (2002), Andersson, Hansen, and Sebestyén (2006), Andersen, Bollerslev, Diebold, and Vega (2007), Hess and Niessen (2008), among others. More closely related are studies on the German bond market that explicitly focus on the liquidity effects of macroeconomic announcements. Most notable are Franke and Hess (2000), Hess and Malinowska (2008) and Malinowska (2008) which, similar to my study, compare trading activity in German bond futures on announcement and non-announcement days. However, Franke and Hess (2000) pool a set of US macroeconomic news and the latter two studies only include the US employment announcement. Thus, they are not able to tell which announcements have the largest effects on financial markets in Germany. Additionally, I decompose the effects on bid-ask spreads into an inventory holding and an information asymmetry component. Such a decomposition better allows me to relate the spread changes to theoretical predictions on market microstructure effects of public news.

I apply the methodology of Fleming and Remolona (1999), Balduzzi, Elton, and Green (2001), and Green (2004) in order to investigate the announcement effects on liquidity. Fleming and Remolona (1999) and Balduzzi, Elton, and Green (2001) study the liquidity dynamics around US macroeconomic news in the US Treasury market by comparing volatility, trading volume, and quoted spreads on announcement days and non-announcement days. Similar analyses have been conducted by Frino and Hill (2001) for Australian stocks, D'Souza and Gaa (2004) for Canadian bonds, and as mentioned above, by Hess and Malinowska (2008) and Malinowska (2008) for German bonds. Green (2004) focuses on the bid-ask spread components, inventory control and information asymmetry, by estimating the Madhavan, Richardson and Roomans (1997) model for announcement and non-announcement periods. I follow the methodology of Green (2004), but instead of pooling all announcements, I distinguish the separate effects on spreads for 38 different announcement types. Thus, my analysis tells which announcements affect information asymmetry and inventory control the most. In addition, I analyze the correlation between price and liquidity effects by calculating rank order correlations. Thus, my analysis reveals that those announcements affect liquidity the most that also induce the largest price movements.

Lastly, my study is related to a number of previous studies that have investigated the effects of US announcements in international financial markets. This includes, among others, King and Wadhwani (1990), Becker, Finnerty, and Friedman (1995), Ahn, Cai, and Cheung (2002), Connolly and Wang (2003), Wongswan (2006), Albuquerque and Vega (2007), and Andersen, Bollerslev, Diebold, and Vega (2007). Some interesting differences between domestic and foreign news effects were found. First, King and Wadhwani (1990) and Albuquerque and Vega (2007) find that UK and Portuguese stock markets do not immediately respond to US macroeconomic news. The price reaction is delayed until one hour later, when the US stock market opens. Second, Albuquerque and Vega (2007) find that liquidity increases on days with a US macroeconomic announcement but decreases on days with domestic Portuguese news. However, there is also contrary evidence in the literature, see for instance Becker, Finnerty, and Friedman (1995) and Andersen, Bollerslev, Diebold, and Vega (2007). Thus, my study provides further evidence that there are no qualitative differences regarding how domestic and foreign economic news is processed.

In summary, my studies offers two important contributions to the literature. First, I offer the first comprehensive depiction of the price and liquidity dynamics in the German stock market around macroeconomic announcements. Second, I include a large number of German and US announcements. Thus, my analyses reveals which announcements induce the largest price and liquidity effects and that both effects are correlated.

3.3 Data

3.3.1 German and US economic news data

I investigate the impact of 17 types of German economic news announcements and 21 types of US economic news. These announcements are subject to very rigorous dissemination procedures in order to prevent any leaks.[2] Thus, they are very exemplary of pure public information, because all market participants learn about the news at the same time.[3] Table 3.1 presents data on the German macroeconomic announcements and Table 3.2 present the US announcements. The announcement data consist of four pieces of information: the release date and time, the announced headline figure, and the market expectation. As in the previous chapter, I standardize the surprise value of each announcement observation by the standard deviation across all observations of the respective announcement type. As before, this is done according to equation (2.1). This procedure facilitates a comparison of estimated coefficients across different news types.

The source and structure of the announcement data is the same as presented in the previous chapter. In this chapter the set of US announcement data additionally includes four announcements (IMP, ISS, IJC, FED) for which data is only available from the late 90s on. The availability of German announcement data varies but almost all German announcements are available for at least 2001 to 2005.

[2]See, for example, Fleming and Remolona (1999) for a description of the release procedure for the US employment report.

[3]One exception is the German employment report. Andersson, Hansen, and Sebestyén (2006) find that the German unemployment report has been made public before its official release time on several occasions.

Table 3.1: German economic news announcement data

Abbr.	Announcment	Obs.	Availability from	until	Source	Time (CET)	Release cycle	Stand. Surprise min	mean	max
PPI	PPI	146	08/93	12/05	SBA	8:00 am	m	-3.82	-0.02	3.40
RTS	Retails Sales	88	04/98	11/05	SBA	8:00 am	m	-4.13	-0.29	2.11
GDP	GDP	40	03/96	11/05	SBA	8:00 am	q	-2.10	0.04	2.40
WPI	Wholesale Price Index	139	03/93	08/05	SBA	8:00 am	m	-2.94	-0.07	3.16
TR1	Current Account Balance	120	11/95	12/05	SBA	8:00 am	m	-2.40	0.08	3.66
TR2	Trade Balance	123	11/95	12/05	SBA	8:00 am	m	-1.87	0.31	5.55
MSP	M3 Money Supply	119	03/93	12/05	BUB	9:30 am	m	-1.94	0.19	7.75
EM1	Unemployment Change	116	05/96	12/05	BAA	9:55 am	m	-2.82	0.06	5.18
EM2	Unemployment Rate	92	02/98	12/05	BAA	9:55 am	m	-3.57	-0.08	2.68
PMI	PMI Manufacturing	82	02/99	12/05	NTC	9:55 am	m	-2.27	-0.10	2.36
PMS	PMI Services	60	10/99	04/05	NTC	9:55 am	m	-2.76	-0.16	2.03
IFO	IFO business climate	113	08/96	12/05	IFO	10:00 am	m	-2.62	0.02	2.97
ZEW	ZEW	51	10/01	12/05	ZEW	11:00 am	m	-2.62	0.11	2.20
MFO	Manufacturing Orders	107	09/96	12/05	SBA	12:00 pm	m	-2.14	0.07	2.98
IND	Industrial Production	107	02/97	12/05	SBA	12:00 pm	m	-3.17	-0.11	2.96
ECB	ECB interest rates	67	10/00	12/05	ECB	1:45 pm	m	-5.42	0.04	2.71
CPI	CPI	57	01/01	11/05	SBA	3:00 pm	m	-2.04	0.17	2.04

This table reports the availability of German economic news announcement data. I report the headline figure, its abbreviation (Abbr.), the number of observations in our sample (Obs.), the availability of our sample, the scheduled release time (in Central European Time, CET) and the release cycle: w(eekly), m(onthly), or q(uarterly). The abbreviations for the releasing agency are: Bundesagentur für Arbeit (BAA), Bundesbank (BUB), European Central Bank (ECB), NTC Research (NTC), Statistisches Bundesamt (SBA), Zentrum für Europäische Wirtschaftsforschung (ZEW). The three right-most columns report summary statistics for the standardized surprise in the announcements, i.e. announced figure minus market expectation according to median analyst expectations, standardized by the sample standard deviation. The announcement M3 money supply (MSP) consists of German data until 1998 and data for the EURO area from 1999. The EURO area data is released by the ECB.

3.3.2 High frequency German stock index futures data

I examine the information processing by German stock traders using high frequency data on the DAX futures (FDAX) from January 1, 1991 to December 31, 2005. I use futures market data for two reasons. First, high frequency futures data is readily available for such a long sample period. Second, the DAX futures might lead the spot index because transaction costs are lower in the futures market, especially for short sales. In fact, Booth,

Table 3.2: US economic news announcement data

Abbr.	Announcment	Obs.	Availability from	until	Source	Time (CET)	Release cycle	Stand. Surprise min	mean	max
E1	Nonfarm Payrolls	180	01/91	12/05	BLS	2:30 pm	m	-2.94	-0.14	3.67
E2	Unemployment Rate	180	01/91	12/05	BLS	2:30 pm	m	-2.77	-0.27	2.77
E3	Hourly Earnings	178	01/91	12/05	BLS	2:30 pm	m	-2.38	0.03	2.85
CPI2	Consumer Price Index	180	01/91	12/05	BLS	2:30 pm	m	-1.83	0.01	3.66
PPI2	Producer Price Index	180	01/91	12/05	BLS	2:30 pm	m	-4.87	-0.14	3.25
RS2	Retail Sales	179	01/91	12/05	BC	2:30 pm	m	-3.04	-0.09	2.53
HS	Housing Starts	175	01/91	07/05	BC	2:30 pm	m	-3.20	0.16	2.91
DGO	Durable Goods Orders	179	01/91	12/05	BC	2:30 pm	m	-2.72	0.03	3.94
PI	Personal Income	179	01/91	12/05	BEA	2:30 pm	m	-3.73	0.14	5.80
BI	Business Inventories	180	01/91	12/05	BC	2:30 pm	m	-3.83	0.15	2.55
TRD	Trade Balance	180	01/91	12/05	BEA	2:30 pm	m	-4.12	-0.14	3.42
GDP	GDP advance report	59	01/91	07/05	BEA	2:30 pm	q	-1.51	0.25	2.14
IJC	Initial Jobless Claims	431	09/97	12/05	ETA	2:30 pm	w	-3.88	-0.01	4.37
IP	Industrial Production	180	01/91	12/05	FRB	3:15 pm	m	-4.01	0.03	3.28
CC	Consumer Confidence	178	07/91	12/05	CB	4:00 pm	m	-2.61	0.06	2.67
ISM	ISM Index	180	01/91	12/05	ISM	4:00 pm	m	-2.35	-0.02	3.62
LI	Leading Indicators	180	01/91	12/05	CB	4:00 pm	m	-2.64	0.10	3.63
CS	Construction Spending	180	01/91	12/05	BC	4:00 pm	m	-2.48	0.03	2.53
IMP	Import Price Index	83	08/98	09/05	BLS	4:00 pm	m	-3.93	-0.09	1.97
ISS	ISM Services	80	01/99	12/05	ISM	4:00 pm	m	-1.78	0.19	2.46
FED	FED interest rates	74	05/97	12/05	FED	8:15 pm	m	-4.34	-0.23	1.10

This table reports the availability of US economic news announcement data. The structure of this table is similar to Table 3.1. The abbreviations for the releasing agency are: Bureau of the Census (BC), Bureau of Economic Analysis (BEA), Bureau of Labor Statistics (BLS), Conference Board (CB), Employment and Training Administration (ETA), Federal Reserve Board (FRB), Federal Open Market Committee (FED), Institute for Supply Chain Management (ISM).

So, and Tse (1999) find that the DAX stock index futures contributes more to price discovery than either the DAX spot index or the DAX index option.

The FDAX is a futures contract on the leading German stock index DAX 30, which contains the 30 largest and most liquid German stocks. It is traded on the fully computerized EUREX[4], which today is the world's most liquid options and futures exchange. Liquidity is provided by traders and voluntary market makers who place limit orders into the

[4]In 1998 the German Futures Exchange (DTB) merged with the Swiss Futures Exchange (SOFFEX) to form EUREX. Before the merger the FDAX was traded on DTB which had the same market structure as the EUREX.

Table 3.3: Trading hours of DAX futures on EUREX

From	Until	First transaction	Last transaction
2/15/1991	5/31/1991	10:30 am	3:00 pm
6/1/1991	5/19/1995	9:30 am	4:00 pm
5/20/1995	9/17/1999	9:00 am	5:00 pm
9/18/1999	6/1/2001	9:00 am	5:30 pm
6/2/2001	11/18/2005	8:45 am	8:00 pm
11/19/2005	12/31/2005	8:45 am	10:00 pm

This table contains trading hours of DAX futures on the EUREX for different periods in the sample. For each sub period I report the approximate time of the first and last transaction. The exact times of first and last transactions on any given day in a sub period might deviate insubstantially by a few minutes from the times reported here.

centralized electronic order book which is open to all market participants. All orders are submitted electronically to the market via a trading terminal where orders are automatically matched, based on strict price and time priority. The minimum transaction size is one contract, and the minimum tick size is half an index point. Trading hours have steadily increased from 10:30 am to 3:00 pm in 1991 to 8:45 am to 10:00 pm in 2005, as can be seen in Table 3.3.

The dataset consists of all best bid and ask quotes, transaction prices, and transaction quantities, time-stamped to the second. My analysis is always based on the most actively traded contract, which is typically the nearby contract. There is no information in the dataset on whether a trade is initiated by a buyer or a seller. Therefore, I classify trades as buyer or seller initiated following the Lee and Ready (1991) procedure. A trade is classified as buyer (seller)-initiated if the transaction price is higher (lower) than the prevailing midpoint of best bid and ask prices (quote rule). If the transaction price is exactly at the quote midpoint, Lee and Ready (1991) apply the tick rule. The tick rule classification is based on price movements relative to previous trades. If the transaction is above (below) the previous price, then it is a buy (sell). If there is no price change it is classified as a buy (sell) if the previous tick was a buy (sell). This procedure leaves no trades unclassified.

The sample spans 15 years and trading characteristics in the DAX futures have evolved considerably during this period. Figure 3.1 reports the mean daily trading volume, mean daily number of trades, volatility of daily log returns and mean 12 pm bid-ask spreads for each year of the sample.

It is evident that during the sample, trading volume as well as the number of transactions in FDAX contracts have increased a lot. In fact, the average daily trading volume has almost multiplied twentyfold from 3,732 in 1991 to 65,566 in 2005. A similar monotonous change in one direction cannot be observed for volatility and quoted bid-ask spreads. However, we can clearly identify a time-variation in these two variables, too. For example, the standard deviation of daily close to close log returns has decreased by almost 70% between 2002 and 2005. The long-term development of quoted spreads (measured at 12 pm) seems to follow a pattern resembling the volatility development.

Besides the long term changes in FDAX trading characteristics there is also an intraday pattern of trading. In European stock markets volume and volatility typically exhibit a U-shape pattern with higher volume and volatility at the beginning of the trading day when markets open and near the end of the trading day when US markets open (see, e.g., Tse (1999) and Abhyankar, Copeland, and Wong (1999)). Such a pronounced pattern in bid-ask spreads is typically not found. Figure 3.2 plots the average intraday trading activity between 9:15 am and 4:45 pm. For each 1-minute interval in that time window, I calculate mean values of trade volume, number of transactions, volatility (measured as absolute log returns) and quoted spreads, averaged across all trading days in the sample. Time of day is given on a 24-hour clock. The plots are based on data from May 5, 1995

Figure 3.1: Long-tern development of FDAX trading

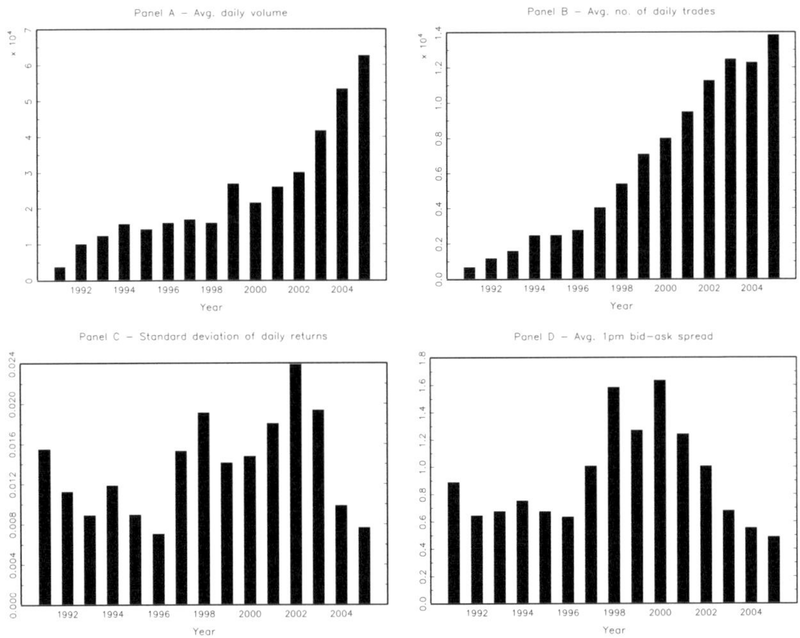

This figure depicts the long-term development of trading activity in DAX futures. For each year of the sample, I plot the average daily trading volume (Panel A), the average no. of daily transactions (Panel B), the standard deviation of daily close-to-close log returns (Panel C) and the average 1 pm bid-ask spread (Panel D).

and later, since trading hours were extended to 9 am to 5 pm on that day. In order to remove the long-term time trend, all values are standardized to correspond to 2005 values using this procedure:

$$Val_{i,y}^{adj} = Val_{i,y} \cdot \frac{Val_{2005}^{avg}}{Val_{y}^{avg}}. \tag{3.1}$$

For each intraday 1-minute interval i, I measure the trading volume, number of trades, absolute log return, and quoted bid-ask spread at the end of the interval. This value is denoted by $Val_{i,y}$, and y denotes the year that this observation occured in. Val_{y}^{avg} refers to either average daily volume, average number of daily trades, standard deviation of daily return, or average bid-ask spread at 1pm during year y, as reported in figure 3.1. As an example, assume we observe a trading volume of 20 in any given 1-minute interval in 1995. Further assume that average daily trading volume in 2005 is four times as high as in 1995. Thus, the adjusted trading volume value for this observation, $Val_{i,y}^{adj}$, is 80.

Trading in FDAX futures exhibits the typical U-shape pattern for trading volume and volatility whereas bid-ask spreads are virtually unchanged throughout the day. Trading intensity is higher at the beginning, then decreases, and sharply increases again at 3:30 pm when US stock markets open. Also, one can clearly identify additional spikes in all trading characteristics at 2:30 pm and a smaller spike at 4:00 pm. These spikes coincide with the release time of major US economic news. The effect of German economic news on FDAX trading is not as clearly visible. This might be attributable to the fact that German economic news releases are scattered throughout the day while almost all US news releases occur at 2:30 pm or 4 pm. Nevertheless, smaller spikes can be found, for example, at 10 am when the German IFO report is released and at 11 am when the German ZEW report

Figure 3.2: Intraday trading patterns

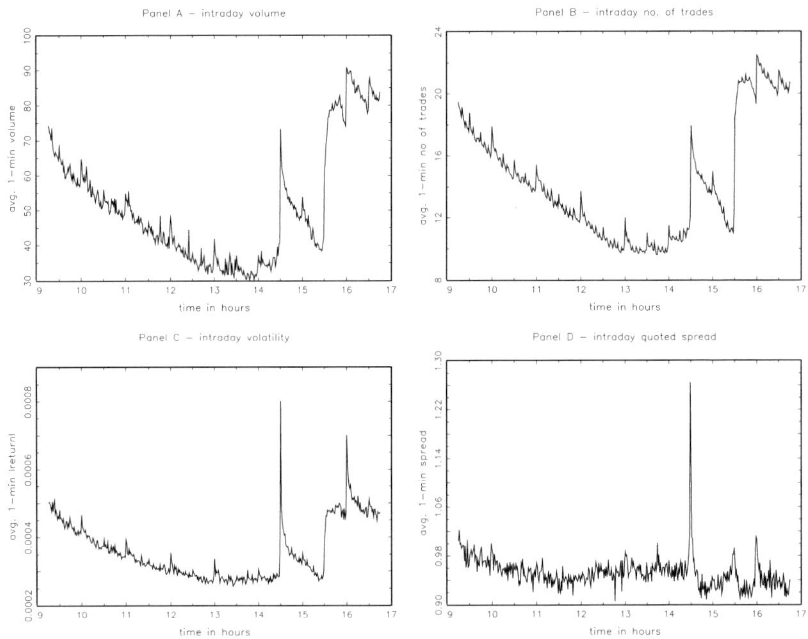

This figure plots the intraday trading activity in DAX futures. In order to remove the long-term time trend, all values are standardized to correspond to 2005 values. Time of day is given on a 24-hour clock as Central European Time. I plot average one-minute trading volume (Panel A), average one-minute number of trades (Panel B), average absolute one-minute log returns (Panel C) and average bid-ask spreads(Panel D). The sample period is May 20, 1995 to December 31, 2005. Average values are calculated as the mean across all trading days in the sample.

is released. Overall, Figure 3.2 hints at significant effects of domestic and US economic news on FDAX trading activity.

To sum up, this section has identified long-term differences in trading activity between different years in the sample, and also intraday differences between different times of the day. I take these findings into account in the empirical analysis.

3.4 Price response to economic news

As a first step I investigate the DAX futures (FDAX) price response to US economic news and compare it to the price impact of German economic news. This analysis is motivated by two objectives. First, I want to assess which economic news types are the most important for German stock prices. Second, I want to examine how quickly economic news is incorporated into FDAX prices.

I analyze the price effects by regressing five-minute FDAX log returns on the surprise value in domestic and US economic news.[5] Specifically, I construct an event window around each announcement observation consisting of two preceding five-minute intervals and twelve intervals following the announcement.[6] The price effects of economic news are estimated using the following econometric model:

$$R_t = c + \sum_{i=1}^{38} \delta_i \cdot S_{i,t} + \epsilon_t. \tag{3.2}$$

[5] Andersen, Bollerslev, Diebold, and Vega (2003, 2007) argue that five-minute returns represent a reasonable balance between confounding market microstructure effects, e.g. price discreteness, by sampling too frequently and blurring specific price reactions when sampling too infrequently.

[6] If an announcement occurs outside of FDAX trading hours, the event window comprises the last two five-minute intervals of the previous trading day and the first twelve intervals at the beginning of the following trading day.

Table 3.4: Price impact of US and German economic news

Rank	Ann	DE	US	Coeff	p-value
1	GDP		x	0.177	0.004
2	E3		x	-0.114	0.001
3	CPI2		x	-0.104	0.000
4	ZEW	x		0.104	0.001
5	CC		x	0.094	0.005
6	PPI2		x	-0.083	0.001
7	MSP	x		-0.079	0.000
8	TRD		x	0.073	0.000
9	RS2		x	0.053	0.016
10	CS		x	0.050	0.085
11	LI		x	0.047	0.005
12	-IJC		x	0.044	0.001
13	IFO	x		0.037	0.043
14	-BI		x	0.034	0.066
15	MFO	x		0.033	0.006
16	IND	x		0.031	0.066
insignif	FED		x	-0.107	0.480
insignif	GDP	x		0.082	0.424
insignif	RTS	x		-0.064	0.249
insignif	ECB	x		-0.056	0.178
insignif	PPI	x		-0.053	0.379
insignif	WPI	x		-0.039	0.593
insignif	ISM		x	0.035	0.247
insignif	DGO		x	0.033	0.301
insignif	TR2	x		0.029	0.627
insignif	IP		x	0.025	0.166
insignif	E1		x	-0.024	0.526
insignif	IMP		x	0.02	0.364
insignif	-EM2	x		-0.02	0.177
insignif	CPI	x		-0.019	0.319
insignif	PMS	x		0.011	0.698
insignif	ISS		x	-0.008	0.768
insignif	PMI	x		-0.005	0.800
insignif	TR1	x		-0.005	0.945
insignif	PI		x	0.003	0.881
insignif	HS		x	-0.002	0.862
insignif	-E2		x	0.002	0.957
insignif	EM1	x		0.002	0.864

(description for Table 3.4)

This table contains regression results of the following equation: $R_t = c + \sum_{i=1}^{38} \delta_i \cdot S_{i,t} + \epsilon_t$ where i indicates the type of economic news. R_t denotes the five-minute log return of the DAX futures. $S_{i,t}$ denotes the standardized surprise component of announcement type i in interval t, if there is an announcement in t. Otherwise $S_{i,t}$ is zero. Robust standard errors are estimated with Newey-West heteroscedasticity and autocorrelation consistent covariance matrix. The middle columns indicate whether an announcement regards US or German economic news.

R_t represents the five-minute log return on the DAX futures between the last price in the interval t-1 and the last price in the interval t. $S_{i,t}$ denotes the standardized surprise component of news type i in interval t if it is released in that interval. Otherwise, if there is no announcement of i in t, $S_{i,t}$ is zero. δ_i denotes the price response coefficient to announcement type i. Standard errors are estimated following Newey and West (1987) to allow for heteroscedasticity and autocorrelation of unknown form.

Table 3.4 reports the estimated price response coefficients δ_i for different German and US economic news types, ordered by the absolute value of δ_i. I reverse the sign of surprises in US and German unemployment rate (E2, EM2), initial jobless claims (IJC) and business inventory (BI) to make them better comparable to other announcement surprises: positive surprise values equal higher than expected economic activity. It is apparent that there are more US than German economic news announcements that are relevant for German stock prices. Also, the most important news type, hourly earnings (E3) and US GDP are both US news. Nevertheless, several types of German economic news also exert a significant price impact on German stocks. For instance, the ZEW announcement ranks fourth among all examined announcement types. The fact that US macroeconomic announcements are that important for German stock prices hints at a large degree of integration between the two economies or the two financial markets. The sign of the price response is similar for US and German news. Surprises in inflation announcements (German/European M3 money supply (MSP), US CPI, PPI, and hourly earnings (E3)) from both countries are negatively related to German stock prices. All other significant economic news types primarily tell about lagged, present or future real activity. Surprises in these news types are all positively linked with German stock prices.

Macroeconomic news, particularly news about real activity, is known to have a state-dependent effect on stock prices (see, e.g. McQueen and Roley (1993) and Boyd, Hu, and Jagannathan (2005)). Thus, I modify Equation (3.2) to allow for a state-dependent effect of US and German economic news on FDAX prices:

$$R_t = c + \sum_{i=1}^{38} \delta_i^{exp} \cdot D_t^{exp} \cdot S_{i,t} + \sum_{i=1}^{38} \delta_i^{rec} \cdot D_t^{rec} \cdot S_{i,t} + \epsilon_t \tag{3.3}$$

where D_t^{exp} (D_t^{rec}) is a dummy variable that takes the value one if the economy is in an expansion (a recession). I define recessions as beginning when there are three consecutive monthly declines in the IFO index, and ending when there are three consecutive monthly increases.[7] All other variables are defined as in equation (3.2). Estimation results are reported in Table 3.5. Different types of economic news are now ranked as follows: First by whether the price response coefficient is significant in both sub samples, then by the sum of absolute price response coefficients, δ_i^{exp} and δ_i^{rec}.

The state-dependent price response analysis reveals a few additional announcements that are relevant in either expansion and/or recession periods. Most notable is the US unemployment rate announcement, which is among the most important announcements in both expansions and recessions but insignificant in the unconditional analysis. Thus, I find the

[7]This approach follows Andersen, Bollerslev, Diebold, and Vega (2007) who use three consecutive increases (decreases) of US nonfarm payrolls to classify the US economy. However, Kunkel (2003) points out that consecutive changes in the IFO index are particularly well suited to classify business cycle states in Germany.

Table 3.5: State-dependent price impact of economic news

Ann	DE	US	Expansion			Recession		
			Coeff	p-value	Rank	Coeff	p-value	Rank
E3		x	-0.101	0.092	6	-0.133	0.002	1
CPI2		x	-0.124	0.002	3	-0.085	0.000	5
-E2		x	-0.119	0.007	4	0.087	0.089	4
ZEW	x		0.088	0.069	8	0.111	0.006	3
PPI2		x	-0.111	0.005	5	-0.061	0.055	10
TRD		x	0.088	0.000	9	0.062	0.006	9
MSP	x		-0.095	0.000	7	-0.051	0.000	13
-IJC		x	0.052	0.020	10	0.044	0.008	15
GDP		x	0.240	0.014	1	0.111	0.101	insignif
FED		x	-0.166	0.001	2	-0.078	0.718	insignif
CC		x	0.061	0.317	insignif	0.118	0.001	2
RS2		x	0.021	0.619	insignif	0.073	0.002	6
ECB	x		-0.030	0.001	11	-0.064	0.226	insignif
DGO		x	-0.022	0.705	insignif	0.063	0.069	8
LI		x	0.024	0.415	insignif	0.055	0.008	11
MFO	x		0.005	0.647	insignif	0.068	0.001	7
IFO	x		0.035	0.267	insignif	0.038	0.081	16
-BI		x	0.035	0.305	insignif	0.035	0.069	17
IND	x		0.001	0.974	insignif	0.051	0.048	12
IP		x	0.000	0.993	insignif	0.049	0.098	14
GDP	x		0.195	0.103	insignif	-0.058	0.703	insignif
TR2	x		-0.021	0.702	insignif	0.101	0.405	insignif
RTS	x		-0.022	0.826	insignif	-0.092	0.152	insignif
PPI	x		-0.004	0.956	insignif	-0.102	0.276	insignif
CS		x	0.030	0.441	insignif	0.064	0.109	insignif
WPI	x		-0.087	0.315	insignif	-0.007	0.952	insignif
ISM		x	-0.007	0.850	insignif	0.057	0.150	insignif
ISS		x	-0.032	0.267	insignif	0.027	0.611	insignif
TR1	x		0.016	0.855	insignif	-0.040	0.716	insignif
E1		x	-0.013	0.825	insignif	-0.040	0.428	insignif
IMP		x	-0.006	0.772	insignif	0.043	0.174	insignif
-EM2	x		-0.018	0.174	insignif	-0.026	0.405	insignif
CPI	x		-0.040	0.251	insignif	0.000	0.978	insignif
HS		x	-0.013	0.369	insignif	0.012	0.577	insignif
PMS	x		0.021	0.333	insignif	0.001	0.984	insignif
PI		x	-0.008	0.878	insignif	0.009	0.572	insignif
-EM1	x		0.012	0.515	insignif	-0.004	0.769	insignif
PMI	x		0.001	0.951	insignif	-0.011	0.766	insignif

(description for Table 3.5)

This table contains regression results of the following equation: $R_t = c + \sum_{i=1}^{38} \delta_i^{exp} \cdot D_t^{exp} \cdot S_{i,t} + \sum_{i=1}^{38} \delta_i^{rec} \cdot D_t^{rec} \cdot S_{i,t} + \epsilon_t$ where i indicates the type of economic news. R_t denotes the five-minute log return of the DAX futures. $S_{i,t}$ denotes the standardized surprise component of announcement type i in interval t, if there is an announcement in t. Otherwise $S_{i,t}$ is zero. D_t^{exp} (D_t^{rec}) is a dummy variable that takes the value one if the economy is in an expansion (a recession) according to the classification rule using the IFO business climate index. Robust standard errors are estimated with Newey-West heteroscedasticity and autocorrelation consistent covariance matrix. The middle columns indicate whether an announcement regards US or German economic news. Alls announcements are ranked by their price impact: First by whether the price response coefficient is significant in both sub samples, then by the sum of the absolute values of price response coefficients, δ_i^{exp} and δ_i^{rec}.

same pattern of response to this announcement in German stock prices as Boyd, Hu, and Jagannathan (2005) find in US stocks: a positive (negative) surprise during a recession leads to an increase (decrease) in stock prices, while the stock price response is reversed during expansions. Another interesting finding is that surprises in nonfarm payrolls (E1) which is often referred to as 'king of announcements' (see Andersen and Bollerslev (1998) and Hautsch and Hess (2007)) do not impact German stock prices in a significant way.[8] Rather, unemployment rate and hourly earnings seem to be the most important headline figures for German stock prices within the US employment report.

Lastly, I analyze the efficiency of the German stock price response to domestic and US economic news. Therefore I expand equation (3.2) into:

$$R_t = c + \sum_{j=-1}^{4} \sum_{i=1}^{38} \delta_i^j \cdot S_{i,t-j} + \epsilon_t. \tag{3.4}$$

This specification tests whether surprises in US and German economic news affect FDAX returns in lead and lag intervals. For example, the impact on the first five-minute interval

[8] However, the importance of the US non-farm payrolls announcement was mostly documented in bond market studies. The impact on stocks is less clear. Becker, Finnerty, and Friedman (1995), for example, find no significant impact of this announcement on US stock prices.

preceding the release corresponds to δ_i^{-1} and the impact on the fifth five-minute interval following the release corresponds to δ_i^4. Assuming efficient markets the price adjustment should be completed after five minutes the latest. Further, this regression reveals whether economic news affects German stock prices before the scheduled release time which would indicate the existence of leakages. Since it is unlikely that the speed of the price response is state-dependent, I do not account for the business cycle in equation (3.4). In Table 3.6 and 3.7 I report the price response in the 30 minutes around the release time. A significant impact on any five-minute return is denoted by ** if the p-value is less than 0.05.

The results in Table 3.6 and 3.7 suggest an almost instantaneous response to both US and German economic news. Significant FDAX price reactions before the release or after the first five-minute interval are very infrequent and show no common pattern. Thus, it can be concluded the the price response in the German stock index futures market is efficient for both domestic and foreign economic news.

I plot the average cumulative return between 30 minutes before the release until 60 minutes after the release for a German announcement (ZEW) and a US announcement (PPI) in Figure 3.3. These announcements are chosen because the ZEW is the most important German announcement and the PPI is one of the most important US announcements. I do not observe any systematic differences between the effects of positive and negative surprises. Therefore the cumulative returns around negative surprises have been reversed for calculating Figure 3.3. The figure again suggests that the German stock index futures market is very efficient and that economic news is incorporated into prices near-instantaneously. Also, it seems that there is no difference in the way US and domestic economic news is incorporated into German stock prices. After the rapid adjustment immediately after the announcement stock prices remain at the new price level on average. Thus, we can rule out a reaction of German traders that resembles that of UK and Portuguese stock

Table 3.6: Speed of price adjustment (German economic news)

Ann	$R_{t-5,t}$	$R_{t,t+5}$	$R_{t+5,t+10}$	$R_{t+10,t+15}$	$R_{t+15,t+20}$	$R_{t+20,t+25}$
ZEW	0.025	0.104 **	-0.044 **	0.017	-0.012	0.009
MSP	0.003	-0.080 **	0.017	0.008	-0.010	-0.007
IFO	-0.006	0.037 **	0.017	-0.019	-0.001	0.006
MFO	0.044	0.033 **	0.024	-0.002	0.004	0.005
IND	-0.004	0.031	0.006	-0.020	0.000	-0.012
GDP	-0.001	0.082	-0.016	0.022	0.050	0.024
RTS	-0.008	-0.064	-0.020	-0.011	0.007	-0.009
ECB	-0.086	-0.056	-0.014	0.063 **	-0.043	-0.011
PPI	0.004	-0.053	-0.007	-0.009	-0.024	0.002
WPI	0.003	-0.039	-0.007	0.009	0.018	0.014
TR2	0.011	0.028	0.004	0.016	-0.012	0.009
-EM2	-0.001	-0.020	0.030	-0.019	0.001	0.030
CPI	0.003	-0.019	-0.009	-0.009	-0.011	-0.008
PMS	-0.033	0.010	-0.044	0.001	-0.044	-0.010
PMI	-0.036	-0.006	0.002	0.024	-0.012	0.025
TR1	0.004	-0.004	-0.011	-0.013	0.003	-0.005
-EM1	-0.002	-0.001	-0.012	0.002	0.018	-0.003

This table contains regression results of the following equation: $R_t = c + \sum_{j=-1}^{4} \sum_{i=1}^{38} \delta_i^j \cdot S_{i,t-j} + \epsilon_t$ where i indicates the type of economic news. R_t denotes the five-minute log return of the DAX futures. $S_{i,t}$ denotes the standardized surprise component of announcement type i in interval t, if there is an announcement in t. Otherwise $S_{i,t}$ is zero. Robust standard errors are estimated with Newey-West heteroscedasticity and autocorrelation consistent covariance matrix. In this table, I report the impact of German economic news surprises on DAX futures log returns in the six five-minute intervals around the news release. The impact in the first five-minute interval preceding the release corresponds to $\hat{\delta_i^{-1}}$ and the impact in the fifth five-minute following the release corresponds to $\hat{\delta_i^4}$. A significant impact on any five-minute return is denoted by ** if the p-value is less than 0.05.

Table 3.7: Speed of price adjustment (US economic news)

Ann	$R_{t-5,t}$	$R_{t,t+5}$	$R_{t+5,t+10}$	$R_{t+10,t+15}$	$R_{t+15,t+20}$	$R_{t+20,t+25}$
GDP	0.001	0.177 **	0.039	0.003	0.026	0.022
E3	0.018 **	-0.114 **	0.003	-0.012	-0.004	-0.009
CPI2	-0.006	-0.104 **	-0.015	-0.004	0.000	-0.004
CC	0.001	0.094 **	0.017	0.017	-0.005	-0.006
PPI2	0.002	-0.083 **	-0.006	-0.014	-0.021	-0.013
TRD	0.004	0.073 **	-0.001	0.000	-0.008	0.004
RS2	-0.011	0.053 **	0.000	-0.010	0.006	0.009
CS	0.005	0.050 **	0.045	-0.008	0.024 **	-0.012
LI	-0.009	0.048 **	-0.006	-0.010	-0.002	0.008
-IJC	-0.004	0.044 **	0.005	-0.007	0.012	0.013
-BI	0.001	0.035	0.037	0.010	0.017	-0.012
FED	-0.046	-0.107	0.050	-0.001	-0.013	0.022
ISM	0.017	0.035	-0.010	0.001	-0.010	-0.011
DGO	0.009	0.033	0.010	0.015	-0.002	0.012
IP	0.003	0.025	0.013	-0.015	-0.030	-0.012
E1	0.020	-0.024	0.019	0.024	0.008	0.008
IMP	-0.020	0.020	-0.023	-0.028	-0.008	-0.017
ISS	0.016	-0.008	-0.016	-0.014	0.015	0.001
PI	0.012	0.003	0.061	-0.005	-0.005	-0.013
HS	0.011	-0.002	0.024 **	0.022 **	0.014	-0.009
-E2	0.010	0.002	-0.014	-0.007	-0.010	0.004

This table reports the impact of US economic news surprises on DAX futures log returns in the six five-minute intervals around the news release. The estimation procedure is as described in Table 3.6.

investors as reported by King and Wadhwani (1990) and Albuquerque and Vega (2007). They find that UK and Portuguese investors respond to US economic news not until US stock markets open one hour after the release. However, since S&P index futures can be traded around the clock, we cannot rule out that German traders are also 'free riding' on the US stock market. The question, what German traders base their price response on, will be investigated in detail in chapter 4.

Figure 3.3: Average cumulative returns around economic news release

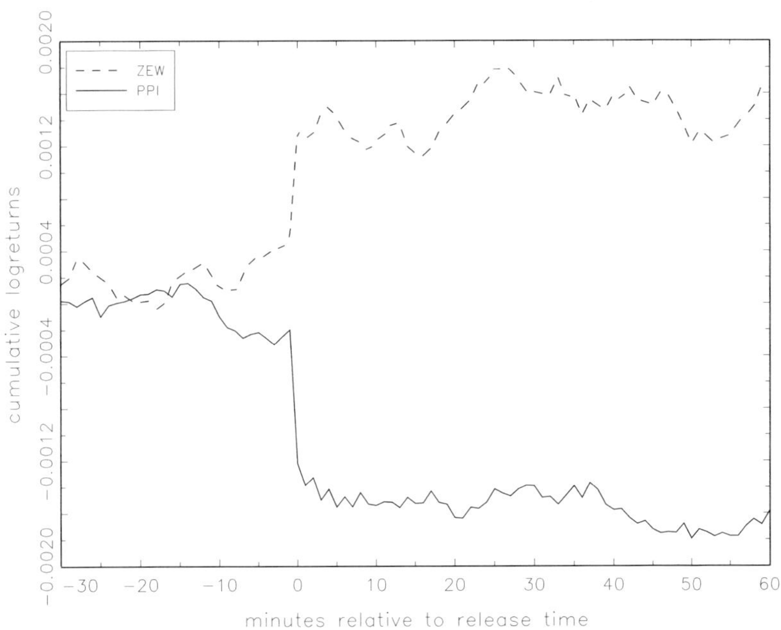

This figure depicts the average cumulative log return of the DAX futures around the release of German ZEW and US PPI news. Cumulative returns around negative surprises have been reversed. Times are given relative to the respective release time.

In summary, this analysis has shown that US economic news is relevant to German stock prices — maybe even more so than German economic news — and that the price adjustment to news from both countries occurs almost instantaneously.

3.5 Trading activity around economic news announcements

I analyze trading activity in DAX futures (FDAX) around the release of US and German economic news. Specifically, I study trading volume, return volatility and bid-ask spreads in a window from 30 minutes before until 90 minutes after the release and compare trading on announcement days with trading on non-announcement days at the same time of day. This approach allows us to assess whether trading activity in DAX futures is affected by the release of German and US economic news. Moreover, since these announcements are associated with large price movements, it is important to understand trading activity patterns in order to trade on the news.

Since I always compare the same time of day on announcement and non-announcement days, I explicitly take the intraday patterns of trading into account. As there is also pronounced long-term changes in FDAX trading activity, I additionally take time-varying non-announcement day levels into account. For each announcement observation, I compare the announcement day value with the mean value on non-announcement days at the same time of day averaged over a period of 42 trading days before until 42 trading days after that observation. This corresponds to roughly four months (two months before and two months after the announcement observation) and it is a compromise between having a large enough window that allows an unbiased comparison value and having a short enough window to take the long-term changes in FDAX trading into account.[9]

[9]Hess and Malinowska (2008) apply a similar standardization method in a comparable study on the US employment report's effect on BUND futures trading. They compare announcement day values of the most actively traded BUND contract with non-announcement day values averaged over the period that this particular contract is the most actively traded contract. Thus, their window is about 3 month in length.

I refer to the difference in announcement and non-announcement day values as the abnormal announcement effect. For example, I calculate the abnormal volume of traded FDAX contracts ($\widetilde{V}$) caused by a release of economic news i (e.g. US employment report) on trading day t in interval τ (e.g. 2:30 to 2:31 pm) as

$$\widetilde{V}_{t,\tau}^{i} = V_{t,\tau}^{i} - MEAN\left(\left\{ V_{s,\tau}^{i} \middle| \, s \in \{t-42, ..., t-1, t+1, ..., t+42\} \wedge D_{s,t}^{j,i} = 0 \right\}\right) \quad (3.5)$$

where $D_{s,t}^{j,i}$ is a dummy variable that takes the value 1 if other relevant[10] economic news $j \neq i$ is released on day s within the event window of -30 ... 90 minutes around the release time of announcement i. Thus, I exclude trading days from the comparison window that are distorted by other economic news. Of course, I cannot completely rule out the release of any other stock market relevant news in the comparison window which might bias the results. Abnormal values for volatility ($|\widetilde{R}|$), computed as the absolute log return between the last price in an interval and the last price in the preceding interval, as well as for quoted bid-ask spreads ($\widetilde{S}$), measured as the first quoted spread in an interval, are calculated likewise. I report the impact of economic news on FDAX trading during pre-announcement intervals in Table 3.8 to 3.13.

These tables report mean values for abnormal trading volume, abnormal volatility, and abnormal spreads, respectively. For each announcement i, I include all release days into the calculation of mean abnormal values that are not distorted by the concurrent[11] release of other relevant economic news. Thus, we can clearly distinguish between the effects of different types of economic news on FDAX trading. I use ** to denote that the abnor-

[10] Relevant economic news is defined as any news type for which there is any significant effects on either FDAX prices, trading or effective spread components.

[11] A concurrent release is defined as any release within one announcement's event window which begins 30 minutes before and ends 90 minutes after the announcement time.

Table 3.8: Pre-announcement effect on volume (German Announcements)

Ann	Obs	-30 to -5	-5 to -4	-4 to -3	-3 to -2	-2 to -1	-1 to 0
ZEW	44	41.9	-6.3	5.0	-8.9	-10.8	5.8
		(1.03)	(0.90)	(1.07)	(0.87)	(0.85)	(1.11)
MSP	94	-8.1	-0.1	2.1	3.2	-2.8	-8.7
		(1.01)	(0.99)	(1.02)	(1.11)	(1.03)	(0.86)
IFO	86	26.0	-6.9	-7.0	2.4	-1.8	3.3
		(1.05)	(0.94)	(0.91)	(1.11)	(1.04)	(1.08)
MFO	105	-118.5	-1.3	6.1	1.3	0.7	0.9
		(0.93)	(1.01)	(1.25)	(1.12)	(1.05)	(1.01)
IND	104	13.3	-3.6	0.8	-0.6	1.8	-2.7
		(1.00)	(0.98)	(1.05)	(1.04)	(1.04)	(1.04)
ECB	9	33.5	14.3	-2.9	1.5	-7.8	1.7
		(1.02)	(1.40)	(0.88)	(1.07)	(0.85)	(1.04)
EM2	98	8.1	-2.6	3.3	4.3	2.9	3.1
		(1.00)	(0.92)	(1.01)	(1.00)	(1.03)	(1.05)
CPI	45	-21.6	-1.3	-6.6	-0.6	-4.0	1.4
		(0.97)	(0.95)	(0.88)	(1.01)	(0.93)	(0.96)
PMS	59	2.4	-2.8	2.5	-7.3	-9.1	-5.8
		(1.02)	(0.98)	(1.07)	(0.90)	(0.87)	(0.92)
PMI	79	-87.6	-5.6	-5.1	-9.6	-7.2	-10.6
		(0.97)	(0.94)	(0.96)	(0.89)	(0.90)	(0.88)

For each announcement type and each release of this announcement, I calculate abnormal trading volume ($\widetilde{V}$) as the value on the announcement day minus the mean value at the same time of day on non-announcement days during the four months around the release day. Mean abnormal values, averaged across all observations of a certain announcement type, are reported in this table for the 30 minutes before the news release, split into six sub periods. For example, -30 to -5 denotes the period beginning 30:00 minutes before each release and ending just before 5:00 minutes prior to the release. I use ** to denote that these means are significantly different from zero with a p-value less than 0.05 based on a two-sided t-test. Further, I report the mean ratio between the values on announcement days and non-announcement days in parentheses. I exclude all announcement observations that are 'distorted' by the concurrent release (i.e. within an event window between -30 to $+90$ minute relative to the release time) of another announcement.

Table 3.9: Pre-announcement effect on volume (US Announcements)

Ann	Obs	-30 to -5	-5 to -4	-4 to -3	-3 to -2	-2 to -1	-1 to 0
GDP	47	-40.6	-2.9	-0.7	0.2	0.9	-7.4
		(0.92)	(0.98)	(1.10)	(0.98)	(1.20)	(0.74)
E3	161	-111.8	0.4	3.6	4.5	7.5 **	16.1 **
		(0.84)	(0.94)	(1.08)	(1.12)	(1.22)	(1.30)
CPI2	58	-23.0	-4.8	1.7	-3.2	-2.4	-1.9
		(0.97)	(0.97)	(1.06)	(0.81)	(0.88)	(1.02)
CC	156	-99.6	-10.7	-13.5	-12.7	-16.6	-12.0
		(0.96)	(0.91)	(0.82)	(0.86)	(0.80)	(0.86)
PPI2	67	13.6	-7.1	-2.1	-4.4	-0.8	1.0
		(0.98)	(0.75)	(0.91)	(0.87)	(0.99)	(1.04)
TRD	102	19.8	-3.3	0.5	-2.4	4.0	-3.4
		(1.11)	(0.96)	(1.04)	(0.96)	(1.23)	(0.82)
RS2	56	-83.9	-6.2	-4.9	-1.0	-5.5	1.8
		(0.82)	(0.82)	(0.82)	(0.89)	(0.84)	(1.10)
CS	112	-242.2	-14.7	-12.7	-24.0	-19.2	-22.7
		(0.87)	(0.81)	(0.85)	(0.72)	(0.76)	(0.74)
LI	159	-15.9	-1.6	-6.2	-11.4	-6.2	-13.4
		(0.94)	(0.94)	(0.91)	(0.77)	(0.82)	(0.89)
IJC	268	161.9 **	8.7	2.2	2.8	2.7	2.3
		(1.18)	(1.22)	(1.05)	(1.08)	(1.07)	(1.07)
BI	80	29.1	-1.5	-1.5	0.2	-3.3	1.4
		(1.00)	(0.95)	(0.97)	(1.02)	(0.94)	(1.09)
DGO	140	97.7	-5.3	-0.1	0.8	-3.5	0.4
		(1.07)	(0.85)	(1.01)	(0.91)	(0.94)	(1.07)
IP	129	123.3	-1.3	0.4	-1.0	-3.7	-3.3
		(1.06)	(0.94)	(1.01)	(0.95)	(0.86)	(0.98)
IMP	76	195.0 **	11.0 **	10.0 **	13.4 **	10.0 **	12.1 **
		(1.10)	(1.13)	(1.13)	(1.15)	(1.09)	(1.17)
ISS	51	9.2	-8.0	-10.6	-17.9	-32.6	-25.9
		(1.02)	(1.00)	(0.93)	(0.90)	(0.73)	(0.77)
PI	126	-133.0	-9.8	-8.7	-8.0	2.9	-7.3
		(0.86)	(0.76)	(0.75)	(0.80)	(1.08)	(0.81)
HS	97	22.4	-3.4	-4.3	-1.3	-4.9	12.4
		(1.02)	(0.93)	(0.88)	(0.96)	(0.82)	(1.41)

This table reports the mean abnormal trading volume ($\widetilde{V}$) during the 30 minutes before US macroeconomic announcements. ** denotes that these values are significantly different from zero with a p-value less than 0.05. The mean ratio of announcement and non-announcement day values is given in parentheses. The estimation method is as described in Table 3.8.

Table 3.10: Pre-announcement effect on volatility (German Announcements)

Ann	Obs	-30 to -5	-5 to -4	-4 to -3	-3 to -2	-2 to -1	-1 to 0
ZEW	44	-0.028	-0.010	0.008	-0.003	-0.006	0.000
		(0.90)	(0.81)	(1.26)	(0.90)	(0.84)	(1.03)
MSP	94	0.036	-0.004	0.002	-0.007	-0.003	-0.003
		(1.24)	(0.88)	(1.08)	(1.01)	(1.03)	(0.94)
IFO	86	-0.025	-0.004	0.000	0.000	-0.010	-0.003
		(0.89)	(0.88)	(0.96)	(0.97)	(0.88)	(0.97)
MFO	105	-0.011	-0.002	0.002	-0.001	0.002	0.006
		(0.92)	(0.89)	(1.03)	(1.01)	(1.01)	(1.24)
IND	104	-0.009	-0.003	0.008	0.009	-0.001	-0.001
		(0.90)	(0.88)	(1.18)	(1.23)	(1.01)	(0.98)
ECB	9	-0.031	0.008	0.016	0.016	0.010	0.050
		(0.82)	(1.13)	(1.38)	(1.32)	(1.32)	(2.80)
EM2	98	0.007	-0.004	0.002	-0.004	0.002	-0.004
		(1.01)	(0.88)	(1.07)	(1.02)	(1.11)	(0.96)
CPI	45	-0.001	0.002	-0.005	0.012	0.019	0.003
		(0.95)	(1.03)	(0.88)	(1.21)	(1.38)	(1.02)
PMS	59	-0.037	0.005	-0.007	-0.003	0.003	0.012
		(0.87)	(1.09)	(0.93)	(0.92)	(0.99)	(1.14)
PMI	79	-0.002	0.001	0.005	-0.002	0.001	-0.007
		(1.07)	(1.05)	(1.04)	(0.91)	(1.09)	(0.92)

This table reports the mean abnormal volatility ($\widetilde{|R|}$) during the 30 minutes before German macroeconomic announcements. ** denotes that these values are significantly different from zero with a p-value less than 0.05. The mean ratio of announcement and non-announcement day values is given in parentheses. The estimation method is as described in Table 3.8.

mal values are significantly different from zero with a p-value less than 0.05 based on a two-sided t-test. Further, I report the average ratio between the respective values on announcement days and on non-announcement days during the 84-days comparison window. These ratios are reported in parentheses. For example, Table 3.9 reports a ratio of 1.30 for trading volume in the last minute leading up to a US employment report announcement. This denotes that trading volume on announcement days is on average 1.30 times as high as on non-announcement days during the comparison window at the same time of day.

Table 3.11: Pre-announcement effect on volatility (US Announcements)

Ann	Obs	-30 to -5	-5 to -4	-4 to -3	-3 to -2	-2 to -1	-1 to 0
GDP	47	-0.027	-0.001	-0.005	0.003	0.001	0.004
		(0.81)	(1.08)	(0.87)	(0.96)	(1.16)	(1.26)
E3	161	-0.019	0.003	0.004	0.003	0.009 **	0.037 **
		(0.83)	(1.06)	(1.19)	(1.28)	(1.40)	(2.60)
CPI2	58	-0.010	-0.005	-0.003	-0.009	0.001	0.011 **
		(0.95)	(0.92)	(0.93)	(0.64)	(1.06)	(1.63)
CC	156	-0.036	-0.003	-0.007	-0.007	-0.010	-0.009
		(0.89)	(0.95)	(0.87)	(0.85)	(0.81)	(0.81)
PPI2	67	0.006	-0.004	0.001	-0.001	0.001	0.015 **
		(1.03)	(0.75)	(0.91)	(0.92)	(1.00)	(1.54)
TRD	102	-0.008	0.000	0.000	-0.005	-0.002	-0.003
		(0.97)	(1.02)	(1.03)	(0.87)	(1.03)	(0.92)
RS2	56	-0.022	-0.006	0.000	-0.012	-0.005	0.002
		(0.86)	(0.87)	(1.00)	(0.67)	(0.85)	(1.11)
CS	112	-0.040	-0.006	-0.008	-0.012	-0.007	-0.010
		(0.83)	(0.92)	(0.89)	(0.85)	(0.86)	(0.82)
LI	159	-0.036	-0.006	-0.002	-0.007	-0.009	-0.007
		(0.83)	(0.89)	(0.91)	(0.75)	(0.79)	(0.86)
IJC	268	0.036 **	0.002	0.002	0.004 **	0.004	0.007 **
		(1.21)	(1.10)	(1.17)	(1.21)	(1.17)	(1.29)
BI	80	0.022	0.002	-0.001	0.006	-0.003	0.007
		(1.16)	(1.06)	(1.00)	(1.17)	(0.90)	(1.19)
DGO	140	-0.013	0.001	-0.002	-0.001	0.000	0.004
		(0.91)	(0.97)	(0.98)	(0.97)	(1.14)	(1.14)
IP	129	-0.007	-0.003	-0.003	-0.004	-0.004	0.001
		(0.99)	(0.89)	(0.91)	(0.80)	(0.84)	(1.08)
IMP	76	0.035	0.001	0.004	0.010	-0.004	-0.006
		(1.16)	(1.06)	(1.10)	(1.23)	(0.94)	(0.91)
ISS	51	-0.004	0.001	-0.006	-0.013	-0.011	-0.013
		(0.99)	(0.95)	(0.93)	(0.73)	(0.78)	(0.78)
PI	126	-0.020	0.003	-0.003	-0.005	-0.002	0.000
		(0.85)	(1.07)	(0.80)	(0.82)	(0.93)	(1.04)
HS	97	-0.007	-0.004	0.001	-0.002	-0.004	0.001
		(0.99)	(0.86)	(1.04)	(0.82)	(0.82)	(1.03)

This table reports the mean abnormal volatility ($\widetilde{|R|}$) during the 30 minutes before US macroeconomic announcements. ** denotes that these values are significantly different from zero with a p-value less than 0.05. The mean ratio of announcement and non-announcement day values is given in parentheses. The estimation method is as described in Table 3.8.

Table 3.12: Pre-announcement effect on spread (German Announcements)

Ann	Obs	-30 to -5	-5 to -4	-4 to -3	-3 to -2	-2 to -1	-1 to 0
ZEW	44	-0.08	0.05	-0.05	-0.08	-0.01	0.10
		(0.93)	(1.09)	(0.93)	(0.88)	(1.01)	(1.20)
MSP	94	0.00	-0.05	0.02	-0.05	0.01	0.02
		(1.01)	(0.95)	(1.00)	(0.97)	(1.00)	(1.07)
IFO	86	0.02	-0.09	0.12	0.03	0.00	0.12
		(0.97)	(0.95)	(1.09)	(1.04)	(1.05)	(1.15)
MFO	105	-0.01	-0.08	0.03	0.03	-0.10	0.05
		(0.98)	(0.93)	(1.05)	(1.03)	(0.94)	(1.08)
IND	104	-0.01	0.05	0.02	0.08	0.01	0.20 **
		(1.00)	(1.02)	(1.00)	(1.06)	(1.04)	(1.21)
ECB	9	0.08	-0.28	0.07	0.16	0.31	0.51
		(1.10)	(0.77)	(1.08)	(1.10)	(1.23)	(1.43)
EM2	98	-0.02	-0.02	-0.08	-0.03	0.04	0.05
		(0.99)	(1.00)	(0.97)	(0.95)	(1.02)	(1.05)
CPI	45	0.02	0.12 **	0.00	0.03	0.05	0.11
		(1.05)	(1.17)	(1.03)	(1.05)	(1.08)	(1.14)
PMS	59	-0.03	-0.02	0.01	0.11	0.13	0.00
		(0.96)	(0.94)	(1.00)	(1.07)	(1.07)	(0.96)
PMI	79	0.14	0.07	0.18 **	0.05	-0.01	0.04
		(1.04)	(1.10)	(1.18)	(1.03)	(1.03)	(1.04)

This table reports the mean abnormal spread ($|\widetilde{S}|$) during the 30 minutes before German macroeconomic announcements. ** denotes that these values are significantly different from zero with a p-value less than 0.05. The mean ratio of announcement and non-announcement day values is given in parentheses. The estimation method is as described in Table 3.8.

Trading activity before German announcements, reported in Tables 3.8, 3.10, and 3.12, is not different from non-announcement day values at the same time of day. The sole exception is an increase in bid-ask spreads in the last minute before a German industrial production announcement. The pre-announcement volume effects of US news are also minor, see Table 3.9. A few US announcements seem to induce an increase in volatility in the last minute before the news release, see Table 3.11. This might reflect the uncertainty that investors face before the announcement. However, for a large number of US news, I

Table 3.13: Pre-announcement effect on spread (US Announcements)

Ann	Obs	-30 to -5	-5 to -4	-4 to -3	-3 to -2	-2 to -1	-1 to 0
GDP	47	-0.04	-0.01	0.08	-0.01	0.18	0.42 **
		(0.97)	(1.00)	(1.08)	(1.01)	(1.18)	(1.42)
E3	161	0.00	0.05	0.11 **	0.21 **	0.34 **	1.44 **
		(0.97)	(1.04)	(1.10)	(1.22)	(1.31)	(2.41)
CPI2	58	-0.10	0.00	0.01	0.09	0.13	0.45 **
		(0.92)	(0.99)	(1.01)	(1.07)	(1.12)	(1.48)
CC	156	-0.09	0.11	-0.01	0.02	0.08	0.26 **
		(0.91)	(1.12)	(0.98)	(1.03)	(1.10)	(1.21)
PPI2	67	0.00	0.04	0.06	-0.01	0.13	0.49 **
		(0.99)	(0.99)	(1.07)	(0.97)	(1.13)	(1.54)
TRD	102	0.05	-0.02	-0.01	0.03	0.06	0.08
		(1.04)	(0.96)	(0.95)	(1.01)	(1.07)	(1.10)
RS2	56	-0.01	0.01	-0.05	0.07	0.07	0.45 **
		(0.98)	(1.02)	(0.96)	(1.06)	(1.09)	(1.43)
CS	112	-0.03	0.05	0.07	0.15 **	0.16 **	0.26 **
		(0.99)	(1.06)	(1.08)	(1.13)	(1.19)	(1.29)
LI	159	-0.12	-0.06	-0.02	-0.02	0.01	0.13 **
		(0.92)	(0.92)	(0.99)	(0.98)	(1.03)	(1.13)
IJC	268	0.01	0.05	0.10 **	0.13 **	0.10 **	0.32 **
		(1.00)	(1.04)	(1.10)	(1.10)	(1.08)	(1.34)
BI	80	0.03	0.04	0.01	0.07	0.06	-0.04
		(1.04)	(1.05)	(1.03)	(1.09)	(1.07)	(0.96)
DGO	140	0.04	0.04	0.00	0.04	0.04	0.29 **
		(1.05)	(1.03)	(1.03)	(1.05)	(1.04)	(1.29)
IP	129	-0.03	0.01	-0.10	0.01	-0.05	0.21 **
		(0.98)	(1.04)	(0.93)	(1.01)	(0.96)	(1.27)
IMP	76	-0.12	0.08	-0.03	0.03	-0.03	0.07
		(0.94)	(1.01)	(0.97)	(1.04)	(0.95)	(1.05)
ISS	51	0.04	-0.06	0.05	0.06	0.08	0.34 **
		(1.06)	(0.96)	(1.10)	(1.05)	(1.13)	(1.35)
PI	126	-0.02	0.05	0.02	0.10 **	0.08	0.10
		(0.97)	(1.04)	(1.02)	(1.07)	(1.08)	(1.12)
HS	97	-0.04	0.02	-0.08	-0.03	0.08	0.16 **
		(0.99)	(1.02)	(0.91)	(1.00)	(1.05)	(1.15)

This table reports the mean abnormal spread ($\widetilde{|S|}$) during the 30 minutes before US macroeconomic announcements. ** denotes that these values are significantly different from zero with a p-value less than 0.05. The mean ratio of announcement and non-announcement day values is given in parentheses. The estimation method is as described in Table 3.8.

find very significant effects on quoted spreads in the last minute before the announcement, see Table 3.13. For example, quoted spreads in the last minute before a US employment report release are higher than usual by 1.44 points on average, which is on average 2.41 times as large as on non-announcement days. My findings are consistent with Fleming and Remolona (1999) and Balduzzi, Elton, and Green (2001) investigations on the US Treasury market. They find the same patterns, increased volatility and wider spreads immediately before the announcement. Fleming and Remolona (1999) relate the widening of the bid-ask spread to the reluctance of market participants to trade prior to the news release given the increased price risk that they face with the announcement.

I now turn to the effects of economic news on trading activity after the release, for which I report results in Tables 3.14 to 3.19. I find a large, instantaneous impact of many US economic news types on FDAX trading in the first post-announcement minute. Volume is as high as four times the normal value of non-announcement days, see Table 3.15. Return volatility increases to up to seven times its normal value, see Table 3.17. The bid-ask spread is comparable to the first minute leading up to the release and significantly larger than on non-announcement days, see Table 3.19. In the following minutes all three variables decrease virtually monotonically. For most US economic news, the widening of bid-ask spreads becomes insignificant as quickly as in the second minute after the announcement. One exception is the US employment report which widens the spread for up to thirty minutes.[12] The effect on volatility mostly lasts between five and thirty minutes and volume is heightened for up to ninety minutes after the news releases. The post-announcement effects of German economic news are much smaller and more short-lived. The spread reaction is only found in response to the ECB and money supply (MSP)

[12] I also find significant abnormal effects on spreads for the Business Inventory (BI) announcement 60 to 90 minutes after the news release, and for the Personal Income (PI) announcement 5 to 30 minutes past the release. However, since these announcements are generally considered less important these findings might be attributable to chance.

Table 3.14: Post-announcement effect on volume (German Announcements)

Ann	Obs	0 to 1	1 to 2	2 to 3	3 to 4	4 to 5	5 to 30	30 to 60	60 to 90
ZEW	44	55.4 **	64.1 **	35.1 **	36.5 **	29.9 **	363.7 **	142.6	-4.6
		(1.60)	(1.76)	(1.39)	(1.47)	(1.43)	(1.20)	(1.09)	(1.02)
MSP	94	15.8 **	20.5 **	22.1 **	22.2 **	16.8 **	163.9 **	23.4	-12.2
		(1.41)	(1.53)	(1.55)	(1.61)	(1.43)	(1.18)	(1.02)	(0.96)
IFO	86	31.7 **	20.9 **	17.8 **	19.0 **	18.4 **	180.7 **	124.1 **	137.1
		(1.44)	(1.30)	(1.30)	(1.34)	(1.32)	(1.12)	(1.07)	(1.07)
MFO	105	18.8 **	5.9	9.9 **	6.4	-0.2	72.3	11.2	-83.1
		(1.32)	(1.10)	(1.17)	(1.14)	(1.03)	(1.09)	(1.02)	(0.94)
IND	104	16.7 **	9.9 **	2.2	6.2	-4.4	-69.0	98.2	-78.2
		(1.31)	(1.22)	(1.10)	(1.17)	(0.93)	(0.95)	(1.10)	(0.93)
ECB	9	24.5	43.0 **	19.8	52.4 **	22.4	534.5 **	618.2	187.5
		(1.54)	(2.14)	(1.49)	(2.47)	(1.61)	(1.47)	(1.42)	(1.18)
EM2	98	0.5	1.3	-3.0	-5.2	-0.4	84.3	34.9	-10.1
		(1.06)	(1.08)	(0.97)	(0.96)	(1.07)	(1.07)	(1.03)	(0.99)
CPI	45	3.4	3.0	2.8	1.4	2.6	-37.6	-96.2	-6.4
		(1.01)	(1.06)	(0.98)	(1.00)	(0.98)	(0.98)	(0.99)	(1.01)
PMS	59	-4.6	-3.6	-2.6	-3.8	0.2	72.7	53.1	-25.2
		(0.92)	(0.94)	(0.98)	(0.97)	(1.02)	(1.06)	(1.02)	(0.97)
PMI	79	-6.4	1.9	-5.9	-10.2	-6.0	-92.9	-136.8	-121.0
		(0.95)	(1.07)	(0.94)	(0.90)	(0.93)	(0.96)	(0.94)	(0.94)

For each announcement type and each release of this announcement, I calculate abnormal trading volume ($\widetilde{V}$) as the value on the announcement day minus the mean value at the same time of day on non-announcement days during the four months around the release day. Mean abnormal values, averaged across all observations of a certain announcement type, are reported in this table for the 90 minutes following the news release, split into eight sub periods. For example, 5 to 30 denotes the period beginning 5:00 minutes after each release and ending just before 30:00 minutes after the release. I use ** to denote that these means are significantly different from zero with a p-value less than 0.05 based on a two-sided t-test. Further, I report the mean ratio between the values on announcement days and non-announcement days in parentheses. I exclude all announcement observations that are 'distorted' by the concurrent release (i.e. within an event window between -30 to $+90$ minute relative to the release time) of another announcement.

Table 3.15: Post-announcement effect on volume (US Announcements)

Ann	Obs	0 to 1	1 to 2	2 to 3	3 to 4	4 to 5	5 to 30	30 to 60	60 to 90
GDP	47	70.1 **	48.6 **	45.0 **	58.2 **	36.6 **	573.9 **	310.5 **	92.5
		(2.93)	(2.19)	(2.26)	(2.65)	(2.16)	(1.68)	(1.28)	(1.07)
E3	161	97.0 **	70.0 **	71.7 **	70.0 **	61.4 **	1090.5 **	574.3 **	356.2 **
		(3.67)	(2.75)	(2.84)	(2.81)	(2.46)	(2.02)	(1.45)	(1.15)
CPI2	58	68.9 **	56.9 **	51.4 **	43.8 **	38.4 **	544.4 **	298.9 **	362.0 **
		(3.35)	(2.78)	(2.49)	(2.14)	(2.08)	(1.63)	(1.22)	(1.14)
CC	156	30.7 **	19.0 **	14.3 **	15.2 **	13.3 **	200.7 **	150.1 **	40.3
		(1.37)	(1.20)	(1.13)	(1.16)	(1.12)	(1.08)	(1.07)	(1.04)
PPI2	67	101.5 **	66.4 **	58.2 **	56.7 **	42.6 **	614.2 **	350.8 **	319.6 **
		(4.00)	(2.84)	(2.59)	(2.68)	(2.28)	(1.75)	(1.38)	(1.20)
TRD	102	29.6 **	22.9 **	20.6 **	24.4 **	16.3 **	260.7 **	43.2	141.2 **
		(1.76)	(1.55)	(1.53)	(1.61)	(1.59)	(1.26)	(1.04)	(1.05)
RS2	56	75.5 **	40.7 **	30.8 **	27.6 **	21.5 **	354.9 **	271.1 **	211.3 **
		(3.03)	(2.02)	(1.91)	(1.64)	(1.45)	(1.35)	(1.29)	(1.10)
CS	112	-9.0	21.7 **	14.3 **	13.3 **	19.7 **	303.4 **	128.4 **	83.5
		(0.85)	(1.28)	(1.20)	(1.12)	(1.20)	(1.11)	(1.03)	(0.99)
LI	159	4.0	5.4	5.4	2.1	5.2	170.3 **	67.1	1.7
		(1.08)	(1.10)	(1.05)	(0.97)	(1.03)	(1.06)	(1.04)	(1.00)
IJC	268	36.6 **	39.8 **	30.6 **	29.0 **	22.6 **	386.8 **	209.0 **	204.7 **
		(1.59)	(1.84)	(1.56)	(1.56)	(1.48)	(1.31)	(1.15)	(1.08)
BI	80	3.9	4.6	7.9	3.8	7.1	50.8	69.6	-29.3
		(1.00)	(1.17)	(1.25)	(1.11)	(1.23)	(1.02)	(1.04)	(0.87)
DGO	140	58.0 **	40.8 **	33.3 **	30.2 **	24.4 **	239.1 **	51.8	44.0
		(2.50)	(2.04)	(2.07)	(1.72)	(1.66)	(1.24)	(1.03)	(1.04)
IP	129	41.4 **	30.6 **	23.7 **	22.3 **	15.9 **	252.5 **	119.1 **	118.0 **
		(2.01)	(1.80)	(1.55)	(1.56)	(1.51)	(1.19)	(1.07)	(1.03)
IMP	76	5.3	1.8	3.0	0.0	-0.4	114.6	107.9	131.4
		(1.07)	(1.02)	(1.07)	(1.01)	(0.99)	(1.06)	(1.05)	(1.02)
ISS	51	-9.1	18.6 **	17.7 **	31.9 **	17.2 **	512.1 **	324.0 **	46.0
		(0.92)	(1.13)	(1.15)	(1.24)	(1.10)	(1.14)	(1.09)	(1.02)
PI	126	7.7	11.8 **	3.2	9.4 **	-2.7	-27.5	-83.1	-171.5
		(1.10)	(1.26)	(1.04)	(1.17)	(0.94)	(0.97)	(0.94)	(0.90)
HS	97	22.3 **	16.5 **	9.0 **	12.7 **	7.2 **	167.5 **	49.4	182.5 **
		(1.49)	(1.36)	(1.20)	(1.31)	(1.14)	(1.21)	(1.06)	(1.07)

This table reports the mean abnormal trading volume ($\widetilde{V}$) during the 90 minutes following US macroeconomic announcements. ** denotes that these values are significantly different from zero with a p-value less than 0.05. The mean ratio of announcement and non-announcement day values is given in parentheses. The estimation method is as described in Table 3.14.

Table 3.16: Post-announcement effect on volatility (German Announcements)

Ann	Obs	0 to 1	1 to 2	2 to 3	3 to 4	4 to 5	5 to 30	30 to 60	60 to 90
ZEW	44	0.046 **	0.007	0.019 **	0.010	0.007	-0.026	-0.009	-0.032
		(2.34)	(1.43)	(1.66)	(1.42)	(1.26)	(0.99)	(1.02)	(0.90)
MSP	94	0.021 **	0.012 **	0.013 **	0.017 **	0.015 **	0.044	-0.014	-0.005
		(1.74)	(1.49)	(1.44)	(1.62)	(1.56)	(1.20)	(0.94)	(1.00)
IFO	86	0.044 **	0.027 **	0.025 **	0.020 **	0.017 **	0.005	-0.003	0.043
		(1.70)	(1.63)	(1.51)	(1.49)	(1.40)	(1.05)	(1.00)	(1.15)
MFO	105	0.023 **	0.005	0.013 **	0.001	0.008 **	0.025	-0.001	-0.020
		(1.53)	(1.21)	(1.26)	(1.06)	(1.24)	(1.10)	(0.96)	(0.86)
IND	104	0.027 **	0.015 **	0.010 **	0.005	0.003	-0.006	0.034	-0.021
		(1.56)	(1.25)	(1.20)	(1.12)	(1.00)	(1.01)	(1.18)	(0.91)
ECB	9	0.165	0.075	0.070	0.085	0.003	0.043	0.128	0.100
		(4.84)	(2.76)	(2.36)	(2.76)	(1.28)	(1.44)	(1.64)	(1.63)
EM2	98	-0.004	-0.002	-0.003	0.003	0.001	0.005	-0.016	0.007
		(0.96)	(0.97)	(1.01)	(1.06)	(1.03)	(1.13)	(1.01)	(1.04)
CPI	45	-0.001	-0.002	0.004	0.003	0.006	0.047	0.023	-0.003
		(1.02)	(0.97)	(1.06)	(1.07)	(1.08)	(1.24)	(1.06)	(0.97)
PMS	59	0.004	-0.004	0.007	0.006	-0.005	0.053	0.020	-0.026
		(1.09)	(0.91)	(1.04)	(1.17)	(0.92)	(1.26)	(1.09)	(0.89)
PMI	79	0.004	0.007	0.001	-0.005	0.006	-0.017	-0.011	-0.001
		(1.13)	(1.18)	(1.00)	(0.89)	(1.22)	(0.99)	(0.92)	(0.95)

This table reports the mean abnormal volatility ($\widetilde{|R|}$) during the 90 minutes following German macroeconomic announcements. ** denotes that these values are significantly different from zero with a p-value less than 0.05. The mean ratio of announcement and non-announcement day values is given in parentheses. The estimation method is as described in Table 3.14.

announcements, see Table 3.18. For return volatility (Table 3.16) and volume (Table 3.14), I find significant effects following the ZEW, MSP, IFO, MFO, and IND announcements. These announcement have been identified in the previous section as the only price-relevant German economic news. The increase in volatility lasts for little more than five minutes and the effect on trading volume disappears after approximately 30 minutes.

My results are mostly similar to Fleming and Remolona (1999) and Balduzzi, Elton, and Green (2001). All three analyzed variables increase following the announcement and then gradually decrease. These results are consistent with popular public information processing models such as Harris and Raviv (1993) and Kim and Verrecchia (1994). In

Table 3.17: Post-announcement effect on volatility (US Announcements)

Ann	Obs	0 to 1	1 to 2	2 to 3	3 to 4	4 to 5	5 to 30	30 to 60	60 to 90
GDP	47	0.163 **	0.048 **	0.039 **	0.021 **	0.027 **	0.049	0.033	0.010
		(5.23)	(2.70)	(2.36)	(1.76)	(1.96)	(1.29)	(1.24)	(1.07)
E3	161	0.204 **	0.073 **	0.063 **	0.050 **	0.055 **	0.125 **	0.049 **	0.065 **
		(6.83)	(3.45)	(3.04)	(2.72)	(2.80)	(1.93)	(1.43)	(1.30)
CPI2	58	0.073 **	0.053 **	0.030 **	0.019 **	0.029 **	0.040	-0.001	0.008
		(3.68)	(3.45)	(2.28)	(1.79)	(2.05)	(1.38)	(1.16)	(1.19)
CC	156	0.088 **	0.022 **	0.010	0.016 **	0.008	0.055	0.024	-0.023
		(2.18)	(1.35)	(1.16)	(1.25)	(1.08)	(1.15)	(1.10)	(0.87)
PPI2	67	0.104 **	0.032 **	0.027 **	0.029 **	0.015 **	0.044 **	0.021	0.028
		(4.24)	(2.16)	(2.15)	(2.13)	(1.52)	(1.32)	(1.22)	(1.19)
TRD	102	0.014 **	0.016 **	0.010 **	0.010 **	0.005	0.008	-0.007	0.009
		(1.59)	(1.65)	(1.36)	(1.39)	(1.24)	(1.05)	(1.01)	(1.15)
RS2	56	0.099 **	0.026 **	0.026 **	0.013 **	0.014 **	0.054 **	0.001	0.042
		(3.71)	(1.96)	(1.99)	(1.52)	(1.44)	(1.33)	(1.01)	(1.20)
CS	112	0.029 **	0.060 **	0.029 **	0.033 **	0.022 **	0.048 **	0.033	0.048 **
		(1.42)	(1.93)	(1.43)	(1.55)	(1.45)	(1.27)	(1.07)	(1.20)
LI	159	0.016 **	0.018 **	0.002	0.006	0.004	0.041	0.050 **	-0.023
		(1.18)	(1.36)	(1.06)	(1.13)	(1.10)	(1.15)	(1.15)	(0.87)
IJC	268	0.043 **	0.025 **	0.018 **	0.016 **	0.011 **	0.039 **	-0.006	-0.002
		(2.21)	(1.77)	(1.57)	(1.48)	(1.39)	(1.32)	(1.00)	(1.00)
BI	80	-0.004	0.010	0.008	0.003	0.006	0.023	0.004	-0.024
		(1.01)	(1.25)	(1.24)	(1.05)	(1.18)	(1.14)	(0.98)	(0.90)
DGO	140	0.074 **	0.030 **	0.027 **	0.019 **	0.007 **	0.028	-0.016	0.011
		(3.17)	(2.25)	(2.04)	(1.70)	(1.30)	(1.08)	(0.88)	(1.05)
IP	129	0.042 **	0.017 **	0.013 **	0.011 **	0.009 **	0.018	-0.020	-0.013
		(2.51)	(1.60)	(1.46)	(1.40)	(1.27)	(1.08)	(0.98)	(1.02)
IMP	76	-0.005	-0.013	-0.006	-0.007	-0.007	0.020	0.016	0.030
		(0.95)	(0.82)	(1.01)	(0.95)	(0.90)	(1.09)	(1.06)	(1.09)
ISS	51	0.047 **	0.037 **	0.035 **	0.010	0.012	0.015	0.025	0.013
		(1.67)	(1.58)	(1.69)	(1.29)	(1.22)	(1.20)	(1.05)	(1.04)
PI	126	0.011 **	0.012 **	0.007 **	0.010 **	0.002	-0.007	-0.029	0.008
		(1.30)	(1.36)	(1.28)	(1.40)	(1.09)	(1.00)	(0.80)	(1.00)
HS	97	0.018 **	0.011 **	0.009 **	0.007 **	-0.002	0.022	-0.001	0.038
		(1.48)	(1.27)	(1.33)	(1.30)	(0.87)	(1.13)	(1.02)	(1.08)

This table reports the mean abnormal volatility ($\widetilde{|R|}$) during the 90 minutes following US macroeconomic announcements. ** denotes that these values are significantly different from zero with a p-value less than 0.05. The mean ratio of announcement and non-announcement day values is given in parentheses. The estimation method is as described in Table 3.14.

Table 3.18: Post-announcement effect on spread (German Announcements)

Ann	Obs	0 to 1	1 to 2	2 to 3	3 to 4	4 to 5	5 to 30	30 to 60	60 to 90
ZEW	44	0.04	-0.06	-0.05	-0.01	0.00	0.03	-0.04	-0.01
		(1.11)	(0.94)	(0.90)	(0.98)	(1.00)	(1.07)	(0.94)	(0.97)
MSP	94	0.16 **	0.14 **	0.11 **	0.02	0.12 **	0.02	-0.04	-0.02
		(1.19)	(1.15)	(1.14)	(1.04)	(1.13)	(1.04)	(0.97)	(1.00)
IFO	86	-0.03	0.11	-0.06	-0.03	0.12	0.03	0.03	0.13
		(0.98)	(1.12)	(0.95)	(0.98)	(1.14)	(0.97)	(1.03)	(1.11)
MFO	105	0.06	0.05	-0.04	0.00	0.03	0.00	0.02	0.02
		(1.05)	(1.04)	(0.93)	(1.04)	(1.02)	(0.99)	(1.02)	(1.06)
IND	104	-0.01	-0.06	0.06	-0.02	-0.04	-0.02	-0.05	-0.01
		(0.99)	(0.95)	(1.04)	(1.01)	(0.96)	(1.00)	(0.97)	(1.02)
ECB	9	0.77 **	0.39	0.18	0.24	0.02	-0.04	-0.09	0.64
		(1.74)	(1.42)	(1.27)	(1.14)	(0.98)	(0.96)	(0.86)	(1.59)
EM2	98	-0.03	-0.05	-0.06	-0.02	-0.02	0.07	-0.08	-0.06
		(1.05)	(0.95)	(0.98)	(0.99)	(0.95)	(1.08)	(0.94)	(0.98)
CPI	45	-0.02	-0.09	-0.03	-0.07	0.01	0.01	-0.06	0.00
		(0.98)	(0.94)	(0.99)	(0.93)	(1.02)	(1.03)	(0.97)	(1.01)
PMS	59	0.05	0.08	0.01	0.05	-0.05	-0.02	0.04	-0.07
		(1.04)	(1.12)	(1.04)	(1.03)	(0.95)	(0.96)	(1.00)	(0.98)
PMI	79	0.01	0.06	0.03	0.05	0.14	0.01	0.00	0.02
		(1.02)	(1.04)	(1.04)	(1.05)	(1.09)	(1.03)	(0.99)	(1.00)

This table reports the mean abnormal spread ($\widetilde{S}$) during the 90 minutes following German macroeconomic announcements. ** denotes that these values are significantly different from zero with a p-value less than 0.05. The mean ratio of announcement and non-announcement day values is given in parentheses. The estimation method is as described in Table 3.14.

these models all traders share common prior beliefs before the public news is revealed. After the release traders are heterogeneous in their interpretation of the public news. As a result, trading volume increases as market participants trade on their differences of opinion regarding the news (see, e.g., Shalen (1993) and He and Wang (1995)).

The only important difference is that in Fleming and Remolona (1999) trading volume in US treasuries does not increase before two minutes after the news announcement while it is even significantly lower at the time economic news is released. In contrast, I find that trading volume usually peaks in the very minute of the release. The same result, that

Table 3.19: Post-announcement effect on spread (US Announcements)

Ann	Obs	0 to 1	1 to 2	2 to 3	3 to 4	4 to 5	5 to 30	30 to 60	60 to 90
GDP	47	0.67 **	0.35	0.21	0.14	-0.04	0.17	-0.01	-0.01
		(1.62)	(1.45)	(1.14)	(1.08)	(0.99)	(1.12)	(0.99)	(0.94)
E3	161	0.71 **	0.41 **	0.29 **	0.32 **	0.22 **	0.23 **	-0.04	0.01
		(1.68)	(1.40)	(1.28)	(1.32)	(1.21)	(1.23)	(0.98)	(1.03)
CPI2	58	0.22 **	-0.09	0.21 **	0.06	0.02	0.06	-0.02	0.04
		(1.27)	(0.94)	(1.21)	(1.05)	(1.04)	(1.08)	(1.01)	(1.04)
CC	156	0.11	0.05	0.03	0.03	0.00	0.03	0.00	-0.03
		(1.08)	(1.06)	(1.04)	(1.01)	(0.99)	(1.03)	(1.01)	(0.99)
PPI2	67	0.47 **	0.09	-0.07	0.03	0.00	0.06	-0.03	-0.04
		(1.58)	(1.17)	(0.91)	(0.96)	(1.03)	(1.09)	(0.98)	(0.93)
TRD	102	0.11 **	0.09	-0.02	-0.03	0.03	-0.03	0.00	-0.07
		(1.11)	(1.09)	(1.01)	(0.96)	(1.04)	(0.98)	(1.01)	(0.95)
RS2	56	0.27	0.09	-0.06	-0.03	-0.10	0.04	-0.01	0.00
		(1.33)	(1.12)	(0.98)	(1.01)	(0.95)	(1.05)	(1.03)	(0.99)
CS	112	0.30 **	0.31 **	0.13 **	0.11	0.14 **	-0.06	0.06	0.03
		(1.30)	(1.31)	(1.12)	(1.10)	(1.16)	(0.93)	(1.12)	(1.00)
LI	159	0.07	-0.04	-0.02	0.02	0.09	-0.01	0.08	-0.03
		(1.05)	(0.98)	(0.97)	(1.02)	(1.08)	(0.99)	(1.07)	(0.99)
IJC	268	0.14 **	0.03	0.05	0.01	0.03	-0.04	-0.04	-0.04
		(1.11)	(1.03)	(1.05)	(1.00)	(1.03)	(0.98)	(1.00)	(0.97)
BI	80	-0.14	0.06	0.03	0.02	0.01	0.00	0.06	0.27 **
		(0.94)	(1.10)	(1.07)	(1.02)	(1.00)	(1.00)	(1.09)	(1.24)
DGO	140	0.11	0.15 **	0.03	0.05	0.03	0.03	0.08 **	0.03
		(1.10)	(1.18)	(1.06)	(1.07)	(1.01)	(1.02)	(1.11)	(1.01)
IP	129	-0.02	-0.02	0.05	0.03	-0.01	-0.05	-0.03	0.00
		(0.98)	(0.98)	(1.06)	(1.06)	(1.00)	(0.97)	(0.96)	(1.00)
IMP	76	-0.08	0.06	0.03	0.11	-0.08	0.10	0.02	0.08
		(0.91)	(1.02)	(0.99)	(1.08)	(0.94)	(1.06)	(1.05)	(1.06)
ISS	51	0.24	-0.02	0.01	0.00	0.11	-0.08	-0.01	-0.04
		(1.25)	(1.00)	(0.96)	(0.99)	(1.13)	(0.95)	(1.05)	(0.99)
PI	126	-0.04	0.14 **	0.12	0.13 **	0.03	0.11 **	-0.03	0.04
		(1.00)	(1.12)	(1.09)	(1.10)	(1.03)	(1.09)	(0.97)	(1.08)
HS	97	0.10	0.05	-0.05	0.12 **	-0.03	-0.02	-0.08	-0.05
		(1.10)	(1.03)	(0.92)	(1.10)	(0.97)	(0.98)	(0.92)	(0.94)

This table reports the mean abnormal spread ($\widetilde{S}$) during the 90 minutes following US macroeconomic announcements. ** denotes that these values are significantly different from zero with a p-value less than 0.05. The mean ratio of announcement and non-announcement day values is given in parentheses. The estimation method is as described in Table 3.14.

trading volume increases as soon as the news is released, is also found by Franke and Hess (2000) and Malinowska (2008) in the BUND futures market.

Table 3.20 ranks all German and US announcements with regard to their effects on FDAX trading activity. The purpose of these rankings is to reveal the relative importance of different types of US and German economic news for FDAX trading. Specifically, the announcements are ranked by how much they increase return volatility in the first post-announcement minute ($|\tilde{R}|_{0...1}$), by how much they increase bid-ask spread in the first pre- and in the first post-announcement minute ($\tilde{S}_{-1...0}$ and $\tilde{S}_{0...1}$), and by how much trading volume is increased in the first post-announcement minute ($\tilde{V}_{0...1}$). The increase is measured as the percentage increase on announcement days compared to average non-announcement day values, that is the numbers in parentheses in Tables 3.8 to 3.19. These rankings, of course, are not the sole objective measure of importance. However, the rankings provide a basic idea of the relative importance of different news types. As in the previous section, in the price effect analysis, I find that the effect of US economic news on FDAX trading is larger than that of German news.

One interesting question is whether there is a relation between the price effect and the liquidity effect. This is analyzed by calculating rank correlation coefficients between the different effects reported in Table 3.20. The Spearman rank correlation coefficient is a non-parametric measure of correlation. It does not assume a linear or any other particular relationship between two variables. For calculating the Spearman rank correlation, all insignificant announcements are assigned a common rank. For example, there are twenty announcements with a significant effect on $|\tilde{R}|_{0...1}$ and seven announcements whose effect is insignificant. Thus, the seven insignificant announcements are collectively assigned the shared last rank, 24.

Table 3.20: Ranking of announcement effects on FDAX trading

Ann	DE	US	Ranks			
			$\widetilde{\lvert R\rvert}_{0...1}$	$\widetilde{S}_{-1...0}$	$\widetilde{S}_{0...1}$	$\widetilde{V}_{0...1}$
E1		x	1	1	2	2
GDP		x	2	5	3	5
PPI2		x	3	2	4	1
RS2		x	4	4	insignif	4
CPI2		x	5	3	6	3
DGO		x	6	8	insignif	6
IP		x	7	10	insignif	7
ZEW	x		8	insignif	insignif	9
IJC		x	9	7	9	10
CC		x	10	11	insignif	14
MSP	x		11	insignif	7	13
IFO	x		12	insignif	insignif	12
ISS		x	13	6	insignif	insignif
TRD		x	14	insignif	8	8
IND	x		15	12	insignif	16
MFO	x		16	insignif	insignif	15
HS		x	17	13	insignif	11
CS		x	18	9	5	insignif
PI		x	19	insignif	insignif	insignif
LI		x	20	14	insignif	insignif
BI		x	insignif	insignif	insignif	insignif
CPI	x		insignif	insignif	insignif	insignif
ECB	x		insignif	insignif	1	insignif
EM1	x		insignif	insignif	insignif	insignif
IMP		x	insignif	insignif	insignif	insignif
PMI	x		insignif	insignif	insignif	insignif
PMS	x		insignif	insignif	insignif	insignif

This table ranks all German and US announcements with regard to their effects on FDAX trading activity. Specifically, the announcements are ranked by how much they increase return volatility in the first post-announcement minute ($\widetilde{\lvert R\rvert}_{0...1}$), by how much they increase bid-ask spread in the first pre- and in the first post-announcement minute ($\tilde{S}_{-1...0}$ and $\tilde{S}_{0...1}$), and by how much trading volume is increased in the first post-announcement minute ($\tilde{V}_{0...1}$). The increase is measured as the percentage increase on announcement days compared to average non-announcement day values, that is the numbers in parentheses in Tables 3.8 to 3.19.

Table 3.21: Rank correlation between trading effects

Spearman	$\widetilde{S}_{-1...0}$		$\widetilde{S}_{0...1}$		$\widetilde{V}_{0...1}$	
$\widetilde{\lvert R\rvert}_{0...1}$	0.87	**	0.88	**	0.85	**
$\widetilde{S}_{-1...0}$			0.75	**	0.75	**
$\widetilde{S}_{0...1}$					0.66	**

Kendall tau	$\widetilde{S}_{-1...0}$		$\widetilde{S}_{0...1}$		$\widetilde{V}_{0...1}$	
$\widetilde{\lvert R\rvert}_{0...1}$	0.66	**	0.58	**	0.66	**
$\widetilde{S}_{-1...0}$			0.55	**	0.54	**
$\widetilde{S}_{0...1}$					0.40	**

This table reports Spearman and Kendall tau rank correlation coefficients between the four variables analyzed in Table 3.20. ** denotes that the correlation coefficient is significantly ($p < 0.05$) different from zero.

The correlation between the first post-announcement minute's price movement, $|\tilde{R}|_{0...1}$, and the three other measures, $\tilde{S}_{-1...0}$, $\tilde{S}_{0...1}$, and $\tilde{V}_{0...1}$ is very large. Since these three variables are measures for liquidity, it can be concluded that there is a relationship between an announcement's effect on prices and liquidity: the larger its price effect, the more does it widen spreads before and after the announcement, and the more does it increase trading volume after the announcement. The correlation between the three liquidity measures is also statistically significant. As a robustness check, I also calculate Kendall tau rank correlations. In contrast to the Spearman correlation, Kendall tau is not based on the difference in ranks. Rather, it only compares whether two measures agree about the relative order of two announcements. Thus, it is even less parametric. All insignificant announcements are ranked according to the value for their respective measures, $|\tilde{R}|_{0...1}$, $\tilde{S}_{-1...0}$, $\tilde{S}_{0...1}$, and $\tilde{V}_{0...1}$. Thus, there are no shared ranked. The correlation values are somewhat lower than for the Spearman correlation, but the qualitative result holds.

As a caveat, it should be noted that this correlation analysis is not able to reveal any causal relationships. Rather it is a descriptive analysis which shows that announcements which on average induce larger price effects also induce larger liquidity effects on average. It is beyond the scope of this study to investigate the causes of this correlation. Holwever, one explanation might be that inventory control is a larger concern before announcements known to move prices a lot. Thus, spreads are wider before more price-relevant announcements. Afterwards, more important types of economic news might be expected to generate a larger variety of private interpretations, for example because more traders pay attention to the news. This in turn induces wider spreads and more trading volume in the aftermath of the news release. This analysis hints at a possible reason why FDAX trading is less affected by the release of German economic news than by the release of US news. It is well conceivable that spreads widen more and volume increases more around US announcements, because US macroeconomic announcement types are often more price-relevant than German announcements.

Finally, in order to illustrate the announcement effects on FDAX trading, Figure 3.4 plots the pattern of FDAX trading activity around the release of a German (ZEW) and a US announcement (PPI). These announcements are chosen because the ZEW is the most important German announcement and the PPI is one of the most important US announcements. The differences in longevity of volume, volatility and spread effects are well visible in the figure. While the increase in bid-ask spreads disappears almost immediately, volatility levels go back to normal only after some ten minutes and trading volume remains elevated for more than an hour. It is also apparent that the general pattern of trading is the same around US and German economic news.

Figure 3.4: Trading activity around economic news releases

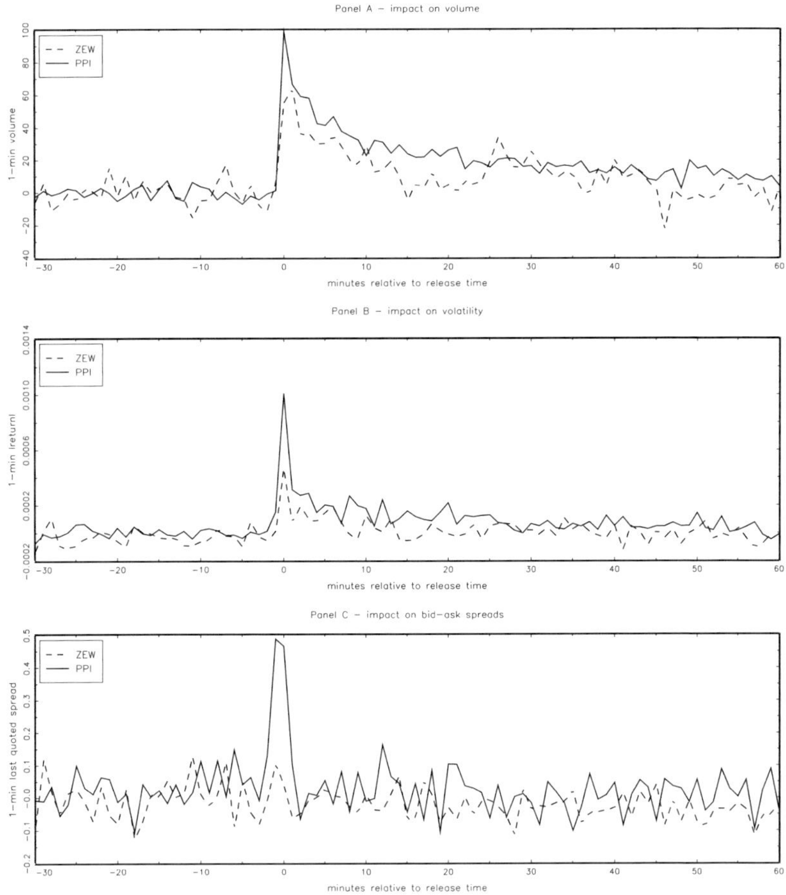

This figure plots abnormal trading activity in DAX futures around the release of ZEW and US PPI news. Abnormal trading activity is defined as the value on announcement days relative to normal, non-announcement day levels. Times are given relative to the respective release time. I plot mean abnormal values of one-minute trading volume (Panel A), average absolute one-minute log returns (Panel B) and average bid-ask spreads at the end of each one-minute interval (Panel C).

3.6 Impact of economic news on information asymmetry and inventory control

This section studies the impact of US and German economic news releases on the components of the effective spread in the German stock index futures market. Theory posits that the spread can be decomposed into an information asymmetry and an inventory holding component (see, e.g., Glosten and Harris (1988) and Stoll (1989)). The former compensates traders who offer liquidity for the risk of trading with a better informed party. The latter compensates traders for offering liquidity and as a result deviating from desired inventory levels. Investigating how these two spread components vary around domestic and US economic news contributes to understanding how the information is processed. Moreover, it helps explaining the patterns in trading activity reported in the previous section.

3.6.1 Methodology

I derive the effective spread components based on the price formation model of Madhavan, Richardson, and Roomans (1997). This model isolates the spread components by examining the relation between transaction prices and signed order flow. It generalizes the trade initiation model of Glosten and Milgrom (1985) by allowing order flow to be autocorrelated. The Madhavan, Richardson, and Roomans (1997) model was previously used by Greene and Smart (1999) to examine stock spreads around earnings announcements and by Green (2004) to study the informational role of trading around US economic news announcements in the US treasury market. Ahn, Cai, Hamao, and Ho (2002) point out that this model is particularly well suited to estimate the spread components on a limit order market, on which FDAX contracts are traded. Moreover, this model is well suited for my analysis because it is able to measure effects on the spread components that are as short-lived as a few minutes.

Madhavan, Richardson and Roomans (1997) derive the estimation equation as follows. Let p_t denote the price of a transaction at time t. μ_t is the underlying fundamental value, and x_t is the buy-sell trade indicator variable: x_t equals $+1$ if the transaction is buyer initiated and -1 if the trade is seller initiated. Further, θ measures the information revealed by a transaction and ϕ denotes the compensation for traders supplying liquidity. Assume that all orders are executed at either the bid or the ask price. Thus, prices follow a standard inventory cost model where the price deviates from the underlying fundamental value by the transitory inventory cost component, ϕ:

$$p_t = \mu_t + \phi x_t. \tag{3.6}$$

For example, if x_t is a buy, then $p_t = \mu_t + \phi$, and if x_t is a sell, then $p_t = \mu_t - \phi$. Assume that order flow is autocorrelated with $E[x_t|x_{t-1}] = \rho x_{t-1}$ and let ρ denote the first-order autocorrelation of x_t. This corresponds to the stylized fact that a buy is more likely to be followed by another buy than by a sell. The fundamental value is assumed to be positively correlated with the unexpected order flow, $x_t - E[x_t|x_{t-1}]$. Thus, the evolution in fundamental values can be described as:

$$\mu_t = \mu_{t-1} + \theta(x_t - \rho x_{t-1}). \tag{3.7}$$

Inserting equation (3.7) into equation (3.6) yields the price change model of Madhavan, Richardson and Roomans (1997):

$$p_t - p_{t-1} = (\phi + \theta)x_t - (\phi + \rho\theta)x_{t-1} + \epsilon_t. \tag{3.8}$$

This model is suited for the purpose of investigating variations in effective spread components around economic news releases, since it can be easily expanded by introducing indicator variables for different periods. We are interested in the differences in spread components between the following periods: non-announcement days (denoted by the indicator variable I^N), the announcement day period before the announcement (I^B), and the period following the announcement. Since we are also interested whether announcement effects disappear quickly, I divide the post-announcement period further into a period immediately following the announcement (I^{A15}) and a second subsequent period (I^{A30}).

In order to account for the direct effect of economic news, I follow Green (2004) and add an independent variable to capture the standardized surprise of the announcement, $S_{j,t}$. If an announcement of type j occured between trades t-1 and t, $S_{j,t}$ is the standardized surprise, otherwise it is zero.[13] Note that I estimate the equation separately for each economic news type j. Therefore j is fixed but changes for each estimation. For economic news types that contain more than a single relevant headline figure, e.g. the employment report which contains three important headline figure, $S_{j,t}$ is a vector containing the standardized surprises for each of the headline figures. The corresponding coefficient for the surprise effect is δ_j, which is a row vector if announcement j contains multiple headline figures. Thus, equation (3.8) is expanded into:

[13] I also follow the methodology of Green (2004) to ensure that the price change spans the announcement release. I aggregate the last two trades before and the first five trades after the announcement unless the trades occured more than two minutes before or after the announcement. Since trade direction is not well defined, x_t and x_{t-1} is set to zero for these aggregated trades.

$$p_t - p_{t-1} = \sum_{i \in \{N,B,A15,A30\}} \left((\phi^i + \theta^i) I_t^i x_t - (\phi^i + \rho^i \theta^i) I_{t-1}^i x_{t-1} \right) + \delta_j S_{j,t} + \epsilon_t. \tag{3.9}$$

In line with Green (2004), I choose an event window from 30:00 minutes before until 30:00 minutes after each announcement. I^B consists of the 30 minutes before each announcement and I^{A15} and I^{A30} encompass the two 15 minutes intervals following each announcement. I^N consists of the entire time period, −30:00 min to +30:00 min, but taken on non-announcement days. Days that are distorted by the release of multiple relevant announcements, i.e. two announcement types are released within 30:00 min of each other, are excluded from the analysis.

The empirical model relates price changes to order flow and economic news at the same time. One disadvantage is that the price impact of economic news is typically measured as a percentage of the price. Since the FDAX price has grown over time during the sample, the results might be biased with regard to the price impact of the economic news. This problem is more severe than in Green's analysis, since Green considers bond prices which are not subject to a long-term time trend. However, I choose to stay with this model because the price impact of US and German economic news has already been investigated in section 3.4. In this analysis, it is more important to measure the changes in the spread components around the announcement. In order to further make the results better comparable across different announcement types, I restrict the sample to the post-October 2001 period because not all announcement types are available before 2001.

Following Madhavan, Richardson and Roomans (1997) and Green (2004), I choose the Generalized Method of Moments (GMM) to estimate the model. Another conceivable estimation method would be Maximum Likelihood (ML). If the distribution of the dependent variable is specified correctly, ML often leads to more efficient parameter estimates. For example, Fuhrer, Moore and Schuh (1995) compare the parameter estimates of GMM and ML for a linear-quadratic inventory model[14], and they find that standard errors are 3 to 15 times smaller for ML than for GMM. However, GMM seems more appropriate in this case, because unlike ML it imposes very weak distribution assumptions. This is especially important because the error term includes rounding errors due to the discreteness of prices. Further, estimation efficiency is not a serious concern given the large number of observations used for the estimation. The GMM procedure also easily accounts for the presence of conditional heteroscedasticity of unknown form. I apply the Newey and West procedure on the variance-covariance matrix of the moment restrictions. The inverse of that matrix is used as the weighting matrix. Letting α represent a constant drift and using the expressions

$$v_t = x_t - \sum_{i \in \{N,B,A15,A30\}} \rho^i I^i_{t-1} x_{t-1} \tag{3.10}$$

and

$$u_t = p_t - p_{t-1} - \sum_{i \in \{N,B,A15,A30\}} \left((\phi^i + \theta^i) I^i_t x_t - (\phi^i + \rho^i \theta^i) I^i_{t-1} x_{t-1} \right) - \delta_j S_{j,t} \tag{3.11}$$

the following population moments implied by equation (3.9) exactly identify the parameters δ_j, α, θ^i, ϕ^i, and ρ^i with $i \in \{N, B, A15, A30\}$:

[14] In this model, a representative firm chooses the level of inventories to minimize the present discounted value subject to its production restrictions. The model is attributed to Holt, Modigliani, Muth and Simon (1960).

$$
\begin{aligned}
E\left[v_t I^i_{t-1} x_{t-1}\right] &= 0, \quad i \in \{N, B, A15, A30\} \\
E\left[u_t - \alpha\right] &= 0 \\
E\left[(u_t - \alpha) I^i_t x_t\right] &= 0, \quad i \in \{N, B, A15, A30\} \qquad (3.12) \\
E\left[(u_t - \alpha) I^i_{t-1} x_{t-1}\right] &= 0, \quad i \in \{N, B, A15, A30\}. \\
E\left[(u_t - \alpha) S_{j,t}\right] &= 0.
\end{aligned}
$$

The first set of moments determines the autocorrelation in order flow during each period of interest, and the remaining equations represent the OLS normal equations.

3.6.2 Results

I separately estimate equation (3.12) for each announcement type j. Table 3.22 for German and 3.23 for US announcements present the results. In the left part of the tables, I report the surprise coefficient estimates, δ_j. These results are very similar to the results presented in section 3.4.[15] In the middle columns of Table 3.22 and 3.23, I report the coefficient estimates for θ, ϕ and ρ for each of the four sub samples. The difference between the different periods' coefficient estimates is of particular interest. I report differences in the right-most columns between the:

[15]The most notable differences compared to the prior analysis are: US CPI is not significant and nonfarm payrolls is the most important figure within the US employment report. In the price-only analysis, as reported in section 3.4, CPI does have a significant effect and hourly earnings are the most important figure within the employment report. These differences are likely due to the different sample period and to the fact that this analysis only captures the price effect within the very fist few trades, whereas the analysis reported in section 3.4 measures the price effect in the first five minutes.

Table 3.22: Effective spread components around German announcements

Ann	Surprise Coeff.			Coefficient estimates					Difference in coefficients							
				N	B	A15	A30		B - N		A15 - B		A30 - A15		A30 - N	
ZEW	1.48	***	θ	0.201	0.198	0.252	0.203	θ	-0.003		0.054	***	-0.049	***	0.002	
			ϕ	0.121	0.122	0.093	0.112	ϕ	0.000		-0.029	***	0.019		-0.010	
			ρ	0.183	0.168	0.198	0.165	ρ	-0.015		0.030		-0.034		-0.019	
MSP	0.69		θ	0.215	0.221	0.221	0.203	θ	0.006		0.000		-0.017		-0.011	
			ϕ	0.129	0.130	0.134	0.131	ϕ	0.000		0.004		-0.002		0.002	
			ρ	0.210	0.196	0.183	0.184	ρ	-0.014		-0.013		0.001		-0.026	
IFO	3.51	***	θ	0.244	0.236	0.304	0.250	θ	-0.008		0.067	***	-0.053	***	0.006	
			ϕ	0.129	0.137	0.125	0.120	ϕ	0.008		-0.012		-0.005		-0.009	
			ρ	0.197	0.191	0.173	0.203	ρ	-0.005		-0.019		0.030		0.006	
MFO	0.68	***	θ	0.216	0.216	0.250	0.233	θ	0.000		0.035	***	-0.017		0.017	
			ϕ	0.129	0.140	0.134	0.144	ϕ	0.011		-0.006		0.010		0.015	
			ρ	0.193	0.190	0.175	0.186	ρ	-0.003		-0.015		0.012		-0.007	
IND	1.72	***	θ	0.215	0.200	0.254	0.216	θ	-0.015		0.054	***	-0.038	***	0.001	
			ϕ	0.131	0.136	0.128	0.126	ϕ	0.005		-0.008		-0.002		-0.005	
			ρ	0.181	0.167	0.190	0.184	ρ	-0.014		0.023		-0.006		0.003	
ECB	-0.37		θ	0.195	0.205	0.316	0.240	θ	0.010		0.111	***	-0.075	***	0.046	***
			ϕ	0.132	0.127	0.091	0.105	ϕ	-0.005		-0.036	***	0.014		-0.027	***
			ρ	0.166	0.174	0.185	0.191	ρ	0.008		0.012		0.005		0.025	
EM1	0.27		θ	0.248	0.270	0.262	0.245	θ	0.022	***	-0.007		-0.017		-0.003	
EM2	-0.27		ϕ	0.122	0.112	0.110	0.103	ϕ	-0.011		-0.002		-0.006		-0.019	***
			ρ	0.179	0.182	0.178	0.200	ρ	0.004		-0.005		0.023		0.021	
PMI	0.19		θ	0.251	0.256	0.262	0.232	θ	0.006		0.006		-0.030		-0.018	
			ϕ	0.127	0.133	0.134	0.112	ϕ	0.006		0.001		-0.022	***	-0.015	
			ρ	0.173	0.165	0.177	0.227	ρ	-0.008		0.012		0.050	***	0.054	***
PMS	0.65	***	θ	0.295	0.299	0.294	0.291	θ	0.004		-0.006		-0.002		-0.004	
			ϕ	0.131	0.116	0.119	0.115	ϕ	-0.014	***	0.002		-0.003		-0.015	
			ρ	0.140	0.153	0.162	0.158	ρ	0.013		0.009		-0.004		0.018	

Ann	Surprise Coeff.		Coefficient estimates N	B	A15	A30		Difference in coefficients B - N	A15 - B	A30 - A15	A30 - N
CPI	0.05	θ	0.257	0.245	0.260	0.285	θ	-0.011	0.015	0.025	0.028
		ϕ	0.119	0.120	0.106	0.111	ϕ	0.001	-0.014	0.005	-0.009
		ρ	0.175	0.171	0.193	0.193	ρ	-0.004	0.023	0.000	0.018

(description for Table 3.22)
This table reports GMM estimates for the following model: $p_t - p_{t-1} = \sum_{i\in\{N,B,A15,A30\}} \left((\phi^i + \theta^i)I_t^i x_t - (\phi^i + \rho^i\theta^i)I_{t-1}^i x_{t-1}\right) + \delta_j S_{j,t} + \epsilon_t$ where i denotes the four sub periods of interest: non-announcement days ($i = N$), the announcement day period before the announcement (B), the minutes 1 to 15 following the announcement ($A15$) and minutes 15 to 30 following an announcement ($A30$). The estimation is done separately for each announcement j. $S_{j,t}$ is the standardized surprise of announcement j if it occured between t-1 and t, otherwise $S_{j,t}$ is zero. p_t denotes the transaction price at time t, x_t the direction of this transaction (1 if buyer-initiated and -1 if seller-initiated) and I_t^i is an indicator variable that takes the value one if t lies in the sub period i. The coefficients in this model are the costs of inventory control (ϕ^i), costs of information asymmetry (θ^i) and the autocorrelation of order flow (ρ^i). Robust standard errors are estimated with Newey-West heteroscedasticity and autocorrelation consistent covariance matrix. This table reports the coefficient estimates for the price effect in the left, and for all other coefficients and for each of the sub samples in the middle columns. The right columns report differences in the respective coefficient estimates between four sub samples. *** denotes that the difference is significant with a p-value less than 0.01 based on a two-sided Wald coefficient test.

Table 3.23: Effective spread components around US announcements

Ann	Surprise Coeff.			Coefficient estimates N	B	A15	A30		Difference in coefficients B - N		A15 - B		A30 - A15		A30 - N	
E1	12.99	***	θ	0.193	0.181	0.435	0.311	θ	-0.012		0.254	***	-0.124	***	0.118	***
E2	-5.51	***	ϕ	0.123	0.143	0.092	0.086	ϕ	0.021	***	-0.052	***	-0.006		-0.037	***
E3	2.64		ρ	0.182	0.148	0.209	0.201	ρ	-0.034	***	0.061	***	-0.009		0.019	
GDP	14.97	***	θ	0.220	0.211	0.385	0.305	θ	-0.009		0.174	***	-0.080		0.085	***
			ϕ	0.146	0.130	0.116	0.112	ϕ	-0.016		-0.014		-0.004		-0.034	
			ρ	0.173	0.174	0.183	0.187	ρ	0.001		0.009		0.004		0.014	
CC	7.45	***	θ	0.293	0.251	0.349	0.295	θ	-0.042	***	0.098	***	-0.054	***	0.002	
			ϕ	0.098	0.109	0.109	0.097	ϕ	0.010		0.001		-0.012		-0.001	
			ρ	0.188	0.188	0.175	0.201	ρ	0.001		-0.013		0.026		0.014	
PPI2	-4.04	***	θ	0.148	0.149	0.210	0.171	θ	0.001		0.061	***	-0.039		0.024	
			ϕ	0.128	0.126	0.140	0.114	ϕ	-0.002		0.014		-0.026		-0.015	
			ρ	0.286	0.270	0.309	0.290	ρ	-0.016		0.039		-0.019		0.004	
CPI2	0.09		θ	0.170	0.169	0.257	0.183	θ	-0.001		0.088	***	-0.074	***	0.013	
			ϕ	0.119	0.141	0.098	0.120	ϕ	0.022	***	-0.043	***	0.022		0.002	
			ρ	0.201	0.155	0.195	0.206	ρ	-0.045	***	0.039		0.011		0.005	
TRD	1.71	***	θ	0.174	0.210	0.200	0.180	θ	0.036	***	-0.010		-0.020		0.006	
			ϕ	0.128	0.135	0.121	0.119	ϕ	0.007		-0.014		-0.002		-0.009	
			ρ	0.231	0.201	0.245	0.254	ρ	-0.030		0.044		0.010		0.024	
RS2	2.53	***	θ	0.244	0.226	0.382	0.299	θ	-0.018		0.155	***	-0.083	***	0.054	***
			ϕ	0.128	0.151	0.155	0.119	ϕ	0.022		0.004		-0.036		-0.009	
			ρ	0.193	0.104	0.121	0.156	ρ	-0.089	***	0.016		0.035		-0.038	
LI	3.20	***	θ	0.281	0.263	0.328	0.273	θ	-0.018	***	0.065	***	-0.056	***	-0.009	
			ϕ	0.092	0.100	0.089	0.091	ϕ	0.008		-0.011		0.002		-0.001	
			ρ	0.184	0.182	0.194	0.173	ρ	-0.002		0.012		-0.021		-0.011	
ISM	0.76		θ	0.275	0.244	0.374	0.286	θ	-0.030	***	0.130	***	-0.088	***	0.011	
CS	3.59	***	ϕ	0.098	0.106	0.098	0.097	ϕ	0.008		-0.008		-0.001		0.000	
			ρ	0.203	0.183	0.202	0.204	ρ	-0.021		0.019		0.002		0.001	

Ann	Surprise Coeff.			Coefficient estimates					Difference in coefficients							
				N	B	A15	A30		B - N		A15 - B		A30 - A15		A30 - N	
IJC	-2.84	***	θ	0.190	0.205	0.271	0.214	θ	0.015	***	0.066	***	-0.057	***	0.024	***
			ϕ	0.124	0.130	0.108	0.116	ϕ	0.006		-0.022	***	0.009		-0.008	
			ρ	0.186	0.178	0.194	0.197	ρ	-0.008		0.016	***	0.002		0.010	
BI	-1.33		θ	0.262	0.211	0.289	0.235	θ	-0.050	***	0.077	***	-0.053	***	-0.026	
			ϕ	0.128	0.134	0.118	0.123	ϕ	0.006		-0.016		0.005		-0.005	
			ρ	0.132	0.138	0.130	0.146	ρ	0.006		-0.007		0.016		0.014	
IP	2.97	***	θ	0.191	0.185	0.218	0.250	θ	-0.007		0.033	***	0.032	***	0.059	***
			ϕ	0.114	0.118	0.123	0.114	ϕ	0.004		0.006		-0.009		0.000	
			ρ	0.192	0.195	0.166	0.169	ρ	0.003		-0.028		0.003		-0.023	
DGO	7.00	***	θ	0.197	0.174	0.268	0.205	θ	-0.023	***	0.094	***	-0.063	***	0.008	
			ϕ	0.117	0.115	0.105	0.105	ϕ	-0.002		-0.009		0.000		-0.011	
			ρ	0.185	0.184	0.180	0.183	ρ	-0.001		-0.004		0.003		-0.002	
HS	1.12	***	θ	0.184	0.178	0.235	0.187	θ	-0.006		0.057	***	-0.048	***	0.003	
			ϕ	0.128	0.126	0.108	0.112	ϕ	-0.002		-0.018		0.004		-0.016	
			ρ	0.168	0.156	0.189	0.216	ρ	-0.013		0.034		0.026		0.047	***
PI	0.78		θ	0.182	0.180	0.224	0.169	θ	-0.003		0.044	***	-0.054	***	-0.013	
			ϕ	0.120	0.142	0.105	0.117	ϕ	0.022	***	-0.036	***	0.011		-0.003	
			ρ	0.187	0.167	0.201	0.172	ρ	-0.020		0.034		-0.029		-0.015	
IMP	0.10		θ	0.342	0.316	0.337	0.306	θ	-0.026	***	0.022		-0.031		-0.036	***
			ϕ	0.102	0.092	0.090	0.101	ϕ	-0.010		-0.002		0.011		-0.001	
			ρ	0.131	0.141	0.127	0.147	ρ	0.010		-0.013		0.020		0.016	
ISS	0.00		θ	0.285	0.261	0.351	0.271	θ	-0.024	***	0.090	***	-0.080	***	-0.014	
			ϕ	0.095	0.104	0.095	0.103	ϕ	0.009		-0.009		0.008		0.009	
			ρ	0.228	0.195	0.218	0.211	ρ	-0.032	***	0.023		-0.007		-0.017	

(description for Table 3.23)

This table reports estimation results for the impact of US macroeconomic announcements on the components of the effective spread in FDAX trading. The estimation procedure is as described in 3.22.

1. pre-announcement (B) and the non-announcement sample (N)
2. first post-announcement sample (A15) and the pre-announcement sample (B)
3. second post-announcement sample (A30) and the first post-announcement sample (A15)
4. second post-announcement sample (A30) and the non-announcement sample (N)

The first value represents pre-release effects of economic news on information asymmetry, inventory control and autocorrelation of order flow. The second difference represents the immediate impact of the news release. The third difference shows whether the immediate effect decreases after 15 minutes. And the last difference assesses whether the values in the A30 sample have returned to normal (i.e. non-announcement day) values. *** denotes that a difference is significant with a p-value less than 0.01 based on a two-sided Wald coefficient test.

Generally, the results for differences in inventory control, ϕ, and autocorrelation coefficients, ρ, are relatively inconsistent. This might be due to the fact that I do not pool the estimates for all announcement types. Thus, my estimates are less efficient than Green (2004). In contrast, the pattern of changes in information asymmetry costs around economic news releases is very pronounced and can be found around almost all US and many German announcements. While pre-announcement information asymmetry is mostly not distinctively different from non-announcement day levels ($\theta^N = \theta^B$), it rises significantly in the first 15 minutes following the announcement ($\theta^{A15} > \theta^B$). Then information asymmetry significantly decreases again in the second post-announcement interval ($\theta^{A30} < \theta^{A15}$) to near non-announcement day levels ($\theta^{A30} = \theta^N$).

These results confirm skilled information processing models such as Kim and Verrecchia (1994, 1997). Trading contains no additional information in the period leading up to the release as there is no private information about the upcoming economic news release. After the public news is released, heterogeneous interpretation skills of market participants lead to private information on implications of the news. Thus, we observe an increased informational role of order flow. However, traders with private information generated by superior interpretation skills are unlikely to possess a monopoly on this kind of expertise. Holden and Subramanyam (1992) show that competition among multiple informed traders leads prices to incorporate private information quickly. In line with this view, I find that the increased information asymmetry decreases significantly in the second post-announcement period.

Table 3.24 visualizes the relative magnitude of each announcement type's impact on information asymmetry in FDAX trading. This is done by ranking the announcements by how much θ increases in the 15 post-announcement minutes compared to the pre-announcement period. The second column ranks the price effect of each announcement type according to the absolute coefficient of the surprise effect. The ranking for the effects on inventory control is not reported since most announcement types don't exert a significant effect on ϕ. The rank order correlation coefficients, Spearman and Kendall tau, reported in the bottom of the table, are significantly positive. This suggests that announcement types known to have a large effect on FDAX prices also have a larger effect on information asymmetry. This is understandable, as it can be assumed that private interpretations about more important news is more valuable than private information about lesser news. This might also explain why information asymmetry is more affected around US announcements than around German economic news, as there are more US economic news that are highly relevant for German stock prices.

In order to further assess the exact duration of the impact of economic news releases on the effective spread components, I now repeat the above analysis separately for each single minute within the event window of -30 min to $+30$ min. I pool together all types

Table 3.24: Ranking of announcement effects on information asymmetry

Ann	DE	US	Ranks $\theta^{A15} - \theta^{B}$	Ranks Abs. Surprise
E1		x	1	2
GDP		x	2	1
RS2		x	3	11
CS		x	4	6
ECB	x		5	insignif
CC		x	6	3
DGO		x	7	4
ISS		x	8	insignif
CPI2		x	9	insignif
BI		x	10	insignif
IFO	x		11	7
IJC		x	12	10
LI		x	13	8
PPI2		x	14	5
HS		x	15	15
IND	x		16	12
ZEW	x		17	14
PI		x	18	insignif
MFO	x		19	16
IP		x	20	9
MSP	x		insignif	insignif
TRD		x	insignif	13
CPI	x		insignif	insignif
EM1	x		insignif	insignif
IMP		x	insignif	insignif
PMI	x		insignif	insignif
PMS	x		insignif	17
Rank correlation				
Spearman:			0.50**	
Kendall tau:			0.40**	

This table ranks all announcement type according to the relative magnitude of each announcement's impact on information asymmetry in FDAX trading. This is done by ranking the announcements by how much θ increases in the 15 post-announcement minutes compared to the pre-announcement period. The second column ranks the price effect of each announcement type according to the absolute coefficient of the surprise effect. In the lower part, I report Spearman and Kendall tau rank order correlation coefficients between these two variables. ** denotes that the correlation coefficient is significantly ($p < 0.05$) different from zero.

of US economic news which exert a significant impact on information asymmetry or inventory control[16], and then proceed likewise with relevant German economic news[17]. This procedure allows for a sufficiently large sample in each minute of the event window. Also, the larger data pool might allow for more efficient estimates. Figure 3.5 plots the results for costs of information asymmetry (θ) and inventory control (ϕ). Autocorrelation does not show a pronounced pattern and is therefore not reported. The solid, dashed and dotted lines denote results for the pool of US, German, and non-announcement day coefficient estimates, respectively. A symbol in the US and German result lines indicates that the value is significantly different (p-value < 0.05) from the non-announcement day value.[18]

The figure confirms conclusions drawn from Table 3.22 and 3.23. The similarity of US and German news effects on information asymmetry is striking. θ sharply increases following the announcement and then gradually returns to normal values. The effect lasts almost 30 minutes for the pool of important US announcements and about 10 minutes for the pool of important German announcements. In addition, the pooled results reveal that in the period immediately before (between -10 and -1 minutes) the news release the informational value of order flow seems to be lower than usual. The larger efficiency of the pooled estimates further allows conclusions regarding inventory holding costs prior to the news release. Before US economic news releases, inventory costs are higher than usual in the approximately 5 minutes before the release, reaching its maximum value immediately before the release. Before German announcements, the increase in inventory costs is less pronounced, but can be observed for approximately 15 minutes before the

[16]Specifically: E1/E2/E3, GDP, CPI2, CC, PPI2, DGO, RS2, IJC, ISM/CS, IP, HS, PI, LI, BI, ISS.

[17]Specifically: ZEW, IFO, MFO, MSP, IND, ECB.

[18]Since I pool together all US and German economic news types the non-announcement day sample now consists of event windows taken at different times of the day. This should not bias the results, as intraday variations in effective spread components on non-announcement days are minor.

Figure 3.5: Effective spread components around economic news releases

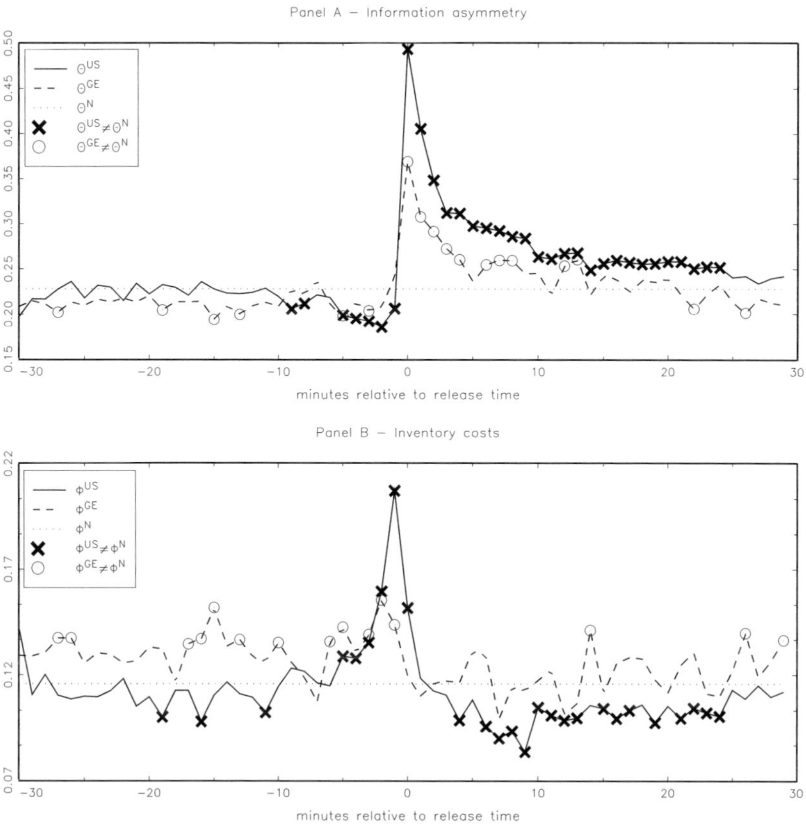

This figure plots coefficient estimates for the components of the effective spread in DAX futures for each one-minute interval in the 60 minutes around the release of US and German economic news, and also for non-announcement days at the same time of day. The estimations are done separately for each one-minute interval. Times are given relative to the respective release time. A cross or circle denotes that the respective announcement day value is significantly (i.e. p-value < 0.05) different from non-announcement day levels. I plot estimates for information asymmetry costs (Panel A) and inventory control costs (Panel B).

announcement. Moreover, the figure reveals that inventory costs are lower than usual in the 15 minutes following US economic news releases. Such a pattern is not visible following German news. These observations support the notion that uncertainty prior to the release makes traders reluctant to supply liquidity and resolved uncertainty following the announcement makes traders more willing to supply liquidity.

These results help us to understand what induces the trading activity patterns revealed in the previous chapter. The first approximately 15 to 30 minutes following an economic news release are characterized by increased levels of information asymmetry caused by private interpretations of the news. This causes increased differences of opinion among market participants on which they trade, which leads to increased levels of trading volume and volatility. In a subsequent period beginning between 15 and 30 minutes after the news release private interpretations have been fully incorporated into prices. Information asymmetry and volatility return to normal levels, yet trading volume remains high as liquidity traders now rebalance their portfolios to account for the just released economic news. The pronounced increases in quoted spreads in the few minutes immediately before and after the announcement can be attributed to different causes. Before the announcement liquidity is scarce due to inventory concerns caused by uncertainty regarding the upcoming news release. After the announcement liquidity is costly as the risk of trading with a better informed trader (i.e. someone with better skills of interpreting the public news) is heightened.

My findings are qualitatively similar to Green's (2004) observations regarding the impact of US economic news on effective spread components in the US treasury market. I extend Green (2004) by differentiating between different types of announcements instead of pooling all news types together. This reveals that on average those announcement types that are known to induce large price effects also exert larger effects on information asymmetry in FDAX trading. In addition, my large dataset allows an exact minute-by-minute examination of the duration of the effects. Most importantly, I compare the effects of domestic and foreign economic news and find that the impact of domestic and US news on the components of the FDAX effective spread is qualitatively very comparable in nature. In a similar effort, Albuquerque and Vega (2007) find that information asymmetry in the Portuguese stock markets decreases following US economic news while it increases after domestic Portuguese news which contradicts my results. However, their analysis is based on a day-by-day analysis and might capture different effects than my analysis which only focuses on the immediate news impact.

3.7 Concluding remarks

This study provides a comprehensive depiction of the price and liquidity dynamics in the German stock market around the release of economic news. The analysis is carried out on the German stock index futures with a dataset consisting of 15 years (1991 – 2005) of high frequency data, and I compare the effects of a large number US and German macroeconomic news types. I investigate the news impact on multiple price and liquidity variables, including: prices, trading volume, volatility, quoted spreads, inventory holding costs and the informational role of trading. I find that the impact of both domestic and US economic news on the German stock index futures is much in line with information processing models regarding the processing of public news. Economic news is almost immediately incorporated into prices and liquidity decreases before and after the announcement. Trading volume and volatility both increase following the news release. Further, I find a strong correlation between the price and liquidity effect of different announcement types. Thus, the larger the price impact of an economic news type, the more does it increase trading volume and decrease liquidity around the release.

The response pattern to domestic news and foreign news is very similar in nature. Interestingly, although Germany is a large economy itself, US economic news affects German stock markets even more than domestic news does. There are more relevant US economic news announcements and most of these have a larger price and liquidity impact. This result highlights the leading role that the US economy has on the world's financial markets. Clearly, the state of the United States' economy also affects German stock prices. From a German investor's point of view, US macroeconomic news releases might very well be the most important recurring news event for the German stock market. My findings imply that German stock traders need to pay attention to both domestic and US economic news releases as these events greatly impact German stock prices. However, traders need to also consider the low liquidity around these news announcements which might make trading in response to the news costly.

Comparing the effects of domestic German and foreign US economic news advances our understanding of how economic news is processed in international financial markets. Previous research suggests that there might be a delayed price response in international financial markets to US macroeconomic announcements. It is argued that foreign traders might prefer to condition their price response on the US price response, because US traders might have a 'home field advantage' in interpreting the news. This chapter has revealed that German stock traders respond to foreign US economic news immediately. They do not wait for the US stock market to open. However, this result cannot rule out that German traders are also conditioning their response on the US stock market's response to the US economic news. The US stock market is closed when most US macro announcements occur at 2:30 pm (CET), but the S&P stock index futures is traded around the clock, although trading volume is very thin outside regular trading hours. In contrast, US bond markets are open at 2:30 and trading volume is high. Therefore the next chapter will deal with information transmission between US and German bond markets and try to answer the question: What do German bond traders condition their price response on – the US macroeconomic announcement itself and/or the US bond price response to the news?

4 The channels of cross bross-border information transmission

4.1 Motivation

This chapter, like the previous chapter, deals with the effects of macroeconomic news on international financial markets. However, in this chapter, I study the channels of cross-border information transmission. I investigate how information is transmitted from the United States' bond market to the German bond market around US macroeconomic announcements. The main research question is: Do German bond traders condition their price reaction on the news announcement itself? Or do German traders condition their response on the US bond price response to the news, or on both? US macroeconomic announcements are suitable for such analysis because, as shown in the previous chapter, they are among the most important scheduled news events for German financial markets. I find that following US macroeconomic announcements, both channels – the news itself and the US price response – contribute to price discovery in German bond prices.

Prior studies have mostly focused on the direct response of foreign security prices to the US economic news itself. In my analysis of the German bond price response to the US news, I additionally account for the US response to the news. The rationale is that the US bond price response to the US economic news release might contain valuable information for pricing German bonds which supplements the information contained in the news release itself. Moreover, I also analyze both the immediate price response in Germany and the German bond price movements in the aftermath of the news release. The immediate price response can be directly associated with the public announcement of US economic news. As shown in the previous chapter, the public news is incorporated into prices almost instantaneously. Afterwards, price movemovements are driven by differential private interpretations of the public news for about 30 minutes (see also Fleming and Remolona (1999) and Green (2004)). Thus, by differentiating between different post-announcement phases in my analysis, I am able to study cross-border transmission of both publicly observable news and private US information that is not observable in the German market.

The relevant literature is mostly concerned with investigating what the foreign price response to US macroeconomic announcements is driven by. On the one hand it might be driven by contagion, i.e. the foreign market only co-moves with the US market *as usual.* On the other hand, it might be driven by a genuine response to the news. There is mixed evidence in the literature. Karolyi and Stulz (1996) and Connolly and Wang (2003) find that the foreign price response on announcement days can be almost completely explained by the usual co-movement. They don't find a separate announcement day effect. In contrast, Andersen, Bollerslev, Diebold, and Vega (2007) find that the foreign price response is driven by both the announcement surprise and the US response to the announcement. However, they don't account for varying levels of cross-market return dependencies. My study takes a slightly different stance. It is well known that there is always international transmission of price movements, especially from the US to other financial markets (see, e.g. Eun and Shim (1989)). Thus, it is important to investigate whether transmission of US bond price movement to German bonds *increases* following US economic news releases.

In order to guide my analysis, I relate the cross-border transmission of economic news to the rational learning model of Chan (1993). Emprirically, I extend the Hasbrouck (1991) quote revision model. I relate price movements in German bonds not only to their own lags and order flow, but also to price movements in US bonds and to the surprise value in US macroeconomic announcements. An empirical model based on high frequency data seems appropriate as information processing occurs very quickly. For example, each price movement in the US bond market is fully incorprorated into German bond prices within about 20 seconds. I find that surprises in macroeconomic announcements lose some of their explanatory power for BUND price movements once lagged US bond price movements are included into the model. At the same time, the level of transmission of US bond price movements to German bond prices is much larger immediately following the announcement of US macroeconomic news than at any other time. Then, after the public news has been fully incorporated into bond prices, price transmission from US to German bond prices is still significantly larger than usual. This effect can be found for up to 60 minutes past the announcement.

My analysis adds to the understanding of how information is transmitted across international financial markets. The previous chapter documented that US economic news induces significant price reactions in German financial markets, too. This chapter shows that this price response can not be explained only by a reaction to the news release itself, but it is also caused by a reaction to the US price response. These results suggest that the US bond price response to the news contains additional information for the valuation of German bonds that is not contained in the news itself. In addition, my findings indicate that German bond traders also try to infer private US interpretations of the news which occur in the 60 minutes following the announcement. Lastly, my results suggest that US economic news is of genuine interest for German bond prices because following these announcements, German bond prices follow US bonds more strongly than usual.

The remainder of this chapter is structured as follows. In section 2 I apply the Chan (1993) model to rational cross-border information flow in order to guide the analysis. Section 3 describes the data used in the empirical investigation. In section 4 I study the price response of German and US bonds to US news releases. Section 5 presents the empirical framework for the information transmission analysis. Section 6 reports the main results on cross-border information flow around US economic news releases. Section 7 concludes the research.

4.2 A simple model of rational cross-border information transmission

The goal of this study is to investigate how US economic news is transmitted to the German bond market. Do German bond prices respond to the news itself or to they (additionally) follow the US price response? In order to guide my analysis, I relate the transmission of economic news to the rational learning model of Chan (1993). In that model two markets receive noisy signals about the value of their respective security. Since each signal additionally contains the same marketwide component, each market learns about its own security price from price movements in the other security price. The model setup resembles the announcement of macroeconomic news. Both markets, the United States' and the German bond market, observe the public announcement of macroeconomic news. Since the news has to be interpreted with regard to its implication for US and German bond prices, each market initially responds to its noisy interpretation of the news. Afterwards, they look at the respective other market's price response which causes corrections of the initial price response.

In a first step, I describe the Chan (1993) model. Then I examine a variation of the model for the case that only one market receives a signal while the other doesn't. This alternative setup corresponds to the case where a signal that contains a global component is observed in only one and not in the other market. Afterwards I discuss in detail how the model setup can be applied to the cross-border transmission of macroeconomic news and price movements. Lastly I demonstrate the model implications with a numerical example and then compare it to other models in the literature.

4.2.1 Both markets receive a noisy signal (Chan (1993))

The following model description follows Chan (1993). Assume two markets a and b in which two securities, V^a and V^b, are traded. The securities are traded over multiple periods t = 1 ... T. A change in the security values occurs whenever information arrives. There are two types of news components, a global component that affects both markets (W_t) and a local component that only affects the local market (S_t^i, $i \in a, b$). The security price in period t is described by equation (4.1):

$$V_{i,t} = \bar{v} + \sum_{\tau=1}^{t} \Delta V_{i,\tau} \tag{4.1}$$

where

$$\Delta V_{i,\tau} = W_\tau + S_{i,\tau}.$$

$\bar{v}$ is a constant, normalized to be the same for each security. W_t and S_t^i are normally distributed with mean zero and variance σ_W^2 and σ_S^2. i denotes the market, a or b. Further, assume that all three news variables are uncorrelated, i.e. $E(S_t^a S_t^b) = 0$ and $E(W_t S_t^i) = 0$. Moreover, all variables are identically distributed over time and serially independent.

There are two market makers, one in each market. The changes in security values cannot be observed directly. Rather, in each period each market maker receives a noisy signal about the value change in his security, $\theta_{i,t} = W_t + S_{i,t} + \epsilon_{i,t}$. Both signals include the common marketwide component W_t, a security specific component $S_{i,t}$, and noise $\epsilon_{i,t}$. Note that market makers do not observe separately the global and the local news component. The noise $\epsilon_{i,t}$ is normally distributed with mean zero and variance σ_ϵ^2. Both $\epsilon_{i,t}$ are mutually uncorrelated, there are no correlations with W_t and $S_{i,t}$, and there are no serial dependencies.

Each period t, the market makers in both markets also observe the series of past prices of both securities $P_{a,t-1}, ..., P_{a,1}, P_{b,t-1}, ..., P_{b,1}$. Let $\Delta P_{i,t}^*$ define the price innovation in security i conditional on its signal $\theta_{i,t}$. Assuming that market makers earn zero expected profits, and given the normality of all variables, the price innovation corresponds to a linear projection of the security value on the signal:

$$\begin{aligned}
\Delta P_{i,t}^* &= E(\Delta V_{i,t}|\theta_{i,t}) \\
&= E(\Delta V_{i,t}) + \frac{Cov(\Delta V_{i,t}, \theta_{i,t})}{Var(\theta_{i,t})}(\theta_{i,t} - E(\theta_{i,t})) \\
&= 0 + \frac{\sigma_W^2 + \sigma_S^2}{\sigma_W^2 + \sigma_S^2 + \sigma_\epsilon^2}\theta_{i,t} \\
&= k\theta_{i,t} \qquad (4.2)
\end{aligned}$$

with k = $\frac{\sigma_W^2+\sigma_S^2}{\sigma_W^2+\sigma_S^2+\sigma_\epsilon^2}$ denoting the signal-to-noise ratio in θ. Information about the series of past price innovations $\Delta P^*_{a,t}$ and $\Delta P^*_{b,t}$ can be retrieved from the series of past actual prices changes $\Delta P_{i,t}$, as will be shown later. The pricing strategy of market maker i in period t can be written as conditional on the current signal, $\theta_{i,t}$ and the series of past $\Delta P^*_{i,t}$:

$$\begin{aligned} P_{i,t} &= E(V_{i,t}|\theta_{i,t}, \Delta P^*_{a,t-1}, ..., \Delta P^*_{a,1}, \Delta P^*_{b,t-1}, ..., \Delta P^*_{b,1}) \\ &= \bar{v} + E(\Delta V_{i,t}|\theta_{i,t}) + \sum_{\tau=1}^{t-1} E(\Delta V_{i,\tau}|\Delta P^*_{a,\tau}, \Delta P^*_{b,\tau}). \end{aligned} \tag{4.3}$$

Equation(4.3) writes $P_{i,t}$ as the sum over periods 1...t of expectations of ΔV. This decomposition is possible because ΔV is serially independent. The expectation of $\Delta V_{i,t}$ is the optimal price change conditional on the signal $\theta_{i,t}, \Delta P^*_{i,t}$. Expectations of past $\Delta V_{i,\tau}$, $\tau = 1...t-1$, can be conditioned on past price innovations $\Delta P^*_{i,\tau}$ as these are available in the information set in t. Since $P_{i,t-1}$ can be similarly expressed, the price change in t can be written as:

$$\Delta P_{i,t} = P_{i,t} - P_{i,t-1} = E(\Delta V_{i,t}|\theta_{i,t}) + E(\Delta V_{i,t-1}|\Delta P^*_{a,t-1}, \Delta P^*_{b,t-1}) - E(\Delta V_{i,t-1}|\theta_{i,t-1}) \tag{4.4}$$

The full price change in equation(4.4) consists of thrre components: (1) $E(\Delta V_{i,t}|\theta_{i,t})$, the initial price innovation conditional on the current signal. (2) $E(\Delta V_{i,t-1}|\Delta P^*_{a,t-1}, \Delta P^*_{b,t-1})$, the optimal price innovations in t-1 conditional on the information about the initital price changes in t-1 which has become available in t. (3) The initial price innovation in t-1, based on the information set available in t-1.

Chan (1993) shows that, using multiple linear regression rules, equation (4.4) can be simplified into:

$$\Delta P_{i,t} = \Delta P^*_{i,t} + \lambda[\Delta P^*_{j,t-1} - (1-m)\Delta P^*_{i,t-1}] \tag{4.5}$$

where

$$\begin{aligned} \lambda &= \frac{(1-k)\sigma_w^2}{k(\sigma_S^2 + \sigma_\epsilon^2 + m\sigma_w^2)} \\ m &= \frac{\sigma_S^2 + \sigma_\epsilon^2}{\sigma_w^2 + \sigma_S^2 + \sigma_\epsilon^2} \end{aligned}$$

and j = b if i = a, and j = a if i = b. The first term, $\Delta P^*_{i,t}$, is the price innovation based on its own signal in t, the second term is the price readjustment based on the past price innovation in the other security j. Reanrranging equation (4.5) shows how the price innovation, $\Delta P^*_{i,t}$, can be retrieved using actually observable price changes, $\Delta P_{i,t}$:

$$\Delta P^*_{i,t} = \Delta P_{i,t} - \lambda[\Delta P^*_{j,t-1} - (1-m)\Delta P^*_{i,t-1}]. \tag{4.6}$$

Through recursive substitutions, all past price innovations can be retrieved, and thus, observing past actual price changes is the same as observing past price innovations. Finally, Chan's main result is that cross-autocovariances between price changes in i and j are positive:

$$Cov(\Delta P_{i,t}, \Delta P_{j,t-1}) = k(1-k)\sigma_W^2 > 0. \tag{4.7}$$

4.2.2 Only one market receives a noisy signal

This subsection discusses a special case of the Chan (1993) model. In the Chan (1993) model, both markets receive a noisy signal about their security value. Both signals contain the same worldwide news component W_t. In this setup only one market, market a, receives a signal. The other market b receives no new information about its security value. Everything else is as described in the Chan (1993) model. The goal is to show that, even if market b receives no signal itself, it will still adjust to price changes in a.

Since there are no news in market b, the security price in market a only adjusts to its own signal, $\theta_{a,t}$:

$$\begin{aligned}
\Delta P_{a,t} &= E(\Delta V_{a,t}|\theta_{a,t}) + \sum_{\tau=1}^{t-1} E(\Delta V_{a,\tau}|\Delta P_{b,\tau}) \\
&= E(W_t + S_{a,t}|\theta_{a,t}) + 0 \\
&= E(W_t + S_{a,t}) + \frac{Cov(W_t + S_{a,t}, \theta_{a,t})}{Var(\theta_{a,t})}(\theta_{a,t} - E(\theta_{a,t})) \\
&= 0 + \frac{\sigma_W^2 + \sigma_S^2}{\sigma_W^2 + \sigma_S^2 + \sigma_\epsilon^2}\theta_{a,t} \\
&= k\theta_{a,t}. \qquad (4.8)
\end{aligned}$$

The security price in market b, on the other hand, only adjusts to the lagged price response in the other market a, since there is no signal in b:

$$
\begin{aligned}
\Delta P_{b,t} &= \sum_{\tau=1}^{t-1} E(\Delta V_{b,\tau}|\Delta P_{a,\tau}) \\
&= E(\Delta V_{b,t-1}|\Delta P_{a,t-1}) \\
&= E(W_{t-1} + S_{b,t-1}|\Delta P_{a,t-1}) \\
&= E(W_{t-1} + S_{b,t-1}) + \frac{Cov(W_{t-1} + S_{b,t-1}, \Delta P_{a,t-1})}{Var(\Delta P_{a,t-1})}(\Delta P_{a,t-1} - E(\Delta P_{a,t-1})) \\
&= \kappa \Delta P_{a,t-1}. \qquad (4.9)
\end{aligned}
$$

where κ is the ratio of the global component's variance to the sum of global and local component variances in the news signal θ

$$
\kappa = \frac{\sigma_W^2}{\sigma_W^2 + \sigma_S^2} > 0.
$$

κ is strictly positive, as long as $\sigma_W^2 > 0$. Thus, market b will adjust to the innovations in W_t even if it doesn't receive a signal about W_t itself, simply by reacting to price movements in a. This result also does not change, if there is additional local news in market b, as long as the the local news component, S_b, is not correlated with the global component W, and thus, not correlated with price movements in a.[1]

Lastly, consider the case that the size of the global component contained in $\theta_{a,t}$ is time-varying. Consider two cases: (1) normal levels of global component (variance of W is σ_W^2) and (2) increased levels of global component in $\theta_{a,t}$ (variance of W is $\tilde{p}\sigma_W^2$, $\tilde{p} > 1$). It follows that the dependency of price movements in market b on price movements in market a is larger in the second case:

[1]In that case, equation (4.9) changes to: $\Delta P_{b,t} = \kappa \Delta P_{a,t-1} + \mu \theta_{b,t}$, where $\theta_{b,t}$ is the local news signal and μ is its signal-to-noise ratio.

$$\tilde{\kappa} = \frac{\tilde{p}\sigma_W^2}{\tilde{p}\sigma_W^2 + \sigma_S^2} > \frac{\sigma_W^2}{\sigma_W^2 + \sigma_S^2} = \kappa. \tag{4.10}$$

This suggests that the cross-market dependencies increase with the relative amount of marketwide information in the signal.

4.2.3 Model implications for cross-border information transmission

The previous subsections describe the Chan (1993) model and detail a special case of the model. Chan (1993) originally used the model to explain cross-autocorrelations between different stocks. He argues that the return in one stock depends on lagged returns of other stocks because these other stock price movements reveal marketwide information which is priced in the first stock. However, the same model can be applied to the information transmission between international financial markets, specifically between the United States' and the German bond market.

In the following discussion, I will only address one-sided information transmission from the US to Germany. This limitation is for two reasons: My analysis focuses on the effects of *US* macroeconomic news on cross-border information flow. It is sensible to assume that during a limited time window around the announcement, the transmission direction is almost entirely one-sided from the US to Germany. In addition, the United States is by far the world's largest financial market. In empirical studies it has frequently been concluded that the US financial market affects almost all other countries' financial markets, while it is virtually unaffected by reverse information flow (see e.g. Eun and Shim (1989), King and Wadhwani (1990), or Albuquerque and Vega (2007)).

First, consider equation (4.9). Equation (4.9) states that returns in one market b will always be positively correlated with returns in a second market a, as long as there is a nonzero global component in the information revealed in the second market a. This result holds even if market b does not receive any signal about the news.

This setup can be applied to information transmission between the US and the German bond market as follows: The US bond market receives information and the US bond price adjusts accordingly. This information might not be available to German market participants. Thus, they don't know what news caused the price change, and whether or not this news is of relevance for German bond prices. What could such news be that is only locally available? For example, it could be a market comment broadcasted on national televison (Think CNBC in the US, or n-tv in Germany), or published on a website that is frequented mostly by market participants of one country and not the other (finance.yahoo.com or finance.yahoo.de). Observing the US price movements, the German bond price adjusts according to changes in expected values, which takes into account that the US price *might* have moved in response to (partly) globally relevant news. Thus, the German bond price follows the US price movement.

I consider this 'normal' price transmission, because it also occurs in the absence of any public news announcements which are observable by both markets. Thus, I formulate this hypothesis as H1.

H1: Normal price transmission

> Each price movement in the US bond futures induces a positively correlated subsequent price movement in the German bond futures.

Second, consider equation (4.10). Equation (4.10) states that the cross-market dependencies vary if the composition of the news signal changes. Applied to US-German return transmission, this suggests that if the global component in price innovations is believed to be high, cross-market dependencies are large. The global component in US price innovations might be particularly large after the announcement of macroeconomic news. It is often argued, see e.g. Karolyi and Stulz (1996), Franke and Hess (2000), or Connolly and Wang (2003), that economic news is of particularly large global relevance. In contrast, a change in US taxation laws is most probably of less global relevance, even if it might strongly affect US bond prices.

For a German market participant, any US price movement in the aftermath of a macroeconomic announcement is considered to be very likely related to that announcement. For instance, Green (2004) argues that in the 30 minutes following a macroeconomic announcement, private interpretations of the news create private information. This private information leads to order flow, and the latter leads to US bond price movements which are observable by German bond traders. It follows that all US bond price movements in the aftermath of a US economic news release are suspected to contain a particularly large global relevance, even if the German market participant does not know what particular news caused the US price change. I formulate H2 as

H2: Transmission of globally information

> For a certain period following US macroeconomic announcements, each US bond price movement has a larger effect on subsequent German bond price movements than usual.

Lastly, consider equation (4.7). Equation (4.7) states that there will be cross-market dependencies, even if both markets receive a news signal that contains the same global component. The news signals in the model, $\theta_a = W + S_a + \epsilon_a$ and $\theta_b = W + S_b + \epsilon_b$, can be viewed as the implications of a public macroeconomic announcement for each of the respective markets. Due to worldwide media coverage, US macroeconomic news is instantaneously made public to everyone at the same time, including German bond traders. However, each country needs to interpret the common signal in terms of its implications for the respective country's bond prices. Therefore, the public news announcement is translated into different signals.

Assume that there is public news which is released to German and US bond traders at the same time. It could, for instance, be the US employment report with the headline 'nonfarm payrolls 100k less than expected'. This common signal might translate into a boost for worldwide bond prices of +0.2, an additional boost for US bonds of +0.3, and no additional boost for German bonds. The price-relevant signal for the US market is a noisy estimate of +0.5, and the price-relevant signal for the German market is a noisy estimate of +0.2. Note, that economic news cannot be deterministically translated into bond price changes.[2] Therefore both markets respond to their noisy estimates of the news implications. Most importantly, it is well conceivable that interpretation errors, i.e. deviations from +0.5 and +0.2 in the interpretations, are not correlated across the two countries. Thus, both markets observe the same announcement but interpret its implications for their respective bond prices differently.

In a first step both markets adjust their bond prices according to their own interpretation. Then, in a second step the initial price change is adjusted to account for the other market's price response. Interpretation errors are likely not correlated across the two markets. Thus, for a German bond trader the US price response contains supplemental information that reduces the uncertainty about his own interpretation of the public announcement. In other words, both transmission channels the macroeconomic announcement itself and the US price response contribute to the price response in German bonds. This is formulated as:

[2]For example, it is well known that economic news implications for stock prices differ between good and bad states of the economy, see e.g. McQueen and Roley (1993) or Boyd, Hu, and Jagannathan (2005).

H3: Transmission of public economic news

> Immediately following a US macroeconomic announcement, German bond futures prices respond to both, surprises in the announcement and lagged price movements of US bond futures.

Hypotheses H1 and H2 are predicted by the special case of the Chan (1993) model in which US news is not observable in Germany, as described in section 4.2.2. The empirical validation is rather straightforward. For H1, I examine a sample during which there is likely little news that is publicly observable by market participants in both Germany and the US. I choose a sample during which there is no public US or German macroeconomic announcement. Then I investigate whether German price movements are positively related to lagged US price changes. For H2, I repeat the analysis for a sample during which US price innovations presumably contain a large global component, but for which there is no direct price effect of macroeconomic announcement surprises. For this I choose the period following US macroeconomic announcements, specifically the period from 1:00 to 30:00 minutes post the announcement. In that sample, I test whether the dependency of German returns on lagged US returns is larger than usual.

Whether or not the transmission of public US economic news to German bond markets follows the Chan (1993) model, as described in section 4.2.1, is more difficult to validate empirically. For this I examine the period during which the announcement surprise immediately affects bond prices, specifically the first post-announcement minute. H3 states that I find both a direct announcement effect on German bond returns and a dependency on lagged US returns. However, the dependency on lagged US returns could also result from normal transmission as predicted by H1. Thus, I also examine whether the depedency is larger than usual, since macroeconomic announcements almost certainly contain an unusually large global component. Admittedly, even if I validate H3 and additionally find the dependency on lagged US returns to be larger than usual, there could still be other explanations. Nevertheless, it is interesting to study the transmission effects immediately during the announcement, as rejecting H3 would strongly suggest that the Chan (1993) does not explain how US economic news is transmitted to Germany. Thus, H3 can be viewed as a necessary, but not sufficient condition for the Chan (1993) model to hold for the transmission of economic news.

4.2.4 Numerical examples

The time-varying dynamics of cross-market dependency are exemplified using three numerical examples. Again, I focus only on one transmission direction, that is from the US to the German bond market.

(1) Normal price transmission

Assume that under normal circumstances the US news components W, S_{US} and ϵ_{US} are normally distributed with mean zero and variance one. Let there be a local US news signal θ. Think of, for instance, a positive market commentary on national television that translates into an increase in US bond prices of +1.0. θ, i.e. the market commentary, is a noisy assesment, since the commentator might be wrong in his assesment. Therefore the US bond price increases by the signal-to-noise ratio: $\Delta P_{US} = k * \theta = \frac{\sigma_W^2+\sigma_S^2}{\sigma_W^2+\sigma_S^2+\sigma_\epsilon^2} * 1.0 = \frac{2}{3} * 1.0 = \frac{2}{3}$. As German bond traders observe the US price movement, they don't observe the news that caused it. Thus, the German bond price adjusts according to the ratio of global to global+local news component: $\Delta P_{GE} = \kappa * \Delta P_{US} = \frac{\sigma_W^2}{\sigma_W^2+\sigma_S^2} * \frac{2}{3} = \frac{1}{2} * \frac{2}{3} = \frac{1}{3}$.

(2) Price transmission following macroeconomic announcements

Assume that in the aftermath of a US macroeconomic announcement, the global news component in US price innovations is relatively larger than usual. ϵ_{US} is distributed as usual with variance of one. But the local news component is smaller than usual, $\sigma_S^2 = \frac{1}{3}$, and the global news component is larger than usual, $\sigma_W^2 = \frac{5}{3}$. Again, let there be a local US news signal that cannot be observed in Germany, which tranlates into an increase in US bond prices of +1.0. The US bond price again adjusts according to the signal-to-noise ratio which as before is $k * \theta = \frac{\sigma_W^2+\sigma_S^2}{\sigma_W^2+\sigma_S^2+\sigma_\epsilon^2} * 1.0 = \frac{2}{3}$. Again, German bond traders don't observe the signal but only observe the US price movement. However, this time they know that price innovations in the aftermath of macroeconomic announcements typically contain a larger global component. Therefore the German price response is larger than usual: $\Delta P_{GE} = \tilde{\kappa} * \Delta P_{US} = \frac{\sigma_W^2}{\sigma_W^2+\sigma_S^2} * \frac{2}{3} = \frac{5}{6} * \frac{2}{3} = \frac{5}{9}$.

(3) Price transmission of macroeconomic news

Assume that during macroeconomic announcements news signals comprise entirely of interpretations of the public news release. There is no news of the kind described in case (1) and (2) that is only observable in the US and not in Germany. Let the variances reflect the generally large importance and the enheightened global relevance of the economic news. Therefore the ratio of the worldwide to local component is the same as in case (2) and all variances are 10 times larger: $\sigma_W^2 = \frac{50}{3}$, $\sigma_S^2 = \frac{10}{3}$, $\sigma_\epsilon^2 = 10$. US macroeconomic announcements are also observable in Germany. Let the variances for the components in the German signal θ_{GE}, i.e. the German interpretation of the same announcement, be the same. But importantly, the German and US interpretation errors, $\sigma_{GE,\epsilon}^2$ and $\sigma_{US,\epsilon}^2$, are not correlated. Assume that there is a US nonfarm payrolls announcement, that is interpreted by the US bond market as +6 for the US bond price, and by the German bond market as +3 for the German bond price.

The model predictions for the price adjustments are given by equation (4.5). In the first period, since there are no past price innovations, both markets directly respond to their respective interpretations of the nonfarm payrolls announcement:

$$\begin{aligned}
\Delta P_{US,1} &= \Delta P^*_{US,1} + \lambda[\Delta P^*_{GE,0} - (1-m)\Delta P^*_{US,0}] \\
\Delta P_{US,1} &= k\theta_{US} \\
\Delta P_{US,1} &= \frac{50/3 + 10/3}{50/3 + 10/3 + 10} * 6 = 4 \qquad (4.11)
\end{aligned}$$

and

$$\Delta P_{GE,1} = \frac{50/3 + 10/3}{50/3 + 10/3 + 10} * 3 = 2.$$

In the second period, both markets revise their initial response according to the respective other market's price response that has become available in the second period. Further assume that there is no new news signal.

$$\begin{aligned}
\Delta P_{US,2} &= \Delta P^*_{US,2} + \lambda[\Delta P^*_{GE,1} - (1-m)\Delta P^*_{US,1}] \\
\Delta P_{US,2} &= 0 + \lambda[\Delta P_{GE,1} - (1-m)\Delta P_{US,1}] \\
\Delta P_{US,2} &= \lambda * (2 - (1-m) * 4) \\
\Delta P_{US,2} &= \frac{45}{112} * (2 - (1 - \frac{4}{9}) * 4) = -\frac{5}{56} \qquad (4.12)
\end{aligned}$$

and

$$\Delta P_{GE,2} = \frac{45}{112} * (4 - (1 - \frac{4}{9}) * 2) = \frac{65}{56}.$$

All three examples are visualized in Figure 4.1. All bond prices are standardized to be zero in period 0.

Figure 4.1: Numerical model examples

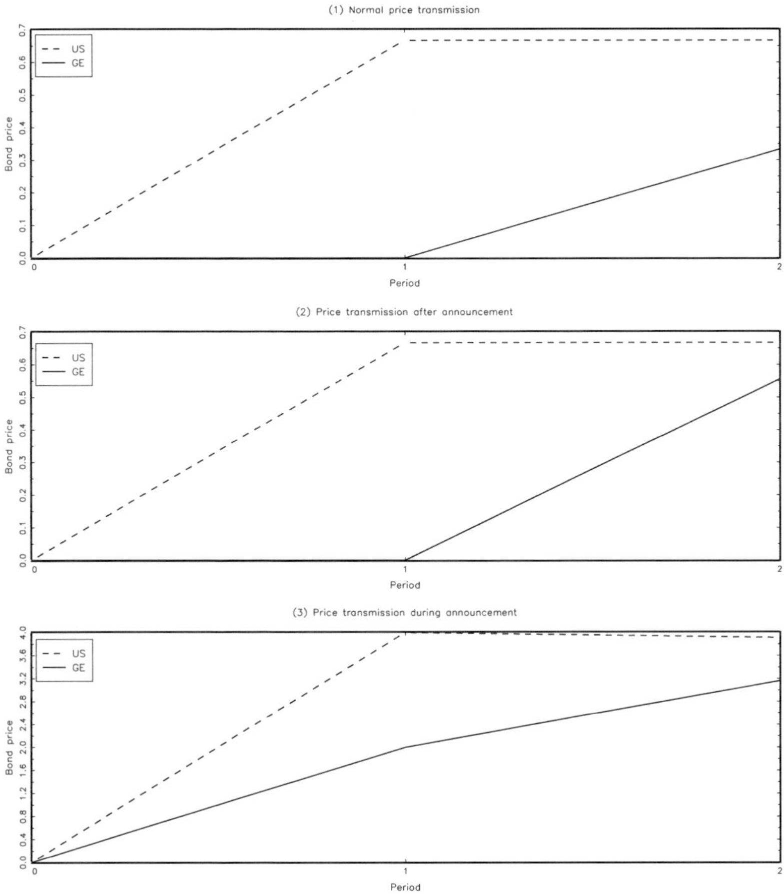

This figure plots the price response of the German and US bond price based on the model described in section 4.2 and the numerical examples described in subsection 4.2.4.

4.2.5 Comparison to other models in the literature

I apply the Chan (1993) model to the transmission of price movements and economic news from the United States' to the German bond market. The news signals in the model represent interpretations of US macroeconomic news implications for the respective market's bond price. The model rests on three main assumptions. First, news signals in both markets contain a positively correlated global component. This seems apparent given that both economies are extensively integrated through financial and trade relationships. Second, noise between the signals is uncorrelated. This is also conceivable, as initial interpretations in both countries are made instantaneously in response to the news release and independent of each other. Third, prices from other markets become available with a period of one lag. This is true if periods are short. In my empirical analysis one period is as short as the time between two trades. In my context, the main implication of the Chan (1993) model is that, although the initial response to the announcement occurs independent of the other market, subsequently the price is revised to account for the other market's price response. In other words, both the economic news itself and the US price response contribute to price discovery in Germany following US macroeconomic announcements.

In a similar effort, King and Wadhwani (1990) model the price change in two stock markets conditional on news observed in the home market and on the foreign market's price response. Like Chan (1993), news is assumed to be either idiosyncratic or of global relevance. The main result is that large return variance in one country also increases variance in the other country. With regard to the price movements, Hypotheses H1 and H2 can both be derived from the King and Wadhwani (1990) model (see their equations (7), (8), and (9)), too. However, there is one main difference: all four news components (local/foreign, idiosyncratic/global) in King and Wadhwani (1990) are assumed to be mutually uncorrelated. Thus, public macroeconomic announcements are difficult to reconcile with the model, because in the model the global factor in one market is uncorrelated with the global factor in the other market. Applied to public economic news releases, this would entail that there is no correlation at all in the interpretations of the public economic news between two markets. This seems unrealistic given the typically positive correlations in US and German bond returns on announcement days (see Franke and Hess (2000)).

Albuquerque and Vega (2007) model the co-movement between Portuguese and US stock returns. In contrast to Chan (1993), Albuquerque and Vega (2007) model prices and liquidity. The model rests on two main assumptions. First, that information transmission is unidirectional, that is only from the US to Portugal and not vice versa. Second, that US investors respond to US economic news first, and Portuguese investors respond not before the US price response becomes observable, too. One of the model's main predictions is that correlation between Portuguese and US stocks is not larger on days with US macroeconomic news than on any other day. Intuitively, US investors filter their private information and combine it with the public news so that the globally relevant news component is fully contained in the US return. Thus, US macroeconomic news does not contribute to price formation in the Portuguese market after accounting for the US return. The reason for this prediction is that the model crucially assumes Portuguese investors to wait for the US response before Portuguese stock prices are adjusted. This assumption seems not to hold for my case, given the finding in chapter 3 that the German stock market responds immediately to US macroeconomic announcements.

Bae, Karolyi, and Stulz (2003) propose an interesting model to study contagion between two markets. They argue that contagion is mainly characterized by the simultaneous occurence of extreme returns. Thus, instead of examining cross-market correlations, they focus on coincidences of large returns. The idea is to examine how often extreme returns in different countries coincide, and if the occurence of an extreme return in one country affects conditional probabilities of simultaneously observing extreme returns in another country. In their empirical investigation of daily stock returns from different countries they find that especially large negative returns tend to coincide in different countries. Further, some regions (e.g. Latin America) are more contagious than other regions (e.g. Asia), i.e. extreme returns in Latin America increase conditional probabilities to find extreme returns in other regions. Unfortunately, Bae, Karolyi, and Stulz (2003) do not account for the announcement of globally relevant news such as US macroeconomic announcements. This would also contribute to the probability of finding coinciding extreme returns, if the announcement effects are highly correlated across different countries and the effects on stock prices are large. However, integrating macroeconomic announcements into the Bae, Karolyi, and Stulz (2003) model is beyond the scope of this research.

4.3 Data

4.3.1 US economic news announcement data

In this chapter I study the transmission of information from the United States' bond market to the German bond market. For the empirical analysis, I employ the same data on US macroeconomic announcements that I used for the analyses in the previous chapter. As before, the announcement data consist of four pieces of information: the release date and time, the announced headline figure, and the market expectation. The surprise value of each announcement is again calculated, as decribed by equation (2.1). However, in this chapter the investigation period is limited by availability of US bond futures data. Therefore the sample is 2001 to 2005. Table 4.1 presents summary statistics for the announcement data used in the empirical analyses in this chapter.

Table 4.1: US macroeconomic news announcement data

Abbr.	Announcment	Obs.	Availability from	until	Source	Time (CET)	Release cycle	Stand. Surprise min	mean	max
E1	**Nonfarm Payrolls**	60	01/01	12/05	BLS	2:30 pm	m	-2.94	-0.14	3.67
E2	**Unemployment Rate**	60	01/01	12/05	BLS	2:30 pm	m	-2.77	-0.27	2.77
E3	**Hourly Earnings**	60	01/01	12/05	BLS	2:30 pm	m	-2.38	0.03	2.85
GDP	**GDP advance report**	19	01/01	07/05	BEA	2:30 pm	q	-1.51	0.25	2.14
CPI2	**Consumer Price Index**	60	01/01	12/05	BLS	2:30 pm	m	-1.83	0.01	3.66
PPI2	**Producer Price Index**	60	01/01	12/05	BLS	2:30 pm	m	-4.87	-0.14	3.25
RS2	**Retail Sales**	60	01/01	12/05	BC	2:30 pm	m	-3.04	-0.09	2.53
DGO	**Durable Goods Orders**	60	01/01	12/05	BC	2:30 pm	m	-2.72	0.03	3.94
IJC	**Initial Jobless Claims**	256	01/01	12/05	ETA	2:30 pm	w	-3.88	-0.01	4.37
TRD	Trade Balance	60	01/01	12/05	BEA	2:30 pm	m	-4.12	-0.14	3.42
HS	Housing Starts	55	01/01	07/05	BC	2:30 pm	m	-3.20	0.16	2.91
PI	Personal Income	60	01/01	12/05	BEA	2:30 pm	m	-3.73	0.14	5.80
BI	Business Inventories	60	01/01	12/05	BC	2:30 pm	m	-3.83	0.15	2.55
IP	Industrial Production	60	01/01	12/05	FRB	3:15 pm	m	-4.01	0.03	3.28
ISM	ISM Index	60	01/01	12/05	ISM	4:00 pm	m	-2.35	-0.02	3.62
CC	Consumer Confidence	60	01/01	12/05	CB	4:00 pm	m	-2.61	0.06	2.67
LI	Leading Indicators	60	01/01	12/05	CB	4:00 pm	m	-2.64	0.10	3.63
CS	Construction Spending	60	01/01	12/05	BC	4:00 pm	m	-2.48	0.03	2.53
IMP	Import Price Index	55	01/01	09/05	BLS	4:00 pm	m	-3.93	-0.09	1.97
ISS	ISM Services	60	01/01	12/05	ISM	4:00 pm	m	-1.78	0.19	2.46

This table reports the availability of US economic news announcement data that we use in our study. We focus on price-relevant 2:30 pm announcements, marked in bold. We report the headline figure, its abbreviation (Abbr.), the number of observations in our sample (Obs.), the availability of our sample, the scheduled release time (in Central European Time, CET) and the release cycle: w(eekly), m(onthly), or q(uarterly). The abbreviations for the releasing agency are: Bureau of the Census (BC), Bureau of Economic Analysis (BEA), Bureau of Labor Statistics (BLS), Conference Board (CB), Employment and Training Administration (ETA), Federal Reserve Board (FRB), Institute for Supply Chain Management (ISM), NTC Research (NTC). The three right-most columns report summary statistics for the standardized surprise in the announcements, i.e. announced figure minus market expectation according to median analyst expectations, standardized by the sample standard deviation.

Some announcements are more important than others. My analysis focuses on the important 2:30 pm announcements which induce a significant price impact on the BUND futures. Those announcemnents are marked in bold in Table 4.1. I am interested in the differences in cross-border information transmission between announcement days and non-announcement days. Thus, I differentiate between 3 types of days in my sample. I define announcement days as days on which any of the seven important announcements occur. Days on which only unimportant announcements (economic news types not marked in bold in Table 4.1) occur are excluded from the sample. The remaining days on which neither an important nor an unimportant announcement occurs constitutes the non-announcement day sample.

4.3.2 US and German bond futures data

I examine cross-border information transmission using high frequency trade-by-trade data on the BUND futures and the ten year T-Note futures in the sample January 2, 2001 to December 31, 2005. All trade observations are time-stamped to the nearest second. I use futures market data because transaction costs are very low and price discovery occurs faster than in the spot market (see, e.g., Booth, So, and Tse (1999)). The BUND is a futures contract on a long-term German government bond ranging from 8.5 years to 10 years in maturity. It is traded on the fully computerized EUREX. The T-Note is traded on the Chicago Board of trade. It is a futures contract on a US government bond with a maturity range from 6.5 to 10 years. T-Note contracts are traded electronically and on the floor. I use T-Note prices from computer trading as throughout most of my sample electronic trading was more liquid than floor trading.

BUND returns are calculated as midquote log returns. T-Note returns are calculated as log returns between transaction prices because quote data is not available for the T-

Note. Transaction prices are advantageous because they might better reflect cross-border information flow in real-time. Given the high speed of information transmission it might be more beneficial for traders to focus their attention on only a single variable, the transaction price, rather than the two quote variables.

Table 4.2 reports descriptive statistics for BUND and T-Note futures data. I study a 40-minute window around the release of 2:30 pm (CET) US macroeconomic announcements.[3] Although there are also US macroeconomic announcements at 3:15 and 4:00, the 2:30 announcements are generally considered by far the most important ones. 2:20:00 to 2:29:59 is the 'before announcement' sample. A longer sample is not possible because regular T-Note trading begins only at 2:20. T-Note computer trading is open virtually around the clock but trading is very thin outside regular trading hours. Public information is processed very quickly on financial markets, yet it takes a few seconds. For example, empirical results of Ederington and Lee (1995) suggest the the processing in the US bond futures market takes 40 seconds. I assume that surprises in macroeconomic announcement need one minute to be processed, and I choose 2:30:00 to 2:30:59 as the 'during announcement' sample.[4] Finally, 2:31:00 to 2:59:59 is the 'after announcement' sample. During this half hour, Green (2004) finds that trading in US bonds contains much private information, presumably generated by private interpretations of the public economic news. The non-announcement day sample contains the entire 40-minute window. Comparing intervals during the same time of day on announcement and non-announcement days avoids biases caused by intraday patterns.

Overall, the non-announcement sample contains 432 trading days vs. 281 announcement days. The remaining days were discarded because they contain unimportant announce-

[3]In order to find out how long announcement effects on cross-border information transmission last, I also analyze alternative windows of up to 100 minutes around the announcment. But most analyses in the results section refer to the 40-minute window.

[4]Results for alternative choices of 30 seconds, 2 minutes, and 5 minutes are presented in the appendix.

Table 4.2: Descriptive statistics for BUND and T-Note futures

Panel A: BUND futures

	Non-ann	Announcement days		
	days	before	during	after
	2:20 pm -	2:20 pm -		2:31 pm -
	2:59 pm	2:29 pm	2:30 pm	2:59 pm
total no. of observations: days	432	281	281	281
total no. of observations: trades	258,877	72,507	14,954	249,853
return std. dev. (*1000)	0.037	0.047	0.137	0.044
avg. time between trades (sec)	3.98	4.18	2.09	2.52

Panel B: 10Y T-Note futures

	Non-ann	Announcement days		
	days	before	during	after
	2:20 pm -	2:20 pm -		2:31 pm -
	2:59 pm	2:29 pm	2:30 pm	2:59 pm
total no. of observations: days	432	281	281	281
total no. of observations: trades	755,741	244,273	141,303	1,428,138
return std. dev. (*1000)	0.045	0.102	0.207	0.055
avg. time between trades (sec)	1.28	1.23	0.22	0.62

This table provides descriptive statistics for the BUND and the 10Y T-Note futures. The data is grouped into intervals on days with and without significant US announcements at 2:30 pm. The announcement sample is further grouped into intervals before (2:20:00 to 2:29:59), during (2:30:00 to 2:30:59) and after (2:31:00 to 2:59:59) the announcement time. We report the number of announcement and non-announcement days, number of trades, the standard deviation of transaction returns, and the average time between two trades. BUND transaction returns are based on mid-quotes and T-Note transaction returns are based on transaction prices. The sample covers January 2, 2001 to December 31, 2005.

ments. The second, third, and fourth row of both panels in Table 4.2 report the total number of trades in the dataset, the standard deviation of transaction returns (defined as change in log prices between two transactions), and the average time in seconds between two trades. Although the 'during announcement' sample (2:30) consist of only one minute per announcement day, it contains a relatively large total number of trade observations: 14,954 for the BUND and 141,303 for the T-Note futures. Thus, the average time between two trades is shorter in the interval immediately following the announcement than before or in the 30 minutes after the announcement. Generally, there are more transactions for T-Note futures than for BUND futures and consequently the average time between two trades is shorter for the T-Note futures. Return standard deviation is also slightly higher for the T-Note, possibly because T-Note prices are based on transaction prices whereas BUND prices are midquotes. The average duration between two trades is very small for both markets. Thus, stale prices should not be a problem. Comparing the announcement day and non-announcement day sample reveals that volatility is higher and more trades occur after a US macroeconomic announcement in both markets. Not too surprisingly, the effect of US announcements is somewhat larger for T-Notes than for the BUND futures. T-Note volatility is notably high in the before announcement sample. This, however, is most probably caused by the beginning of the trading day, rather than by the macroeconomic announcement.

Table 4.3 reports descriptive statistics for each year in my sample to illustrate changes over time. For BUND and T-Note returns, I report the total number of observations, standard deviation, and the average duration between trades for the 'during announcement' sample (2:30:00 to 2:30:59) in each year. While there is no apparent trend in the volatility, the number of trades has increased during the sample. This is particularly apparent for the T-Note. The most obvious implication on my analysis is that in the earlier

Table 4.3: Descriptive statistics over time (during announcement sample, 2:30 pm)

	BUND			T-Note		
	Obs.	std. dev.	avg. trd. dur.	Obs.	std. dev.	avg. trd. dur.
2001	2333	0.112	2.81	3137	0.198	2.26
2002	2388	0.126	2.71	13569	0.152	0.48
2003	2570	0.133	2.26	33986	0.163	0.17
2004	3343	0.195	1.82	53415	0.250	0.11
2005	4320	0.097	1.46	37196	0.192	0.17

This table reports descriptive statistics for each year in my sample to illustrate changes over time. For BUND and T-Note returns, I report the total number of observations, standard deviation, and the average duration between trades for the 'during announcement' sample (2:30:00 to 2:30:59) in each year.

years of my sample, the screen-traded T-Note might have been less liquid than today, and price innovations might have been of less importance to German traders. They might have instead chosen to follow floor-traded T-Note price movements for which I do not account in my analysis. However, if that were the case, it would bias my results towards not finding a dependency of German returns on lagged US returns. Thus, if I still find a dependency, it is safe to assume that this is not caused by the increasing importance of T-Note prices from screen-trading over time. One more concern is that, since my empirical analysis is based on trade-by-trade data, my results are much more representative for the more recent years. This, however, is not a serious concern because time periods in my analysis correspond to trades in the BUND futures market, and the number of trades in the BUND futures is relatively stable over time during my sample.

4.4 Price impact of US economic news on German and US bond futures

This section analyzes price effects of US macro announcements on German and US bond futures prices. The objective is to show how quickly the public news is processed, what the relative importance of different announcement types is, and to illustrate the price adjustment process. Cross-border transmission of price movements is not included for now.

In order to measure how long it takes until surprises in US announcements are fully incorporated into US and German bond prices, I follow Balduzzi, Elton, and Green (2001). The idea is to regress the 30-minute return between 2:30 and 3:00 on the announcement surprise, but discarding the first τ seconds immediately following the announcement. For example, if it takes 10 seconds to fully incorporate the public news then the return between 2:30:10 and 2:59:59 ($R^{10,1800}$)should not be related to the announcement surprise, whereas $R^{\tau,1800}$ should significantly be related to the 2:30 announcement surprise for $\tau = 0, 1, . . .$, 9 seconds. Therefore, for each announcement type, I run the regressions

$$R_m^{\tau,1800} = c + \beta S_m + \epsilon_m \tag{4.13}$$

where S_m is the surprise in the headline figure in month m. For the employment report, S is a vector containing the surprises for E1, E2, and E3. If two announcements occur at the same time, those observations are removed. Equation (4.13) is estimated for a number of different time horizons: $\tau = 0, 1, 2, ..., 60$ seconds, and 120, 180, ..., 1740 seconds.

Figure 4.2: Speed of BUND futures price response

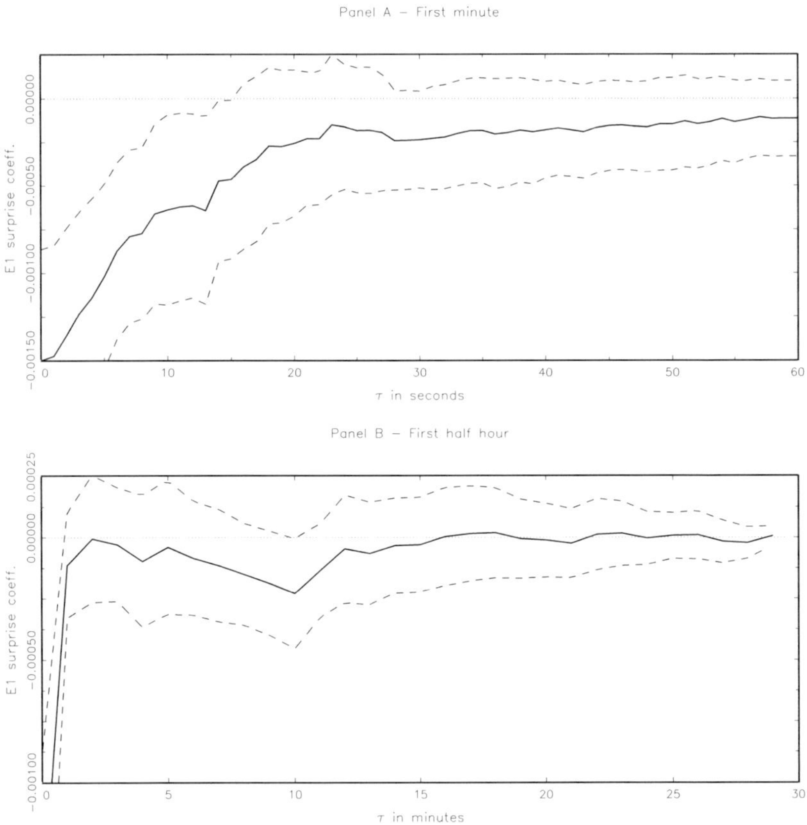

I run the regression $R_m^{\tau,1800} = c + \beta S_m + \epsilon_t$ where S_m is a vector containing the surprises in the employment report's headline figures (E1, E2, E3) in month m. $R^{\tau,1800}$ is the BUND futures price change from τ seconds past the announcement to 30 minutes past the announcement. A number of different time horizons τ are chosen: $\tau = 0, 1, 2, ..., 60, 120, ..., 1740$ seconds. This figure depicts how the coefficient estimates for the nonfarm payrolls (E1) surprise and its 95% confidence bands vary as τ is increased. Panel A depicts regression results for $\tau = 0, 1, . . ., 60$ seconds, and Panel B depicts regression results for $\tau = 0, 1, . . ., 29$ minutes.

The results for the nonfarm payrolls announcement is reported in Figure 4.2. This figure illustrates the high efficiency of the price response. Panel A depicts regression results for $\tau = 0, 1, \ldots, 60$ seconds, and Panel B depicts regression results for $\tau = 0, 1, \ldots,$ 29 minutes. The solid line is the coefficient estimate and the dashed lines are the 95% confidence bands. It is apparent that the larger τ is, i.e. the more of the immediate post-announcement seconds are discarded, the smaller the remaining announcement effect on the total price response is. If τ is set to values larger than 15 seconds I find no significant announcement effects at all. This means that, for instance, the price response between the 16th second and 30 minutes past the announcement cannot be significantly explained by the announcement surprise.

Table 4.4 reports the main results for the seven 2:30 US announcements that have a significant price impact on BUND prices. The first two columns report the BUND price response coefficient and the t-stat for $\tau = 0$ seconds. The results for $R^{0,1800}$ include the entire price response to US macroeconomic announcements for BUND and T-Note futures. The columns 3 and 4 report the maximum τ for which I find a significant price impact, i.e. for which β is significant at the 0.01 and 0.05 significance level. Columns 5 to 8 report these results for the T-Note regressions.

The most important announcement for both bond futures based on the coefficient estimate is the employment report, but only the nonfarm payrolls headline figure (E1) is highly significant for both markets. Unemployment figures (E2) are typically also considered a major component of the US employment report. For example, Hautsch and Hess (2002) show that surprises in the unemployment headline figure significantly affect two-minute US bond price returns. In my sample, unemployment surprises are significantly related to the T-Note price response at the 0.05 significance level, but do not significantly affect the BUND futures price response. The reason why I find weaker effects might be that I

Table 4.4: US announcment price impact on BUND and T-Note

	BUND				T-Note			
	$R^{0,1800}$		signif. effect lasts τ sec		$R^{0,1800}$		signif. effect lasts τ sec	
Ann	$\beta_i * 100$	t-stat	(0.01)	(0.05)	$\beta_i * 100$	t-stat	(0.01)	(0.05)
E1	-0.150	4.615	8	15	-0.259	4.380	5	11
E2	0.040	1.547	— *insignif* —		0.122	2.524	*insignif*	13
E3	-0.055	1.249	— *insignif* —		-0.058	0.815	— *insignif* —	
GDP	-0.121	6.075	8	16	-0.153	4.843	4	6
CPI2	-0.071	5.206	54	240	-0.080	3.527	1	120
PPI2	-0.039	4.594	1	3	-0.034	2.320	*insignif*	0
RS2	-0.056	2.530	*insignif*	2	-0.106	2.524	*insignif*	1
DGO	-0.064	3.268	1	2	-0.100	3.321	1	2
IJC	0.033	5.289	22	50	0.037	3.775	4	7

For each announcement we run the regression $R_m^{\tau,1800} = c + \beta S_m + \epsilon_t$ where S_m is the surprise in the headline fuigure in month m. For the employment report, S is a vector containing the surprises for E1, E2, and E3. If two announcements occur at the same time, those observations are removed. $R^{\tau,1800}$ is the price change from τ seconds past the announcement to 30 minutes past the announcement. A number of different time horizons τ are chosen to measure the price impact: τ = 0, 1, 2, ..., 60 seconds, and 120, 180, ..., 1740 seconds. The first two columns report the BUND price response coefficient (*100) and the t-stat for $\tau = 0$ seconds. The columns 3 and 4 report the maximum τ for which we find a significant price impact, i.e. for which β is significant at the 0.01 and 0.05 significance level. Columns 5 to 8 report the results for the T-Note regression. The sample covers January 2, 2001 to December 31, 2005.

study the response of the 30-minute return, which is noisier than the two-minute returns studied by Hautsch and Hess (2002). My results are consistent with Becker, Finnerty, and Kopecky (1995) who study 15-minute returns and find only a weakly significant US bond price response at the 0.10 significance level. The main result, however, is that the nonfarm payrolls headline figure (E1) is by far the most important component of the employment report. Therefore the two other headline figures in the employment report will be excluded from the analysis from hereon. The highest t-stat for both bond markets is found for the GDP announcement. Nevertheless, each announcement reported here has a significant impact on both markets, and all t-stats are at least 2.32. The price response direction is identical for BUND and T-Note futures. This indicates that US announcements might contain a common component that affects US and German interest rates into the same direction. Not surprisingly, the T-Note response is stronger in magnitude, indicating that part of the US news is not relevant for valuing German bonds.

I interpret the maximum τ for which equation (4.13) yields a significant estimate for β as the time it takes the bond futures markets to fully incorporate the US economic news into bond prices. Generally, both markets are very efficient in processing the news. T-Note prices generally incorporate the news a few seconds earlier than BUND futures prices. Except for the CPI and initial jobless claim (IJC) announcement, all US announcements are processed within no more than 16 seconds. IJC and CPI announcements take longer, up to two minutes, to be fully processed. Thus, the time it takes to process economic news can be narrowed down to somewhere between a few seconds and a few minutes. Since Ederington and Lee (1995) estimate this time at 40 seconds, I will assume 1 minute in my empirical analysis. In addition, I conduct the analyses assuming alternative durations for processing the news and report the alternative results in the appendix.

In order to better visualize the price response process in US and German bond futures I plot two exemplary price responses in Figure 4.3 and 4.4. Figure 4.3 plots the cumulative return for BUND and T-Note futures during the first 120 seconds following the nonfarm payrolls announcement on March 7, 2003 at 2:30 pm CET. As shown before, nonfarm payrolls is the most important US economic news for both markets, and this particular announcement is the largest absolute surprise in my sample.[5] The announced figure was 3.0 standard deviations lower than expected. The price response pattern in this example is similar to what Ederington and Lee (1995) find. There is no single large price movement

[5]This, of course, does not necessarily mean that the price response has to be the largest, since other considerations such as the announcement's precision also plays a role (see e.g. Hautsch and Hess (2007) and Hautsch, Hess, and Müller (2008)).

Figure 4.3: BUND and T-note price response – an example (large NFP surprise)

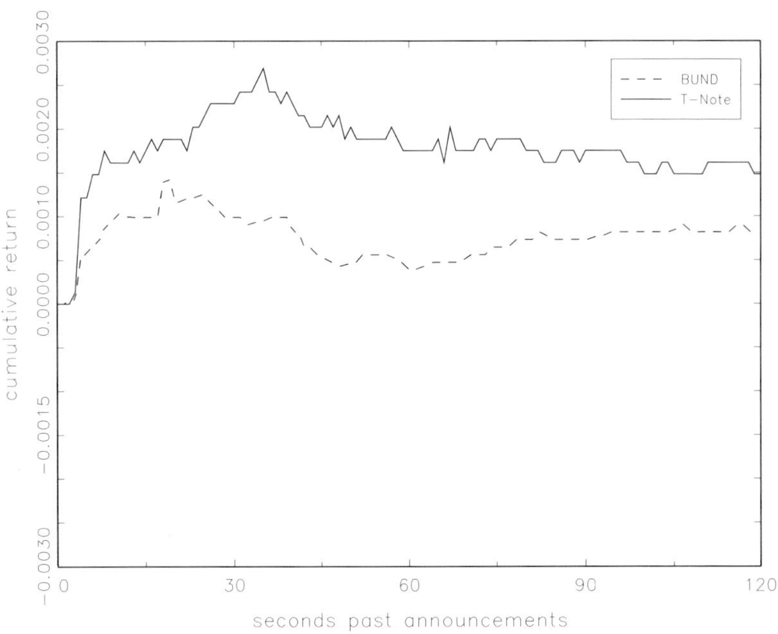

This figure plots the cumulative return for BUND and T-Note futures during the first 120 seconds following the nonfarm payrolls announcemnet on March 7, 2003 at 2:30 pm CET. This is the largest absolute surprise in the nonfarm payrolls announcement in my sample. The announced figure was 3.0 standard deviations lower than expected.

Figure 4.4: BUND and T-note price response – an example (small NFP surprise)

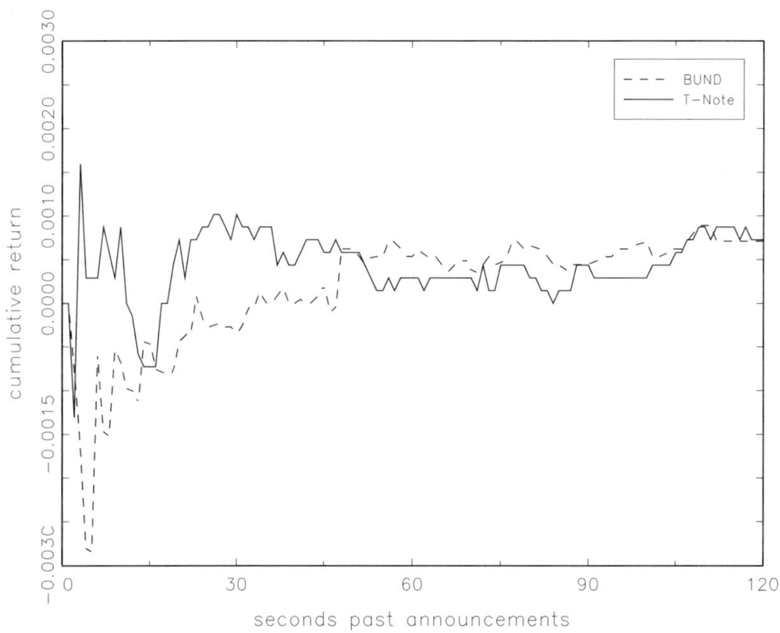

This figure plots the cumulative return for BUND and T-Note futures during the first 120 seconds following the nonfarm payrolls announcemnet on June 4, 2004 at 2:30 pm CET. This is the smallest absolute surprise in the nonfarm payrolls announcement in my sample. The announced figure was less than 0.1 standard deviations lower than expected.

that fully incorporates the news, but there is a series of numerous, but small price changes. As an example, if the cumulative repsonse was 0.1% then it would be much more likely to find ten price increases of 0.01% instead of one price increase of 0.1%.

Figure 4.4 plots the US and German bond futures price response to the nonfarm payrolls announcement on June 4, 2004. This is the smallest absolute surprise in my sample and the cumulative price response after 120 seconds is very small for both US and German bonds. However, there is considerable price movements immediately following the announcement for this example, too.

I draw three conclusions from the price response analysis. First, US macroeconomic announcements are processed very quickly in US and German bond futures. I consider one minute as the period during which the news is processed. Although this might be more than it takes for highly efficient futures markets to process the news, this period ensures that announcements that occured later than exactly at 2:30:00 are accounted for. Secondly, the analysis shows that some announcements are consistently more important than others. The two most important announcements are the nonfarm payrolls and the GDP announcement. Lastly, I confirm that the price response occurs not in one large price movement, but in a series of smaller price adjustments.

4.5 Measuring information transmission in trade-by-trade data

This section presents the empirical framework for measuring transmission of price movements from one market to a second market. The previous section has shown that public information is fully processed very quickly, wihtin about 15 seconds. The high efficiency of financial markets necessitates a model that can capture information flow that occurs within a few seconds. Using returns based on intervals of a fixed duration seems inpractical, as even for intervals as short as ten seconds most of the cross-market transmission would occur during simultaneous intervals. Therefore, I opt to base my analysis on transaction returns, that is price changes between two trades. A similar approach, likewise based on transaction returns, has been previously utilized by Finucane (1999) and Zebedee (2001). For my analysis, I choose an augmented version of Hasbrouck (1991). Hasbrouck constructs a vector autoregressive system to study the impact of trades on the price process. In particular, he specifies a system with two equations. The first equation of the system models the trading process, while the second equation models the price revision process. Specifically, trade-by-trade price changes are regressed on lagged price changes and the unexpected component of the current trade's and lagged trades' order flow.

My model focuses on the price revision process of German BUND futures prices. In addition to lagged price changes and order flow, I additionally include lagged US T-Note price changes into the regression. I only model one type of cross-border information flow: Transmission of US bond price movements to German bond prices. In particular, I do not model the transmission of US order flow and the reverse transmission of German information to the US market. The purpose is to keep the model parsimomious and focus on the cross-border transmission of US price movements. The ommission of US order flow is defensible as US price data is much more easily available than order flow information to non-exchange members such as German bond traders, especially given the high frequency nature of my model. Not modeling reverse transmission from Germany to the US seems justifiable since the US market is much larger and presumably contains much more globally relevant information. Further, I focus on a narrow time window around US macroeconomic announcements when it is even more unlikely that US traders look at other markets to a large extent. The empirical model is:

$$r_t^{GE} = c + \sum_{i=0}^{5} \gamma_i r_{t-i}^{US} + \sum_{i=0}^{5} \delta_i x_{t-i}^{GE} + \sum_{i=1}^{5} \lambda_i r_{t-i}^{GE} + \epsilon_t \tag{4.14}$$

where r_t^{GE} is the BUND futures transaction return of trade t. r_t^{US} is the return of the T-Note futures between clock time of trade t and clock time of t-1, i.e. the last T-Note price available to BUND traders before t, minus the last T-Note price available to BUND traders before t-1. x_t is the unexpected order flow of transaction t. In order to calculate the unexpected order flow, I follow Underwood (2007) and Albuquerque and Vega (2007) and, in a first step, relate actual order flow to its on its own lags, and lags of r^{US} and r^{GE}:

$$q_t = c + \sum_{i=1}^{5} \zeta_{1,i} q_{t-i} + \sum_{i=0}^{5} \zeta_{2,i} r_{t-i}^{US} + \sum_{i=1}^{5} \zeta_{3,i} r_{t-i}^{GE} + x_t^{GE}. \tag{4.15}$$

q_t is a trade indicator variable that takes the value 1 for a buy and -1 for a sell. The unexpected order flow x_t is first calculated as the residual of equation (4.15) and then, in a second step, used in equation (4.14).[6] Following Hasbrouck (1991), I truncate all models after 5 lags.

[6]This procedure might be subject to an 'error in variables' problem. However, given the large number of observations in my dataset this problem is negligible.

Figure 4.5: Data integration for measuring trade-by-trade transmission

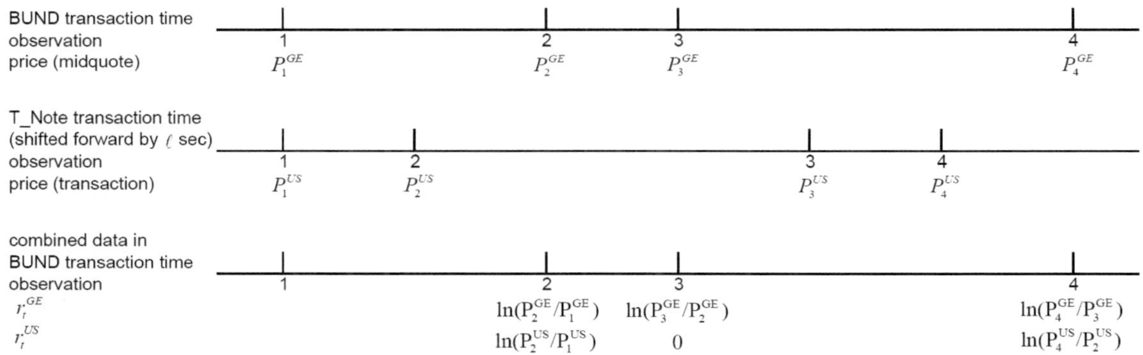

This figure illustrates how non-synchronous transactions of BUND and T-Note futures are integrated into a combined transaction time using an example of BUND and T-Note trades. Since BUND transaction returns are the dependent variable BUND transactions are chosen as the combined transaction time. The T-Note clock time is shifted forward by ℓ seconds. This is based on the assumption that BUND traders need ℓ seconds to learn about T-Note price movements. The first two lines present BUND and T-Note transactions in terms of clock time. The trades in both markets do not necessarily line up as they are recorded as they occur. The procedure for integrating T-Note prices with BUND prices is to observe the last recorded T-Note price given a newly recorded BUND transaction. For example, the last available T-Note price when the second BUND trade occurs in t_2 is P_2^{US}. When the third BUND trade occurs P_2^{US} is still the most recent T-Note price since there are no T-Note trades between t_2 and t_3. Consequently, the T-Note return between t_2 and t_3 is zero. Between t_3 and t_4 there are two T-Note transactions. Therefore the T-Note return r_4^{US} is calculated as $ln(P_4^{US}/P_2^{US})$. BUND prices are calculated using midquotes, and T-Note prices are calculated using transaction prices.

The procedure for integrating German BUND and US T-note returns is illustrated in Figure 4.5. This figure illustrates how non-synchronous transactions of BUND and T-Note futures are integrated into a combined transaction time using an example of BUND and T-Note trades. Since BUND transaction returns are the dependent variable BUND transactions are chosen as the combined transaction time. The first two lines present BUND and T-Note transactions in terms of clock time. The trades in both markets do not necessarily line up as they are recorded as they occur. The procedure for integrating T-Note prices with BUND prices is to observe the last recorded T-Note price given a newly recorded BUND transaction. For example in Figure 4.5, the last available T-Note price when the second BUND trade occurs in t_2 is P_2^{US}. When the third BUND trade occurs P_2^{US} is still the most recent T-Note price since there are no T-Note trades between t_2 and t_3. Consequently, the T-Note return between t_2 and t_3 is zero. Between t_3 and t_4 there are two T-Note transactions. Therefore the T-Note return r_4^{US} is calculated as $ln(P_4^{US}/P_2^{US})$.

A problem occurs when a BUND and a T-Note trade occur at the exact same second. Then it is impossible to tell which trade occured first. I try to mitigate this problem by shifting the T-Note clock time forward by ℓ seconds. This is based on the assumption that BUND traders need ℓ seconds to learn about T-Note price movements. The German return in t is now regressed on US returns occuring in $t - \ell$ or earlier. This assures that all US returns, used as independent variables, occured before the German return in t which is the dependent variable. Since it is likely that T-Note prices are readily available in real-time to BUND traders, I choose $\ell = 1$ second as the base specification. Moreover, $\ell = 1$ second seems sensible considering the fast price response to macroeconomic announcements (see the previous section) and considering the increasing use of algorithmic trading strategies (see, e.g., Hendershott, Jones, Menkveld (2008)). However, my analyses are also repeated with alternative specifications of ℓ for which I report results in the appendix.

Table 4.5 reports estimation results for equation (4.14). Values that are significantly ($p < 0.01$) different from zero are denoted by '*'. The sample includes the time window 2:20:00 to 2:59:59 on non-announcement days only, because this section investigates normal price transmission that can be found between international markets at any time. This tests hypothesis H1, that US bond price movements always contain a global component. The first column in Table 4.5 contains estimates for the Hasbrouck (1991) specification, i.e. lagged US returns are ommitted from equation (4.14). Similar to Hasbrouck's analysis of US stocks I find a positive impact of lagged order flow which indicates that buys reveal good private information and sells reveal bad private information. The coefficients for lagged returns are negative which Hasbrouck explains with inventory control motives. When prices go up it is usually accompanied by a buy. Thus, liquidity providers try to elicit a sell and clear inventories by reducing quoted prices. All variables are highly significant for all five lags which can be related to a lagged response.

The next rows contain estimation results for equation (4.14) based on shifting the T-Note clock forward by ℓ seconds. The second column, $\ell = 1$ second, contains the basic specification. The coefficents for lagged US return can be interpreted as follows. A unit increase in T-Note prices leads to a 0.045 increase in BUND prices for the next BUND transaction. This T-Note impulse also positively impacts the next five subsequent BUND trades. The second coefficient is slightly larger than the first one, and then the coefficients gradually decrease. This indicates that some BUND traders immediately, that is within one trade, respond to each price movement in the US market. However, most traders respond between the first and second subsequent trade, and fewer and fewer BUND traders respond to the initial T-Note impulse after more subsequent trades. The sum of the six US

Table 4.5: Trade-by-trade cross-border information transmission

	no r^{US}	$\ell = 1$ sec	2 sec	5 sec	10 sec	20 sec	30 sec
r_t^{US}		0.045*	0.049*	0.027*	0.005*	0.004*	0.000
r_{t-1}^{US}		0.058*	0.054*	0.025*	0.004*	0.002	0.001
r_{t-2}^{US}		0.047*	0.041*	0.017*	0.008*	0.004*	0.003
r_{t-3}^{US}		0.032*	0.026*	0.011*	0.004*	0.003	0.001
r_{t-4}^{US}		0.021*	0.017*	0.009*	0.006*	0.002	0.000
r_{t-5}^{US}		0.013*	0.012*	0.006*	0.003	0.002	0.000
$\sum_{i=0}^{5} \gamma_i$		0.215*	0.200*	0.094*	0.029*	0.017*	0.004
x_t^{GE}	0.011*	0.011*	0.011*	0.011*	0.011*	0.011*	0.011*
x_{t-1}^{GE}	0.008*	0.007*	0.008*	0.008*	0.008*	0.008*	0.008*
x_{t-2}^{GE}	0.004*	0.004*	0.004*	0.004*	0.005*	0.004*	0.004*
x_{t-3}^{GE}	0.002*	0.002*	0.002*	0.002*	0.003*	0.002*	0.002*
x_{t-4}^{GE}	0.002*	0.002*	0.002*	0.002*	0.002*	0.001*	0.001*
x_{t-5}^{GE}	0.002*	0.002*	0.002*	0.002*	0.002*	0.001*	0.001*
r_{t-1}^{GE}	-0.208*	-0.226*	-0.225*	-0.216*	-0.212*	-0.206*	-0.206*
r_{t-2}^{GE}	-0.097*	-0.118*	-0.116*	-0.104*	-0.096*	-0.092*	-0.091*
r_{t-3}^{GE}	-0.051*	-0.070*	-0.069*	-0.058*	-0.048*	-0.044*	-0.044*
r_{t-4}^{GE}	-0.038*	-0.053*	-0.053*	-0.045*	-0.036*	-0.031*	-0.030*
r_{t-5}^{GE}	-0.025*	-0.035*	-0.035*	-0.031*	-0.024*	-0.019*	-0.018*
adj. R^2	0.134	0.149	0.150	0.147	0.146	0.147	0.147
Coeff-test: $\gamma_0 = ... = \gamma_6 = 0$							
p(F-stat)	—	0.000	0.000	0.000	0.000	0.001	0.598

We run the regression: $r_t^{GE} = c + \sum_{i=0}^{5} \gamma_i r_{t-i}^{US} + \sum_{i=0}^{5} \delta_i x_{t-i}^{GE} + \sum_{i=1}^{5} \lambda_i r_{t-i}^{GE} + \epsilon_t$ where r_t^{GE} is the BUND futures transaction return of trade t. r_t^{US} is the return of the T-Note futures between clock time of trade t and clock time of t-1, i.e. the last T-Note price available to BUND traders before t minus the last T-Note price available to BUND traders before t-1. While integrating BUND and T-Bond data we account for a transmission lag of ℓ seconds, i.e. we assume that T-note trade prices take ℓ seconds before they are known to BUND traders. We accomplish this by shifting the T-note clock time forward by ℓ seconds. x_t is the unexpected order flow of a transaction. Let q_t be a trade indicator variable that takes the value 1 for a buy and -1 for a sell. Then x_t is calculated as the residual of regressing q on its own five lags, and five lags of r^{US} and r^{GE}. This table reports coefficient estimates for different transmission lags ℓ: 1, 2, 5, 10, 20, and 30 seconds. Significant results ($p < 0.01$) are denoted by *. The coefficients for x_{t-i}^{GE} are multiplied with 1,000. The sum of the r_t^{US} coefficients is reported in the seventh row (marked by a line above and below that row). For each regression, I test whether all coeffcients for r^{US} are zero, i.e. $\gamma_0 = \;\; = \gamma_6 = 0$. The p-value of the F-statistics is reported in the bottommost row of the table.

return coefficients, $\sum_{i=0}^{5} \gamma_i$, can be interpreted as the cumulative impact of a unit impulse in T-Note prices on BUND futures prices. For convenience, this number is separately reported in row seven.

In order to assess how long it takes until a US price movement is fully incorporated into German bond prices, I also estimate equation (4.14) based on shifting the T-Note clock forward by $\ell = 2$, 5, 10, 20, and 30 seconds. For instance, $\ell = 30$ means that BUND transaction returns are regressed on T-Note price movements that occured at least 30 seconds earlier. If there is no response after ℓ seconds, the hypothesis $\gamma_0 = \gamma_1 = ... = \gamma_6 = 0$ cannot be rejected. As ℓ increases the cumulative T-Note price transmission decreases rapidly. For example, when BUND returns are regressed on T-Note returns lagged by at least 5 seconds, each unit increase in T-Note prices only affects cumulative subsequent BUND price movements by less than half as much as for $\ell = 1$. For $\ell = 10$ the effect is only about an eighth. This means that US price movements are transmitted to German bond prices very quickly. Most of the transmission occurs within the first 10 seconds. After 30 seconds I find no more price transmission effects. The model fit, as indicated by the adjusted R^2, increases after incorporating US returns into the model. The difference compared to the original Hasbrouck (1991) specification is small, though.

I interpret $\sum_{i=0}^{5} \gamma_i$ as the cumulative impact of a unit impulse in T-Note prices for the purpose of testing significance levels. However, this interpretation does not account for the negative autocorrelation in BUND returns. If a positive US price movement causes a positive German price change this price response will be partly reversed in the next transaction due to negative autocorrelation in BUND transaction returns. Table 4.6 illustrates the dynamic impact of a unit T-Note impulse on German bond prices throughout the next ten trades. This table is based on the model and coefficient estimates described in Table 4.5 for $\ell = 1$. Most of the response occurs during the first three subsequent

Table 4.6: Dynamic impact of T-Note price movements on BUND prices

Transactions	$\sum_{i=0}^{t} r_i^{GE}$	r_t^{GE}	r_t^{US}	x_t^{GE}
0	0.045	0.045	1	0
1	0.092	0.048	0	0
2	0.123	0.030	0	0
3	0.139	0.016	0	0
4	0.147	0.008	0	0
5	0.150	0.003	0	0
6	0.144	-0.006	0	0
7	0.143	-0.001	0	0
8	0.142	0.000	0	0
9	0.143	0.000	0	0
10	0.143	0.000	0	0

This table illustrates the cumulative quote revision for BUND futures prices subsequent to a unit impulse of the T-Note futures, based on the model and coefficient estimates described in Table 4.

BUND trades. The long-term permanent impact of a unit T-Note impulse, accounting for negative return autocorrelation, is 0.143.

This section has shown that even when there is no public US economic news, each price movement in the US bond market positively affects subsequent German bond price movements. Thus, hypothesis H1 is supported. The price transmission occurs very quickly. It begins in the first second following the US price movement and most of the transmission occurs within about 10 seconds. After less than 30 seconds the US price change is fully incorporated into German bond prices. An explanation for this might be that each US price movement reveals US information that is not observable in Germany but possibly contains a globally relevant component. German bond traders try to infer this global news component and respond to the US price movement.

4.6 Cross-border information transmission around US economic news releases

4.6.1 Main results

This section analyzes the channels of cross-border information transmission around US economic news releases. The analysis is based on the empirical model presented in the previous section in equation (4.14). In order to account for time-varying effects around the announcement, I divide the sample into 4 subsamples: the non-announcement day interval between 2:20:00 and 2:59:59 (n), the interval before an announcement between 2:20:00 and 2:29:59 (b), during an announcement between 2:30:00 and 2:30:59 (d), and after an announcement between 2:31:00 and 2:59:59 (a). The choice of one minute as the during announcement sample is motivated by the findings in section 4.4, that it takes about a minute until the public news is fully incorporated into prices.

As an additional regressor compared to equation (4.14), I also include the announcement surprise S into the regression for the intervals (d) and (s). This specification assumes that the total announcement effect is not incorporated through one single price movement, but that it is equally distributed among each transaction return in the respective subsample. This assumption is in line with the findings of Ederington and Lee (1995) and with my analysis in section 4.4. The surprise is additionally included in the after announcement sample to verify that the announcement surprise is fully processed after no more than one minute. The final empirical specification (Model C) is:

Table 4.7: Cross-border information transmission around US macro announcements

	Model A: no US information				Model B: include US news releases				Model C: full model			
	Non-ann days	Announcement days before	Announcement days during	Announcement days after	Non-ann days	Announcement days before	Announcement days during	Announcement days after	Non-ann days	Announcement days before	Announcement days during	Announcement days after
E1							-0.039*	0.000			-0.014	0.000
GDP							-0.029*	-0.001			-0.018	-0.001
CPI2							-0.011*	0.000			-0.006	0.000
PPI2							-0.009*	0.000			-0.004	0.000
RS2							-0.011*	0.000			-0.005	0.000
DGO							-0.011*	0.000			-0.008*	0.000
IJC							0.006*	0.000			0.001	0.000
r_t^{US}									0.045*	0.088*	0.188*	0.069*
r_{t-1}^{US}									0.058*	0.087*	0.138*	0.082*
r_{t-2}^{US}									0.047*	0.060*	0.116*	0.059*
r_{t-3}^{US}									0.032*	0.037*	0.069*	0.037*
r_{t-4}^{US}									0.021*	0.036*	0.045*	0.022*
r_{t-5}^{US}									0.013*	0.030*	0.033*	0.012*
$\sum_{i=0}^{5} \gamma_i$									0.215*	0.337*	0.588*	0.281*
$\sum_{i=0}^{5} \delta_i$	0.029*	0.030*	0.000	0.033*	0.286*	0.296*	0.003	0.033*	0.028*	0.033*	0.060*	0.033*
$\sum_{i=1}^{5} \lambda_i$	-0.419*	-0.304*	-0.210*	-0.303*	-0.419*	-0.304*	0.141	-0.303*	-0.502*	-0.455*	-0.776*	-0.431*
adj. R^2	0.112				0.114				0.174			
Coefficient tests												
		difference	F-stat	p(F-stat)		difference	F-stat	p(F-stat)		difference	F-stat	p(F-stat)
$\sum_{i=0}^{5} \gamma_i^b = \sum_{i=0}^{5} \gamma_i^n$		—	—	—		—	—	—		0.122	6.4	0.012
$\sum_{i=0}^{5} \gamma_i^d = \sum_{i=0}^{5} \gamma_i^a$		—	—	—		—	—	—		0.307	40.1	0.000
$\sum_{i=0}^{5} \gamma_i^a = \sum_{i=0}^{5} \gamma_i^n$		—	—	—		—	—	—		0.067	140.1	0.000

(description for Table 4.7)
I run three regressions:
Model A: $r_t^{GE} = c + \sum_{v\in\{d,a\}} I_t^v \sum_{i=1}^{8} \beta_i^v S_i + \epsilon_t$.
Model B: $r_t^{GE} = c + \sum_{v\in\{d,a\}} I_t^v \sum_{i=1}^{8} \beta_i^v S_i + \sum_{v\in\{n,b,d,a\}} I_t^v \sum_{i=0}^{5} \gamma_i^v r_{t-i}^{US} + \epsilon_t$.
Model C: $r_t^{GE} = c + \sum_{v\in\{d,a\}} I_t^v \sum_{i=1}^{8} \beta_i^v S_i + \sum_{v\in\{n,b,d,a\}} I_t^v \sum_{i=0}^{5} \gamma_i^v r_{t-i}^{US} + \sum_{v\in\{n,b,d,a\}} I_t^v \sum_{i=0}^{5} \delta_i^v x_{t-i}^{GE} + \sum_{v\in\{n,b,d,a\}} I_t^v \sum_{i=1}^{5} \lambda_i^v r_{t-i}^{GE} + \epsilon_t$.
I_t^v is an indicator variable that takes the value 1 if trade t occured in interval v. v is either the non-announcement day interval between 2:20:00 and 2:59:59 (n), the interval before an announcement between 2:20:00 and 2:29:59 (b), during an announcement between 2:30:00 and 2:30:59 (d), or after an announcement between 2:31:00 and 2:59:59 (a). r_t^{GE} is the BUND futures transaction return of trade t. S_i is the surprise in the headline figure i that is announced at 2:30 on that day. If two or more headline figures are announced simultaneously, we only account for the more important announcemend and set the other announcement surprise to zero. r_t^{US} is the return of the T-Note futures between clock time of trade t and clock time of t-1, i.e. the last T-Note price available to BUND traders before t minus the last T-Note price available to BUND traders before t-1. While integrating BUND and T-Bond data we account for a transmission lag of 1 second, i.e. we assume that T-note trade prices take 1 second before they are known to BUND traders. We accomplish this by shifting the T-note clock time forward by 1 second. x_t is the unexpected order flow of a transaction. If q_t is a trade indicator variable that takes the value 1 for a buy and -1 for a sell, then x_t is calculated as the residual of regressing q on its own five lags, and five lags of r^{US} and r^{GE}.
This table reports the coefficient estimates for the announcement surprises (β_i^v) and the lagged US return (γ_i^v) for each model and each interval v. In addition, I report the sum of the lagged T-note return, order flow, and BUND return coefficients ($\sum_{i=0}^{5} \gamma_i$, $\sum_{i=0}^{5} \delta_i$, $\sum_{i=1}^{5} \lambda_i$) for each model and each interval v. In the bottom part of each panel, I report coefficient tests for the T-note return coefficients. I test whether the sum of all six lagged US return coefficients is equal in the interval before the announcement and on non-announcement days, during the announcement and after the announcement, and after the announcement and on non-announcement days.

$$
\begin{aligned}
r_t^{GE} &= c + \sum_{v\in\{d,a\}} I_t^v \sum_{i=1}^{7} \beta_i^v S_i + \sum_{v\in\{n,b,d,a\}} I_t^v \sum_{i=0}^{5} \gamma_i^v r_{t-i}^{US} \\
&+ \sum_{v\in\{n,b,d,a\}} I_t^v \sum_{i=0}^{5} \delta_i^v x_{t-i}^{GE} + \sum_{v\in\{n,b,d,a\}} I_t^v \sum_{i=1}^{5} \lambda_i^v r_{t-i}^{GE} + \epsilon_t
\end{aligned}
\tag{4.16}
$$

where I_t^v is an indicator variable that takes the value 1 if trade t occured in interval v, $v \in \{n, b, d, a\}$. S_i is the surprise in the headline figure i that is announced at 2:30 on that day. If two or more headline figures are announced simultaneously, I only account for the more important announcement according to Table 4.4 and set the other announcement surprise to zero. All other variables are as explained for equation (4.14). Table 4.7 reports estimation results for equation (4.16).

In addition to the full Model C, I also estimate two reduced versions, Model A and B. Model A only includes lagged domestic information, that is lagged BUND returns and lagged BUND order flow. For the sake of brevity, I do not report each lagged coefficient separately for the two domestic information variables, but rather the sum of all lags. Significant coefficients ($p < 0.01$) are denoted by '*'. Model B additionally includes the announcement surprise for the during and after announcement subsamples. As expected all announcement surprises are significant for the first minute, but not for the post announcement sample.

Estimates for the full specification Model C, as described by equation (4.16), are reported in the right-most columns. Comparing the adjusted R^2 of the full specification with Model A which contains only domestic information reveals that German bond price changes are much better described when lagged US price movements are included. Recall that the addition of US price movements in the analysis of non-announcement day BUND price changes, as reported in Table 4.5, does not improve model fit by a lot. Thus, it seems that lagged US bond price movements are especially important for explaining BUND price movements around the announcement of US economic news.

When comparing the coefficient estimates for lagged BUND returns (λ) and BUND order flow (δ) during the first minute following the announcement for the full Model C with the reduced Model A, it is evident that not accounting for US returns might lead to biased estimates. Model A yields that order flow does not contribute to price discovery in interval (d) and that BUND returns are relatively weakly negatively autocorrelated. The full specification, on the other hand, reveals that the informational value of order flow and the negative autocorrelation of BUND returns are both the largest among all subsamples during the announcement (interval (d)). The latter results seem to be easier to reconcile with intuition. During the announcement much information needs to be processed so that private interpretations of the information, which are revealed through order flow, contain a lot of value. Similarly, since BUND prices move so strongly, inventory control concerns are the largest, hence the highly negative autocorrelation. The biases during the other subsamples are less pronounced. Most notable is that the negative return autocorrelation is larger once US price movements are accounted for.

The level of price transmission from T-Note price movements to German bond futures prices varies around US announcements. In order to test if differences are significant, I conduct three coefficient tests using the sum of all six price transmission coefficients, $\sum_{i=0}^{5} \gamma_{t-i}$. I interpret $\sum_{i=0}^{5} \gamma_{t-i}$ as the cumulative impact of a unit T-Note impuls and ignore the negative autocorrelation of BUND returns for now. First, I test whether price transmission is higher during the ten minutes before an announcement compared to non-announcement days. Second, I test whether transmission is higher during the announcement, i.e. in the first minute following the announcement, compared to the subsequent 29 minutes. Lastly, I compare price transmission during the after announcement sample to the non-announcement sample.

While $\sum_{i=0}^{5} \gamma_{t-i}$ is relatively high before US announcements it is not significantly larger than on non-announcement days. Price transmission coefficients in the 30 minutes following the announcements (interval (a)), on the other hand, are highly significantly larger than during the non-announcement day sample. It is well known that public US economic news releases induce differential private interpretations about the news (see Fleming and Remolona (1999) or Green (2004)). This private information about the US economy presumably carries a high degree of globally relevant information, and is thus highly valuable to German bond traders. While this information is not directly observable it is revealed to German bond traders through US bond price movements. Therefore German bond prices follow US bond prices more strongly than at other times. Hence, hypothesis H2, that price transmission increases following a US macroeconomic announcement, is strongly supported.

Interestingly, price transmission coefficients during the first minute after the announcement (interval (d)), when the public news is processed, are the highest among all subsamples. They are even significantly higher than during the after announcement sample. Thus, we can support hypothesis H3. German bond prices do not solely respond directly to the public economic news itself. Rather, German traders additionally also follow the US price response to the public news. Interestingly, it seems that not accounting for US price movements produces upwardly biased estimates of the announcement surprise coefficients. In fact, comparing Model B and C it can be seen that many announcement surprises become insignificant at the one percent level once lagged US returns are accounted for.[7] According to the Chan (1993) model, the interpretation of the economic news is uncorrelated

[7] At the five percent level, DGO, E1, GDP, and RS2 are significant, though.

between German and US bond traders. Thus, German traders condition their bond price response first on the news itself and then also on the US response in order to diversify the noise, and come up with a more precise estimate of the news' implication for German bond prices.

Figure 4.6 illustrates the varying levels of price transmission around US macroeconomic announcements. This figure plots the dynamic impact of a unit T-Note impulse on German bond prices throughout the next trades. The calculation is based on Model C estimates for different subsamples as reported in Table 4.7. BUND autocorrelation is accounted for in this calculation. Results for the before announcement sample are ommited in order to focus on the more important subsamples (d), (a), (n). The general order of price transmission levels remains unchanged after accounting for autocorrelation in BUND returns. The highest impact of US bond price movements on subsequent German bond price changes is found during the first minute following an announcement. A unit T-Note impulse results in a cumulative BUND price response of 0.33 throughout the next trades in the during announcement sample (d). For the subsequent 29 minutes of the after announcement sample (a), a unit T-Note impulse causes BUND prices to increase by 0.19, whereas the same impulse only causes a 0.14 BUND price increase during the non-announcement day sample (n).

The price transmission results also suggest that correlation between German and US bond futures might be higher following US announcements than otherwise. Figure 4.7 plots the correlation of 5-min returns between the T-Note and BUND futures during the 40-min time window around US macroeconomic announcements. The solid line denotes 5-minute return correlation for the respective interval on announcement days and the dashed line denotes the 5-minute return correlation on non-announcement days. On non-announcement days, I don't differentiate between the different 5-minute intervals as there

Figure 4.6: Transmission of T-Note price movements around US announcements

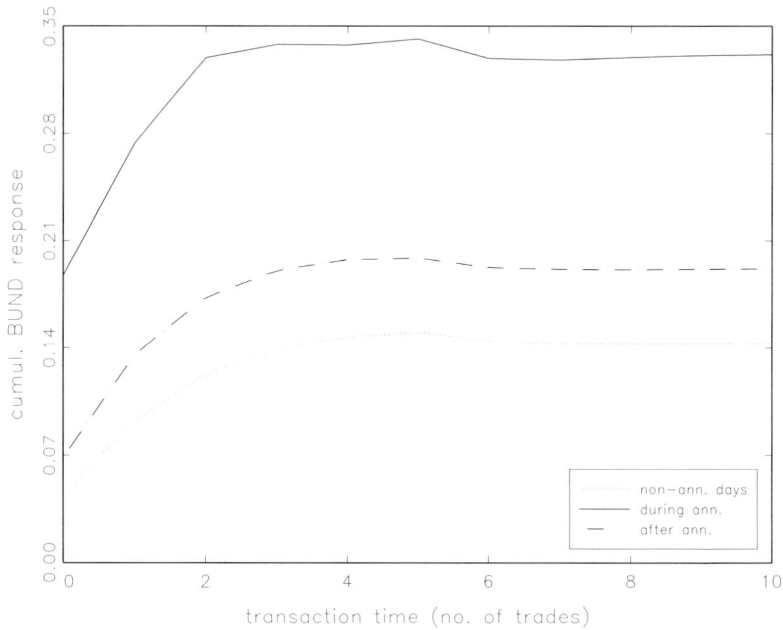

This figure depicts the cumulative quote revision for the BUND futures subsequent to a unit impulse of the T-Note futures, based on the model and coefficient estimates described in Table 5 Model C. I differentiate 3 intervals and allow for different response pattern. The intervals are: non-announcement day intervals between 2:20:00 and 2:59:59, the interval during an announcement between 2:30:00 and 2:30:59, and after an announcement between 2:31:00 and 2:59:59.

is no pronounced difference. The sample size is 508 observations for each 5-minute interval on announcement days and 4907 5-minute returns on non-announcement days. An 'X' in the solid line denotes that this value is significantly ($p < 0.01$) different from the non-announcement day value.

Before the announcement, correlation on announcement days is not significantly different from normal values on non-announcement days. This is in accordance with the price transmission results which indicate that there is not a significantly higher global component in US price innovations. After the announcement correlation increases. Correlation is significantly higher on announcement days for all six post-announcement intervals until 3:00. The highest correlation is found during the first interval when the public news is processed in both markets. In line with conventional wisdom this suggests that US economic news carries information which is relevant to bond prices worldwide. In subsequent intervals, correlation is still abnormally high although the public news only needs about one minute to be fully incorporated. This finding might indicate that there is a large global component in US returns as US investors continue to interpret the public news.

My results regarding correlation of five-minute US and German bond returns are qualitatively in line with Franke and Hess (2000). They likewise investigate return correlation between US and German bonds for the sample 1992 to 1996. They also find that post-announcement correlation is abnormally large following US macroeconomic announcements. However, in their analysis correlation returns to normal non-announcement day levels after 15 minutes. Thus, the fact that correlation stays abnormally large for longer in my more recent sample might indicate that international bond markets have become more integrated.

Figure 4.7: 5-minute BUND and T-Note return correlation around US macro announcements

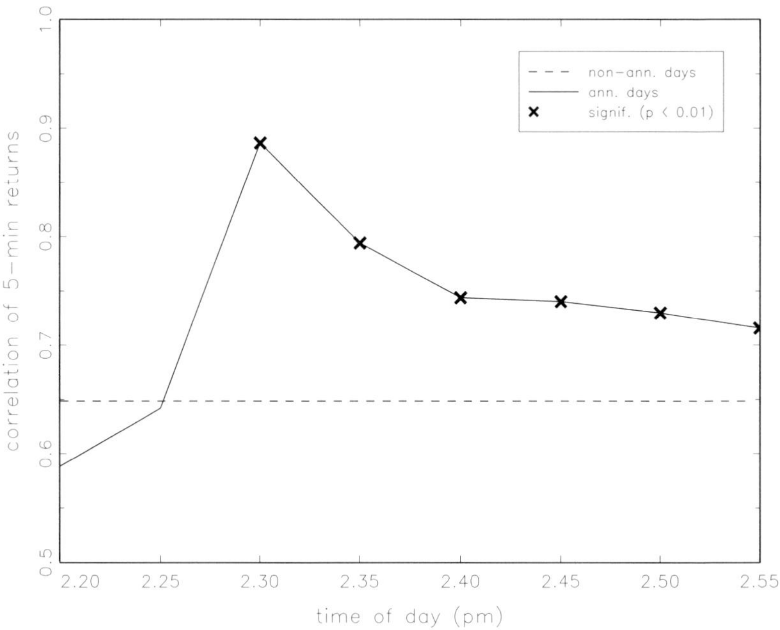

This figure plots the correlation of 5-minute BUND and T-Note returns on announcement days between 2:20 and 2:55 (solid line). The correlation at this time of day on non-announcement day is depicted by the dashed line. An 'X' in the solid line denotes that the correlation on announcement days is significantly different from non-announcement day correlation at the 0.01 significance level.

4.6.2 Differences between news types

The prior analyses pool the price transmission effects for different types of US macroeconomic announcements. Since the price effect is not equally large across different announcement types, there also might be differences in the cross-border price transmission for different announcement types. It is interesting to analyze whether more important announcements, that is those which have a larger price impact, also induce higher levels of price transmission. This would be an indication that these more important announcements also carry a relatively larger global component. The alternative hypothesis is that more important announcements carry a relatively large local component which is only relevant for pricing US bonds. In that case there should not be higher levels of price transmission following more important announcements compared to less important announcements. I reestimate equation (4.16), but only include one type of announcement at a time. Table 4.8 reports the results.

Each panel contains the estimates for one announcement type. The non-announcement day results are repeated in the first panel to facilitate comparison. I only report the sum of all US return, BUND order flow, and autocorrelation lags to conserve space. As in Table 4.7, I conduct three coefficient tests regarding the time-varying level of price transmission. The general pattern is that more important announcements induce higher levels of cross-border price transmission. For example, the two most important announcements, nonfarm payrolls and GDP, induce by far the highest levels of price transmission. This relationship is strongest for the first minute immediately following the announcement (interval (d)) and less pronounced for the subsequent 29 minutes of interval (a).

Table 4.8: Differences between announcement types

Non-Announcement days

	14:00 - 14-59	
$\sum_{i=0}^{5}\gamma_i$	0.215*	
$\sum_{i=0}^{5}\delta_i$	0.028*	
$\sum_{i=1}^{5}\lambda_i$	-0.458*	
adj. R^2	0.036	
Coefficient tests	difference	p(F-stat)
$\sum_{i=0}^{5}\gamma_i^b = \sum_{i=0}^{5}\gamma_i^n$	—	—
$\sum_{i=0}^{5}\gamma_i^d = \sum_{i=0}^{5}\gamma_i^a$	—	—
$\sum_{i=0}^{5}\gamma_i^a = \sum_{i=0}^{5}\gamma_i^n$	—	—

only E1 Announcement

	before	during	after
E1		-0.009	0.000
$\sum_{i=0}^{5}\gamma_i$	0.476*	1.007*	0.305*
$\sum_{i=0}^{5}\delta_i$	0.042*	0.135*	0.042*
$\sum_{i=1}^{5}\lambda_i$	-0.458*	-1.692*	-0.460*
adj. R^2		0.089	
Coefficient tests		difference	p(F-stat)
$\sum_{i=0}^{5}\gamma_i^b = \sum_{i=0}^{5}\gamma_i^n$		0.261	0.006
$\sum_{i=0}^{5}\gamma_i^d = \sum_{i=0}^{5}\gamma_i^a$		0.702	0.000
$\sum_{i=0}^{5}\gamma_i^a = \sum_{i=0}^{5}\gamma_i^n$		0.090	0.000

only GDP Announcement

	before	during	after
GDP		-0.010	-0.001
$\sum_{i=0}^{5}\gamma_i$	0.296*	0.884*	0.312*
$\sum_{i=0}^{5}\delta_i$	0.027*	0.087*	0.035*
$\sum_{i=1}^{5}\lambda_i$	-0.367*	-1.178*	-0.485*
adj. R^2		0.044	
Coefficient tests		difference	p(F-stat)
$\sum_{i=0}^{5}\gamma_i^b = \sum_{i=0}^{5}\gamma_i^n$		0.081	0.271
$\sum_{i=0}^{5}\gamma_i^d = \sum_{i=0}^{5}\gamma_i^a$		0.572	0.000
$\sum_{i=0}^{5}\gamma_i^a = \sum_{i=0}^{5}\gamma_i^n$		0.097	0.000

only CPI2 Announcement

	before	during	after
CPI2		-0.010*	0.000
$\sum_{i=0}^{5}\gamma_i$	0.171*	0.455*	0.270*
$\sum_{i=0}^{5}\delta_i$	0.035*	0.071*	0.031*
$\sum_{i=1}^{5}\lambda_i$	-0.603*	-0.869*	-0.437*
adj. R^2		0.049	
Coefficient tests		difference	p(F-stat)
$\sum_{i=0}^{5}\gamma_i^b = \sum_{i=0}^{5}\gamma_i^n$		-0.044	0.456
$\sum_{i=0}^{5}\gamma_i^d = \sum_{i=0}^{5}\gamma_i^a$		0.185	0.000
$\sum_{i=0}^{5}\gamma_i^a = \sum_{i=0}^{5}\gamma_i^n$		0.055	0.000

only PPI2 Announcement

	before	during	after
PPI2		-0.007*	0.000
$\sum_{i=0}^{5}\gamma_i$	0.223*	0.508*	0.279*
$\sum_{i=0}^{5}\delta_i$	0.034*	0.073*	0.032*
$\sum_{i=1}^{5}\lambda_i$	-0.536*	-0.918*	-0.465*
adj. R^2		0.050	
Coefficient tests		difference	p(F-stat)
$\sum_{i=0}^{5}\gamma_i^b = \sum_{i=0}^{5}\gamma_i^n$		0.008	0.828
$\sum_{i=0}^{5}\gamma_i^d = \sum_{i=0}^{5}\gamma_i^a$		0.229	0.000
$\sum_{i=0}^{5}\gamma_i^a = \sum_{i=0}^{5}\gamma_i^n$		0.064	0.000

only RS2 Announcement

	before	during	after
RS2		-0.005	0.000
$\sum_{i=0}^{5}\gamma_i$	0.205*	0.539*	0.314*
$\sum_{i=0}^{5}\delta_i$	0.029*	0.060*	0.032*
$\sum_{i=1}^{5}\lambda_i$	-0.549*	-0.698*	-0.481*
adj. R^2		0.046	
Coefficient tests		difference	p(F-stat)
$\sum_{i=0}^{5}\gamma_i^b = \sum_{i=0}^{5}\gamma_i^n$		-0.010	0.747
$\sum_{i=0}^{5}\gamma_i^d = \sum_{i=0}^{5}\gamma_i^a$		0.226	0.000
$\sum_{i=0}^{5}\gamma_i^a = \sum_{i=0}^{5}\gamma_i^n$		0.099	0.000

only DGO Announcement

	before	during	after
DGO		-0.011*	0.000
$\sum_{i=0}^{5} \gamma_i$	0.204*	0.527*	0.265*
$\sum_{i=0}^{5} \delta_i$	0.034*	0.077*	0.031*
$\sum_{i=1}^{5} \lambda_i$	-0.576*	-0.960*	-0.450*
adj. R^2		0.048	
Coefficient tests		difference	p(F-stat)
$\sum_{i=0}^{5} \gamma_i^b = \sum_{i=0}^{5} \gamma_i^n$		-0.011	0.655
$\sum_{i=0}^{5} \gamma_i^d = \sum_{i=0}^{5} \gamma_i^a$		0.262	0.000
$\sum_{i=0}^{5} \gamma_i^a = \sum_{i=0}^{5} \gamma_i^n$		0.051	0.000

only IJC Announcement

	before	during	after
IJC		0.004*	0.000
$\sum_{i=0}^{5} \gamma_i$	0.197*	0.414*	0.280*
$\sum_{i=0}^{5} \delta_i$	0.033*	0.053*	0.032*
$\sum_{i=1}^{5} \lambda_i$	-0.521*	-0.677*	-0.414*
adj. R^2		0.071	
Coefficient tests		difference	p(F-stat)
$\sum_{i=0}^{5} \gamma_i^b = \sum_{i=0}^{5} \gamma_i^n$		-0.018	0.223
$\sum_{i=0}^{5} \gamma_i^d = \sum_{i=0}^{5} \gamma_i^a$		0.134	0.000
$\sum_{i=0}^{5} \gamma_i^a = \sum_{i=0}^{5} \gamma_i^n$		0.065	0.000

(description for Table 4.8)

This table reports the coefficient estimates for the announcement surprise, lagged T-Note return (γ_i), BUND order flow (δ_i), and lagged BUND return (λ_i). For the sake of brevity, I only report the sum of lagged T-Note return, BUND order flow, and lagged BUND return coefficients ($\sum_{i=0}^{5} \gamma_i$, $\sum_{i=0}^{5} \delta_i$, $\sum_{i=1}^{5} \lambda_i$). Estimates are based on the regression $r_t^{GE} = c + \sum_{v\in\{d,a\}} I_t^v \beta_i^v S_i + \sum_{v\in\{n,b,d,a\}} I_t^v \sum_{i=0}^{5} \gamma_i^v r_{t-i}^{US} + \sum_{v\in\{n,b,d,a\}} I_t^v \sum_{i=0}^{5} \delta_i^v x_{t-i}^{GE} + \sum_{v\in\{n,b,d,a\}} I_t^v \sum_{i=1}^{5} \lambda_i^v r_{t-i}^{GE} + \epsilon_t$. I_t^v is an indicator variable that takes the value 1 if trade t occured in interval v. v is either the non-announcement day sample (n), the sample before (b), during (d), or after (a) the respective announcement i. All other variables are as described in Table 4.7. The regression for the non-announcement day results is $r_t^{GE} = c + I_t^n \sum_{i=0}^{5} \gamma_i r_{t-i}^{US} + I_t^n \sum_{i=0}^{5} \delta_i x_{t-i}^{GE} + I_t^n \sum_{i=1}^{5} \lambda_i r_{t-i}^{GE} + \epsilon_t$. In the bottom part of each panel, I report coefficient tests for the T-note return coefficients. I test whether the sum of all six lagged US return coefficients is equal in the interval before the announcement and on non-announcement days, during the announcement and after the announcement, and after the announcement and on non-announcement days.

It is also interesting to note that for nonfarm payrolls, the most important announcement, price transmission already increases before the announcement. It is improbable that nonfarm payrolls announcements are leaked before the scheduled release time at 2:30, given the rigid release procedure.[8] However, it is conceivable that German traders suspect US traders to posses some information that allows a better forecast of the value that is to be released. Alternatively, given the importance of the nonfarm payroll announcement the attention of German bond traders might be generally turned towards the US market already before the release, even if US traders do not possess more globally relevant private information than at other times.

[8] A detailed description of the procedure can be found in Fleming and Remolona (1999).

Overall, these results give some indication that more important results induce a higher level of cross-border price transmission and support the hypothesis that more important US economic news carries relatively more globally relevant information compared to local information.

4.6.3 Duration of increased price transmission

I find higher levels of price transmission in the after announcement sample compared to non-announcement days. I interpret this as an indication that German traders try to infer US interpretations of the public news that are not directly visible for German traders, but can be inferred from US bond price movements. In order to assess how long this effect lasts I extend my sample beyond 3:00. I further investigate the intervals 3:00 - 3:29 and 3:30 - 3:59 in order to compare price transmission on announcement and non-announcement days. The goal is to find out whether price transmission is still significantly higher on announcement days beyond the first 30 minutes past the announcement. For this, I estimate

$$\begin{aligned} r_t^{GE} = {} & c + \sum_{v \in \{ad,nad\}} I_t^v \sum_{i=0}^{5} \gamma_i^v r_{t-i}^{US} + \sum_{v \in \{ad,nad\}} I_t^v \sum_{i=0}^{5} \delta_i^v x_{t-i}^{GE} + \sum_{v \in \{ad,nad\}} I_t^v \sum_{i=1}^{5} \lambda_i^v r_{t-i}^{GE} \\ & + \epsilon_t \end{aligned} \tag{4.17}$$

for the intervals 3:00 - 3:29 and 3:30 - 3:59. In this equation, ad and nad denote intervals on announcement and non-announcement days respectively. All other variables are as described for equation (4.16).

During the 3:00 - 3:29 interval the sum of all six price transmission coefficients on announcement days is still significantly larger than on non-announcement days, although

Table 4.9: Duration of increased transmission

	15:00 - 15:29		15:30 - 15:59	
	AD	NAD	AD	NAD
r_t^{US}	0.056*	0.044*	0.056*	0.046*
r_{t-1}^{US}	0.074*	0.061*	0.062*	0.059*
r_{t-2}^{US}	0.058*	0.052*	0.052*	0.051*
r_{t-3}^{US}	0.040*	0.040*	0.036*	0.036*
r_{t-4}^{US}	0.029*	0.027*	0.027*	0.027*
r_{t-5}^{US}	0.019*	0.018*	0.018*	0.020*
$\sum_{i=0}^{5}\gamma_i$	0.276*	0.242*	0.251*	0.237*
$\sum_{i=0}^{5}\delta_i$	0.031*	0.030*	0.033*	0.033*
$\sum_{i=1}^{5}\lambda_i$	-0.610*	-0.552*	-0.603*	-0.585*
adj. R^2	0.151		0.160	
Coefficient test	difference	p(F-stat)	difference	p(F-stat)
$\sum_{i=0}^{5}\gamma_i^{ad} = \sum_{i=0}^{5}\gamma_i^{nad}$	0.033	0.000	0.013	0.075

This table reports estimation results for the model: $r_t^{GE} = c + \sum_{v\in\{ad,nad\}} I_t^v \sum_{i=0}^{5} \gamma_i^v r_{t-i}^{US} + \sum_{v\in\{ad,nad\}} I_t^v \sum_{i=0}^{5} \delta_i^v x_{t-i}^{GE} + \sum_{v\in\{ad,nad\}} I_t^v \sum_{i=1}^{5} \lambda_i^v r_{t-i}^{GE} + \epsilon_t$, where ad and nad denote intervals on announcement and non-announcement days respectively and all other variable are as described in Table 4.7. The estimation is done separately for the intervals 3:00 - 3:29 and 3:30 - 3:59. For the sake of brevity, I only report the sum of lagged BUND order flow and lagged BUND return coefficients ($\sum_{i=0}^{5}\delta_i$, $\sum_{i=1}^{5}\lambda_i$). Significant results ($p < 0.01$) are denoted by *. The coefficients for x_{t-i}^{GE} are multiplied with 1,000.

the difference is not as pronounced as during the first half hour after an announcement (2:31 to 2:59). But during the interval 3.30 - 3.59 the difference is not significant anymore. These results suggest that German bond prices follow US bond prices more closely after US announcements for about an hour. One likely explanation is that German traders expect it to take an hour until all private US interpretations of the news have been fully revealed.

4.6.4 Discussion of results

In this section, I report three main empirical findings. The main results are validated with a series of extensive robustness analyses which are reported in the appendix. First and foremost, both surprises in the economic news itself and lagged US bond price movements contribute to price discovery in German bonds after a US macroeconomic announcement. Second, the level of transmission of US bond price movements to German bond prices varies, and it is the largest immediately (i.e. first minute) following the announcement of US macroeconomic news, larger than at any other time. Third, even after the public news is fully processed, price transmission from US to German bond prices is still significantly larger than usual for up to an hour. These findings allow for some new insights into how information is transmitted across international financial markets. Most importantly, they indicate that German bond traders learn about the implications of US macroeconomic announcements not only through the public news itself, but also through following the US price response.

One interesting further finding is that US announcement surprises do not carry much additional information over US returns in explaining the German bond price response to US economic news. This confirms the stock market results of Connolly and Wang (2003). However my interpretation is different. Connolly and Wang (2003) conclude that the foreign price response is due to contagion, that is *normal* co-movement which is always present between international financial markets. In other words, foreign investors do not care so much about the information conveyed in US macroeconomic announcements, they just follow the US market to the same degree as they always do. In contrast, I find that the level of price transmission increases significantly after the announcement, especially immediately following the announcement. This result in accodance with the rational learning model suggests a different explanation. The news itself and the US price response are two complementary channels for transmitting the economic news to German bond markets. It is beneficial for German traders to condition their price response first on the surprise and then subsequently also on the US price response in order to gain a more precise estimate of the news implications for bond prices.

The finding that price transmission and correlation is higher following US macroeconomic announcements compared to non-announcement days conflicts with the results of Karolyi and Stulz (1996) and Albuquerque and Vega (2007). Karolyi and Stulz find that correlation between daily Japanese and US stock returns is not different on days with and without US macroeconomic announcements. Albuquerque and Vega regress daily Portuguese stock returns on contemporaneous US returns, US announcement surprises, and Portuguese order flow. They likewise don't find a stronger dependency between Portuguese and US stock returns on US announcement days. The main difference of my methodology is that I focus on a narrow time window around the US announcement where the global component in US returns is presumably the largest. In addition I focus on price transmission that occurs within a few trades whereas the two other studies investigate daily returns. Given my result that most of the price transmission effects is complete after about 10 seconds, a trade by trade analysis seems like the more sensible choice. Lastly, I focus my analysis on bond prices and not on stock prices. Since bond prices react more strongly to economic news than stock prices (see, e.g., McQueen and Roley (1993) and Jones, Lamont, and Lumsdaine (1998)), there might be a larger global component in US economic news for valuing bonds than stock. These considerations are supported by findings of Franke and Hess (2000) who study the same markets as I do. They also find an increase in intraday return correlations which disappears quickly. However, I extend on Franke and Hess (2000) by accounting for varying levels of cross-market dependency and the public news at the same time.

A further main finding is that price transmission is still enheightened for up to an hour following the announcement, even after the public news is fully processed. This indicates that German bond traders are aware that US traders generate differential private interpretations about the public news in the aftermath of an announcement. Since these interpretations carry a presumably large global component, they are of particular value to pricing German bonds. Hence, German bond traders infer US interpretations on the just released news by following US bond price movements particularly strongly after a US macroeconomic announcement.

4.7 Concluding remarks

This chapter investigates the channels of cross-border information transmission. Specifically, I study what drives the price discovery process in German bond futures around the release of US macroeconomic news. Do German bond traders condition their price response only on the news itself? Or do they also take the US bond price response to the news into account? I find that both channels – the US news itself and also the US bond price response – are important for explaining the German bond price movements in the post-announcement phase.

In order to guide my analysis, I relate the cross-border transmission of economic news to the rational learning model of Chan (1993). The empirical analysis is carried out on trade-by-trade data of German and US bond futures. I relate transaction returns in German bonds to lagged trade-by-trade price movements in US bonds and also to surprises in US macroeconomic announcement. The main finding is that US information is transmitted through both, the announcement surprise itself and through US price movements. Interestingly, once lagged US returns are accounted for, public US announcement surprises lose some of their explanatory power for German bond prices. The level of price transmission, as measured by how much US bond price movements explain subsequent German returns, is the highest immediately following the announcement. But even after the public news is fully processed, price transmission is still elevated for up to an hour past the announcement.

This study adds to the understanding of cross-border information flow. I examine how publicly released economic news and other news which is not observable from outside the US is transmitted across international financial markets. German bond traders not only directly respond to public US news, but also indirectly to the US price response to that news. Even after the news is fully incorporated into prices, price transmission is elevated as German traders try to infer private US interpretations of the news. Moreover, I apply the Chan (1993) model on cross-border transmission of price movements. This yields that the level of cross-border price transmission is not always the same but follows predictable patterns. When the global component in US price innovations is presumably high, German bonds follow US bond price movements more strongly than otherwise. Empirically, I find a particularly large dependence of German bond returns on lagged US returns in the post-announcement period.

My findings also contribute to the discussion whether US economic news is fundamentally relevant to international asset prices or whether the reaction is due to contagion. The results strongly favor the economic fundamentals hypothesis and cast doubt on the contagion hypothesis. German and US bond futures do not simply co-move *as usual* following a US macroeconomic announcment. Rather, there is a significant *increase* in the transmission of price movements. I relate this increase to the fact that US price innovations following US macroeconomic announcements reveal private interpretations about globally relevant US economic news.

5 Conclusion

Macroeconomic announcements are among the most important news for financial markets. Surprises in the announcements have large effects on security prices and liquidity. Research has mostly focused on the news effects on domestic stock and bond markets. This dissertation investigates the effects of macroeconomic announcements on three financial markets, namely the commodity futures market and international stock and bond markets. My research is guided by three main research questions:

1. How do commodity futures prices respond to macroeconomic news?
2. What are the price and liquidity effects of domestic and foreign US economic news in the German stock index futures market?
3. What are the channels of information transmission from the US to German bond markets around the release of US economic news?

The dissertation consists of an introduction, the main part, and this conclusion. The main part devotes one chapter to each of the three main research questions. My analyses offer three major contributions to the understanding of how macroeconomic news is processed on financial markets.

First, I conduct the first empirical analysis on how commodity futures indices respond to macroeconomic news. In recent years commodities have become an increasingly attractive alternative investment. Prior research has only studied the price response of individual commodity futures types. However, correlation between different types of commodity futures is low. Therefore an index much better represents most commodity investors' portfolios. Most importantly, I allow for an asymmetric price response dependent on the state of the economy. I find that the commodity futures price response is state-dependent. During recessions, news about higher (lower) inflation and real activity lead to positive (negative) adjustments of commodity futures prices. In contrast, I find no significant reactions during economic expansions. These results help to explain price movements caused by macroeconomic news in the commodity futures market. In addition, they provide further evidence that the impact of economic news on financial markets can be dependent on the state of the economy. This was previously only known from the stock market.

Secondly, I offer a comprehensive depiction of the price and liquidity effects of economic news. The analysis is conducted on German stock index futures data and includes a large number domestic German and foreign US macroeconomic announcements. I find that both domestic and foreign economic news affect the German stock index futures on multiple dimensions, including: prices, trading volume, volatility, quoted spreads, inventory holding costs and the informational role of trading. There seems to be a strong correlation between price and liquidity effects, as those announcement types that induce large price movements also affect liquidity. Contrary to some prior evidence, there is no qualitative difference in how domestic and foreign economic news is processed. However, the impact of US news on prices and liquidity in the German stock market is considerably larger than the impact of domestic German news. This result highlights the outstanding worldwide importance of the US economy. Moreover, my findings are valuable for investors in the German stock market to better adjust trading strategies around important events such as macroeconomic news releases.

As a third major contribution, I investigate the channels of cross-border information transmission from the US to the German bond futures market. I focus on the period around the release of US macroeconomic news, because economic news is considered to be of relatively large global relevance compared to other kind of news. I consider two channels: the direct response of German bond prices to the news and the indirect German response to the US response to the news. Prior research has been done only on data with lower frequencies, and thus, has not been able to give a clear answer which channels are used for cross-border information transmission. I conduct my analysis on a trade-by-trade dataset and I find that information around economic news is transmitted to the German bond market via both channels. In addition, I analyze how the level of price movement transmission varies. When the public news is processed during the first minute following the announcement, price transmission is the highest. It is much higher than usual because US economic news is of large relevance for German bond prices, too. Subsequently, when presumably there is much private information in the US market caused by private interpretations of the news, German bond prices still follow US bond prices more strongly than usual. This suggests that German investors use US bond price movements as an information transmission channel for both publicly observable US information and US information that is not observable from Germany.

In conclusion, this dissertation contributes to the understanding of how macroeconomic news is processed. Specifically, my analyses reveal how macroeconomic announcements are processed in the commodity futures market and in German stock and bond futures markets. Moreover, my thesis answers research questions that are specific to information processing on these markets. Finally, my findings are also valuable for traders in these markets because they help them to adjust their trading strategies to better account for the important effects of macroeconomic news.

Appendix

In chapter 4, I report three main empirical findings:

1. Surprises in macroeconomic announcements lose much of their explanatory power for BUND price movements once lagged US bond price movements are included into the model.

2. At the same time, the level of transmission of US bond price movements to German bond prices is larger immediately (e.g. first minute) following the announcement of US macroeconomic news than at any other time. This is measured by how much German transaction returns can be explained by lagged US price movements.

3. After the public news is fully processed, price transmission from US to German bond prices is still significantly larger than usual.

The first two findings indicate that German bond traders learn about public US economic news through both the news itself and through following the US price response to the news. The third finding indicates that German bond traders try to infer private US interpretations of the news through observing US bond price movements. In this appendix, I test the robustness of my major empirical findings by applying alternative methodologies to reproduce the main Table 4.7. Results for Model A is not reported for the following analyses, as Model A is not affected by the alternative approaches.

A.1 Length of the 'during announcement' interval

In my main analysis I assume that US economic news takes one minute to be processed. This assumption is derived from regressing the return between τ seconds and 30 minutes past the announcement on the announcement surprise. This approach has previously been used by Balduzzi, Elton, and Green (2001) to measure the speed of the price response. For τ larger than about 20 seconds almost all announcement surprises become insignificant which indicates that processing the news does not take much more than 20 seconds. Based on this analysis, I choose one minute as the 'during announcement' period. This ensures that I include the entire period given that the release for some announcements might be delayed and not occur at exactly 2:30:00.

The first subsection tests whether I can derive the same duration for processing the news using an alternative methodology. The second subsection tests whether my main results hold for varying assumption about the 'during announcement' interval.

A.1.1 Speed of price response

An alternative approach to measure the duration it takes to process the news is to regress $R^{-600,\tau}$ on the announcement surprises for different values of τ. $R^{-600,\tau}$ denotes the US or German bond futures return from 600 seconds before the announcement until τ seconds after the release. Starting with $\tau = 0$, the t-stat of the announcement surprise coefficient should increase with larger values of τ as long as the news is not fully processed. I regress $R^{-600,\tau}$ on the surprises in each of the analyzed announcements and report results in Table A.1. Panel A reports results for the BUND price response and Panel B reports results for the T-Note price response.

Table A.1: Duration of price response

Panel A: BUND price response

	BUND					
	$R^{-600,5}$		$R^{-600,\tau}$ largest t-stat in $\tau \leq 60$ sec		$R^{-600,\tau}$ largest t-stat in $\tau \leq 1800$ sec	
Ann	$\beta_i * 100$	t-stat	τ	t-stat	τ	t-stat
E1	-0.122	4.73	4	5.18	28min	5.50
E2	— *insignif* —		1	2.13	1	2.13
E3	— *insignif* —		— *insignif* —		— *insignif* —	
GDP	-0.089	5.99	31	9.37	31	9.37
CPI2	-0.016	2.23	52	4.19	4min	4.84
PPI2	-0.015	3.95	56	8.03	56	8.03
RS2	-0.029	7.02	42	7.32	42	7.32
DGO	-0.033	3.06	20	6.62	20	6.62
IJC	0.017	7.23	38	10.66	38	10.66

Panel B: T-Note price response

	T-Note					
	$R^{-600,5}$		$R^{-600,\tau}$ largest t-stat in $\tau \leq 60$ sec		$R^{-600,\tau}$ largest t-stat in $\tau \leq 1800$ sec	
Ann	$\beta_i * 100$	t-stat	τ	t-stat	τ	t-stat
E1	-0.339	5.56	7	5.72	7	5.72
E2	-0.089	2.20	0	3.06	0	3.06
E3	— *insignif* —		— *insignif* —		— *insignif* —	
GDP	-0.166	4.60	55	5.69	1min	6.89
CPI2	-0.056	3.94	52	5.24	3min	6.29
PPI2	-0.051	4.32	47	6.85	47	6.85
RS2	-0.046	5.76	43	6.61	43	6.61
DGO	-0.070	4.45	47	7.23	47	7.23
IJC	0.038	8.60	46	11.64	46	11.64

For each announcement, I run the regression $R_m^{-600,\tau} = c + \beta S_m + \epsilon_t$ where S_m is the surprise in the headline fuigure in month m. For the employment report, S is a vector containing the surprises for E1, E2, and E3. If two announcements occur at the same time, those observations are removed. $R^{-600,\tau}$ is the price change from 600 seconds before to τ seconds past the announcement. A number of different time horizons τ are chosen to measure the price impact: τ = 0, 1, 2, ..., 60 seconds, and 120, 180, ..., 1740 seconds. Panel A reports estimation results for BUND returns, and Panel B reports results for T-Note returns. The first two columns report the price response coefficient (*100) and the t-stat for τ = 5 seconds. Columns 3 reports the $\tau \leq 60$ value for which the regression yields the largest t-stats for the price response coefficient. Column 4 reports that t-stat. Columns 5 and 6 report the same values for $\tau \leq 1800$. The sample covers January 2, 2001 to December 31, 2005.

The first two columns report the announcement surprise coefficients along with the respective t-stats for regressing $R^{-600,5}$, i.e. the return from 600 seconds before until 5 seconds after the announcement, on the surprises. These values can be interpreted as the instantaneous price response that occurs during the first five seconds. I further repeat the analysis for $R^{-600,\tau}$ with $\tau = 0, 1, ..., 1800$ seconds. The third and fourth columns report the coefficients and t-stats for those value of $\tau <= 60$ that yield the largest t-stat. In other words, after how many seconds is the price response the largest. The last two columns report the same values for $\tau <= 1800$, that is the maximum price response within the first half hour.

Generally, the maximum price response is completed after 30 to 60 seconds and most of it occurs within the first 5 seconds. For example, the t-stat for regressing the BUND return $R^{-600,5}$ on the GDP surprises is 5.99. Regressing $R^{-600,31}$ on GDP surprises yields a larger t-stat of 9.37. However, there is no $\tau <= 1800$ for which regressing $R^{-600,\tau}$ on GDP surprises yields a larger t-stat than for $\tau = 31$. This indicates that the GDP announcement is fully processed after half a minute, but more than half of the price response occurs within the first 5 seconds. After half a minute, BUND prices have assumed a new fair value based on the announcement. Any further price movements are due to private opinions that are not systematically related to the announcement surprise. Interestingly, the price response to the employment report seems to occur considerably faster than for any other announcement. This might be related to the large importance of this announcement.

Due to the differential methodology, it is not surprising that this analysis yields larger estimates for the time it takes to fully process public economic news compared to the analysis in section 4.4. More importantly, this analysis reassures that macroeconomic announcements take between 20 to 60 seconds to be fully incorporated into prices.

A.1.2 Varying 'during announcement' intervals

I test whether the main results hold when I vary the 'during announcement' sample. I repeat the analysis reported in Table 4.7 for 'during announcement' intervals of 30 seconds, 2 minutes, and 5 minutes in addition to the choice of 1 minute in my main analysis. The results are reported in Table A.2, Table A.3 and Table A.4.

1. For all three alternative 'during announcement' intervals, all announcement surprises are significant in Model B which does not include lagged US returns. Once lagged US returns are included in Model C the coefficients decrease compared to Model B and most coefficients become insignificant.

2. $\sum_{i=0}^{5} \gamma_i^d = \sum_{i=0}^{5} \gamma_i^n$ can be significantly rejected in each case.

3. $\sum_{i=0}^{5} \gamma_i^a = \sum_{i=0}^{5} \gamma_i^n$ can also be significantly rejected in each case.

My results hold for varying 'during announcement' intervals.

A.2 Transmission lag between US and German bond price movements

In my main analysis I explain German bond price movements with lagged US bond price movements by regressing BUND transaction returns on lagged US returns. When matching German and US prices I shift forward the clock time of the US data by one second (the 'transmission lag' ℓ). This procedure assumes that some BUND traders process US price movements as quickly as in one second. Obviously, some traders need more time than one second to react to US price movements. This is accounted for, as I include US

Table A.2: Transmission of US macro announcements (30sec 'during announcement' interval)

	Model B: include US news releases					Model C: full model				
	Non-ann		Announcement days			Non-ann		Announcement days		
	days	before	0, 30s	30, 60s	after	days	before	0, 30s	30, 60s	after
E1			-0.070*	-0.007	0.000			-0.026	-0.004	0.000
GDP			-0.060*	0.001	-0.001			-0.039*	0.003	-0.001
CPI2			-0.017*	-0.007	0.000			-0.007	-0.005	0.000
PPI2			-0.015*	-0.006	0.000			-0.007	-0.003	0.000
RS2			-0.015*	-0.007*	0.000			-0.004	-0.006*	0.000
DGO			-0.021*	-0.005	0.000			-0.015*	-0.004	0.000
IJC			0.011*	0.001	0.000			0.003	0.000	0.000
r_t^{US}						0.045*	0.088*	0.210*	0.085*	0.069*
r_{t-1}^{US}						0.058*	0.087*	0.158*	0.092*	0.082*
r_{t-2}^{US}						0.047*	0.060*	0.142*	0.057*	0.059*
r_{t-3}^{US}						0.032*	0.037*	0.086*	0.050*	0.037*
r_{t-4}^{US}						0.021*	0.036*	0.050*	0.040*	0.022*
r_{t-5}^{US}						0.013*	0.030*	0.036*	0.028*	0.012*
$\sum_{i=0}^{5} \gamma_i$						0.215*	0.337*	0.683*	0.351*	0.281*
$\sum_{i=0}^{5} \delta_i$	0.029*	0.030*	-0.008	0.035*	0.033*	0.028*	0.033*	0.072*	0.054*	0.033*
$\sum_{i=1}^{5} \lambda_i$	-0.419*	-0.283*	0.159	-0.205*	-0.333*	-0.394*	-0.496*	-1.000*	-0.578*	-0.468*
adj. R^2			0.115					0.178		
Coefficient tests			**Model B**					**Model C**		
			difference	F-stat	p(F-stat)		difference	difference	F-stat	p(F-stat)
$\sum_{i=0}^{5} \gamma_i^{b} = \sum_{i=0}^{5} \gamma_i^{n}$			—	—	—			0.122	6.4	0.012
$\sum_{i=0}^{5} \gamma_i^{0,30} = \sum_{i=0}^{5} \gamma_i^{n}$			—	—	—			0.468	71.7	0.000
$\sum_{i=0}^{5} \gamma_i^{30,60} = \sum_{i=0}^{5} \gamma_i^{n}$			—	—	—			0.136	21.0	0.000
$\sum_{i=0}^{5} \gamma_i^{a} = \sum_{i=0}^{5} \gamma_i^{n}$			—	—	—			0.067	140.1	0.000

For this table, I repeat the analysis done for Table 4.7. The only difference is that this time the 'during announcement' sample (d) only spans the first 30 post-announcement seconds instead of 60. Thus, interval (d) ranges from 2:30:00 to 2:30:29 and interval (a) ranges from 2:30:30 to 2:59:59. Everything else is as described in Table 4.7.

Table A.3: Transmission of US macro announcements (2min 'during' interval)

	Model B: include US news releases				Model C: full model			
	Non-ann	Announcement days			Non-ann	Announcement days		
	days	before	0, 2m	after	days	before	0, 2m	after
E1			-0.022*	0.000			-0.010*	0.000
GDP			-0.017*	-0.001			-0.011	0.000
CPI2			-0.006*	0.000			-0.003	0.000
PPI2			-0.004*	0.000			-0.002	0.000
RS2			-0.005*	0.000			-0.002	0.000
DGO			-0.006*	0.000			-0.004	0.000
IJC			0.003*	0.000			0.001	0.000
r_t^{US}					0.045*	0.088*	0.170*	0.067*
r_{t-1}^{US}					0.058*	0.087*	0.124*	0.081*
r_{t-2}^{US}					0.047*	0.060*	0.100*	0.059*
r_{t-3}^{US}					0.032*	0.037*	0.058*	0.037*
r_{t-4}^{US}					0.021*	0.036*	0.039*	0.022*
r_{t-5}^{US}					0.013*	0.030*	0.030*	0.012*
$\sum_{i=0}^{5} \gamma_i$					0.215*	0.337*	0.520*	0.278*
$\sum_{i=0}^{5} \delta_i$	0.029*	0.030*	0.012	0.033*	0.028*	0.033*	0.050*	0.032*
$\sum_{i=1}^{5} \lambda_i$	-0.419*	-0.304*	0.103	-0.306*	-0.502*	-0.455*	-0.631*	-0.429*
adj. R^2		0.111				0.172		
Coefficient tests			**Model B**				**Model C**	
		difference	F-stat	p(F-stat)		difference	F-stat	p(F-stat)
$\sum_{i=0}^{5} \gamma_i^b = \sum_{i=0}^{5} \gamma_i^n$		—	—	—		0.122	6.4	0.012
$\sum_{i=0}^{5} \gamma_i^d = \sum_{i=0}^{5} \gamma_i^a$		—	—	—		0.242	31.1	0.000
$\sum_{i=0}^{5} \gamma_i^a = \sum_{i=0}^{5} \gamma_i^n$		—	—	—		0.063	129.7	0.000

For this table, I repeat the analysis done for Table 4.7. The only difference is that this time the 'during announcement' sample (d) is not the first 60 post-announcement seconds. Instead, interval (d) spans the first 120 post-announcement seconds. Everything else is as described in Table 4.7.

price movements that occured between the last five BUND trades into the model (r_{t-1}^{US}, ..., r_{t-5}^{US}). The choice of one second as the minimum response time is motivated by results reported in Table 4.5. If for example I choose a transmission lag of $\ell = 5$ seconds or larger, the explanatory power of lagged US returns is considerably diminished.

In this section, I test whether my main results hold when I vary the assumed transmission lag, that is the minimum time German traders are assumed to need to respond to US

Table A.4: Transmission of US macro announcements (5min 'during' interval)

	Model B: include US news releases				Model C: full model			
	Non-ann	Announcement days			Non-ann	Announcement days		
	days	before	0, 5m	after	days	before	0, 5m	after
E1			-0.009*	0.000			-0.004*	0.000
GDP			-0.008*	0.000			-0.005	0.000
CPI2			-0.003*	0.000			-0.002	0.000
PPI2			-0.001	0.000			-0.001	0.000
RS2			-0.003*	0.000			-0.001	0.000
DGO			-0.002*	0.000			-0.002	0.000
IJC			0.001*	0.000			0.001*	0.000
r_t^{US}					0.045*	0.088*	0.150*	0.066*
r_{t-1}^{US}					0.058*	0.087*	0.113*	0.079*
r_{t-2}^{US}					0.047*	0.060*	0.086*	0.057*
r_{t-3}^{US}					0.032*	0.037*	0.048*	0.037*
r_{t-4}^{US}					0.021*	0.036*	0.032*	0.021*
r_{t-5}^{US}					0.013*	0.030*	0.025*	0.012*
$\sum_{i=0}^{5} \gamma_i$					0.215*	0.337*	0.455*	0.272*
$\sum_{i=0}^{5} \delta_i$	0.029*	0.030*	0.020*	0.032*	0.028*	0.033*	0.040*	0.032*
$\sum_{i=1}^{5} \lambda_i$	-0.419*	-0.304*	0.037	-0.313*	-0.502*	-0.455*	-0.506*	-0.429*
adj. R^2		0.107				0.168		
Coefficient tests		**Model B**				**Model C**		
		difference	F-stat	p(F-stat)		difference	F-stat	p(F-stat)
$\sum_{i=0}^{5} \gamma_i^b = \sum_{i=0}^{5} \gamma_i^n$		—	—	—		0.122	6.4	0.012
$\sum_{i=0}^{5} \gamma_i^d = \sum_{i=0}^{5} \gamma_i^a$		—	—	—		0.183	24.2	0.000
$\sum_{i=0}^{5} \gamma_i^a = \sum_{i=0}^{5} \gamma_i^n$		—	—	—		0.057	99.9	0.000

For this table, I repeat the analysis done for Table 4.7. The only difference is that this time the 'during announcement' sample (d) is not the first 60 post-announcement seconds. Instead, interval (d) spans the first 300 post-announcement seconds. Everything else is as described in Table 4.7.

price movements. For this, I repeat the analysis conducted for Table 4.7 and now assume $\ell = 2$, 5, 10, and 20 seconds.

1. For all transmission lags ℓ, announcement surprise coefficients strictly decrease once lagged US returns are included in Model C compared to Model B. However, for $\ell >= 10$ the decrease is relatively small compared to smaller ℓ's, and most announcements are still significant even in Model C

2. $\sum_{i=0}^{5} \gamma_i^d = \sum_{i=0}^{5} \gamma_i^a$ can be significantly rejected for $\ell <= 10$, although only weakly significantly for $\ell = 10$.

3. $\sum_{i=0}^{5} \gamma_i^a = \sum_{i=0}^{5} \gamma_i^n$ can only significantly be rejected for $\ell = 2$.

Generally, the larger ℓ, the weaker the results get. This is understandable since Table 4.5 suggests that much of the price movement transmission occurs within the first 5 seconds. Moreover, when ℓ increases, the adjusted R^2 for Model C decreases. This also indicates that US price movements occuring immediately before each BUND trade are essential for explaining German bond price movements.

A.3 Cumulative price response error

In my main analysis I assume that German bond traders learn about US macroeconomic news through observing immediately lagged US price movements. This implicitly assumes that information about US price movements is efficiently processed by German traders: US price movements are immediately incorporated into German bond prices within a few trades. US price movements lagged by more than a few trades do not explain German bond price movements.

Table A.5: Transmission of US macro announcements (different transmission lags)

Panel A: Transmission lag ℓ = 2sec

	Model B: include US news				**Model C: full model**			
	Non-ann	Announcement days			Non-ann	Announcement days		
	days	before	during	after	days	before	during	after
E1			-0.041*	0.000			-0.018*	0.000
GDP			-0.029*	-0.001			-0.019	-0.001
CPI2			-0.011*	0.000			-0.006	0.000
PPI2			-0.009*	0.000			-0.005	0.000
RS2			-0.011*	0.000			-0.006	0.000
DGO			-0.011*	0.000			-0.009*	0.000
IJC			0.005*	0.000			0.002	0.000
r_t^{US}					0.049*	0.082*	0.173*	0.072*
r_{t-1}^{US}					0.054*	0.056*	0.127*	0.071*
r_{t-2}^{US}					0.041*	0.045*	0.095*	0.045*
r_{t-3}^{US}					0.026*	0.036*	0.044*	0.027*
r_{t-4}^{US}					0.017*	0.036*	0.046*	0.016*
r_{t-5}^{US}					0.012*	0.021*	0.019	0.010*
$\sum_{i=0}^{5} \gamma_i$					0.200*	0.276*	0.504*	0.241*
$\sum_{i=0}^{5} \delta_i$	0.029*	0.032*	0.017	0.034*	0.028*	0.034*	0.066*	0.033*
$\sum_{i=1}^{5} \lambda_i$	-0.421*	-0.313*	0.070	-0.311*	-0.498*	-0.427*	-0.778*	-0.422*
adj. R^2		0.121				0.172		
Coefficient tests			**Model B**				**Model C**	
		difference	F-stat	p(F-stat)		difference	F-stat	p(F-stat)
$\sum_{i=0}^{5} \gamma_i^b = \sum_{i=0}^{5} \gamma_i^n$		—	—	—		0.076	2.6	0.104
$\sum_{i=0}^{5} \gamma_i^d = \sum_{i=0}^{5} \gamma_i^a$		—	—	—		0.228	11.8	0.001
$\sum_{i=0}^{5} \gamma_i^a = \sum_{i=0}^{5} \gamma_i^n$		—	—	—		0.041	54.6	0.000

Panel B: Transmission lag ℓ = 5sec

	Model B: include US news				**Model C: full model**			
	Non-ann	Announcement days			Non-ann	Announcement days		
	days	before	during	after	days	before	during	after
E1			-0.043*	0.000			-0.024*	0.000
GDP			-0.028*	-0.001			-0.022*	-0.001
CPI2			-0.011*	0.000			-0.007	0.000
PPI2			-0.008*	0.000			-0.005	0.000
RS2			-0.010*	0.000			-0.007	0.000
DGO			-0.011*	0.000			-0.009*	0.000
IJC			0.004*	0.000			0.002	0.000
r_t^{US}					0.027*	0.036*	0.120*	0.035*
r_{t-1}^{US}					0.025*	0.029*	0.065*	0.023*

r_{t-2}^{US}					0.017*	0.018	0.058*	0.014*
r_{t-3}^{US}					0.011*	0.015	0.016	0.013*
r_{t-4}^{US}					0.009*	0.011	0.023*	0.008*
r_{t-5}^{US}					0.006*	0.015	0.013	0.007*
$\sum_{i=0}^{5} \gamma_i$					0.094*	0.123*	0.294*	0.101*
$\sum_{i=0}^{5} \delta_i$	0.030*	0.035*	0.055*	0.036*	0.029*	0.035*	0.073*	0.035*
$\sum_{i=1}^{5} \lambda_i$	-0.417*	-0.318*	-0.207	-0.315*	-0.454*	-0.364*	-0.666*	-0.363*
adj. R^2		0.138				0.160		
Coefficient tests			**Model B**				**Model C**	
		difference	F-stat	p(F-stat)		difference	F-stat	p(F-stat)
$\sum_{i=0}^{5} \gamma_i^b = \sum_{i=0}^{5} \gamma_i^n$		—	—	—		0.029	1.0	0.323
$\sum_{i=0}^{5} \gamma_i^d = \sum_{i=0}^{5} \gamma_i^a$		—	—	—		0.171	8.8	0.003
$\sum_{i=0}^{5} \gamma_i^a = \sum_{i=0}^{5} \gamma_i^n$		—	—	—		0.006	1.3	0.256

Panel C: Transmission lag ℓ = 10sec

	Model B: include US news releases				Model C: full model			
	Non-ann	Announcement days			Non-ann	Announcement days		
	days	before	during	after	days	before	during	after
E1			-0.041*	0.000			-0.027*	0.000
GDP			-0.027*	-0.001			-0.022*	-0.001
CPI2			-0.010*	0.000			-0.007	0.000
PPI2			-0.008*	0.000			-0.006	0.000
RS2			-0.009*	0.000			-0.007*	0.000
DGO			-0.011*	0.000			-0.009*	0.000
IJC			0.004*	0.000			0.002	0.000
r_{t}^{US}					0.005*	0.001	0.080*	0.002
r_{t-1}^{US}					0.004*	0.015*	0.037	0.007*
r_{t-2}^{US}					0.008*	0.008	0.005	0.009*
r_{t-3}^{US}					0.004*	0.013	0.003	0.009*
r_{t-4}^{US}					0.006*	0.009	0.009	0.005*
r_{t-5}^{US}					0.003	0.016*	0.013	0.005*
$\sum_{i=0}^{5} \gamma_i$					0.029*	0.062*	0.147*	0.037*
$\sum_{i=0}^{5} \delta_i$	0.030*	0.036*	0.076*	0.036*	0.030*	0.036*	0.075*	0.036*
$\sum_{i=1}^{5} \lambda_i$	-0.409*	-0.307*	-0.414*	-0.309*	-0.416*	-0.317*	-0.514*	-0.318*
adj. R^2		0.150				0.158		
Coefficient tests			**Model B**				**Model C**	
		difference	F-stat	p(F-stat)		difference	F-stat	p(F-stat)
$\sum_{i=0}^{5} \gamma_i^b = \sum_{i=0}^{5} \gamma_i^n$		—	—	—		0.033	1.9	0.164
$\sum_{i=0}^{5} \gamma_i^d = \sum_{i=0}^{5} \gamma_i^a$		—	—	—		0.086	3.9	0.049
$\sum_{i=0}^{5} \gamma_i^a = \sum_{i=0}^{5} \gamma_i^n$		—	—	—		0.008	2.4	0.121

Panel D: Transmission lag ℓ = 20sec

	Model B: include US news releases				Model C: full model			
	Non-ann	Announcement days			Non-ann	Announcement days		
	days	before	during	after	days	before	during	after
E1			-0.038*	0.000			-0.036*	0.000
GDP			-0.027*	-0.001			-0.026*	-0.001
CPI2			-0.009*	0.000			-0.009*	0.000
PPI2			-0.007*	0.000			-0.007*	0.000
RS2			-0.009*	0.000			-0.008*	0.000
DGO			-0.011*	0.000			-0.010*	0.000
IJC			0.003*	0.000			0.003*	0.000
r_t^{US}					0.004*	0.005	0.013	0.004*
r_{t-1}^{US}					0.003	0.003	0.004	0.006*
r_{t-2}^{US}					0.004*	0.008	-0.004	0.004*
r_{t-3}^{US}					0.003	0.002	0.008	0.005*
r_{t-4}^{US}					0.002	-0.003	-0.005	0.003
r_{t-5}^{US}					0.002	-0.002	0.000	0.005*
$\sum_{i=0}^{5} \gamma_i$					0.018*	0.013	0.015	0.027*
$\sum_{i=0}^{5} \delta_i$	0.030*	0.036*	0.083*	0.036*	0.030*	0.036*	0.084*	0.036*
$\sum_{i=1}^{5} \lambda_i$	-0.408*	-0.305*	-0.490*	-0.308*	-0.410*	-0.306*	-0.499*	-0.310*
adj. R^2		0.153				0.153		
Coefficient tests			**Model B**				**Model C**	
		difference	F-stat	p(F-stat)		difference	F-stat	p(F-stat)
$\sum_{i=0}^{5} \gamma_i^b = \sum_{i=0}^{5} \gamma_i^n$		—	—	—		-0.005	0.1	0.705
$\sum_{i=0}^{5} \gamma_i^d = \sum_{i=0}^{5} \gamma_i^a$		—	—	—		0.002	0.0	0.932
$\sum_{i=0}^{5} \gamma_i^a = \sum_{i=0}^{5} \gamma_i^n$		—	—	—		0.009	2.8	0.097

(description for Table A.5)

For this table, I repeat the analysis done for Table 4.7. There is only one difference. This time the transmission lag ℓ, i.e. the time by which the T-Note clock time is shifted forward when integrating BUND and T-Note data, is not 1 second. Instead, it is 2 seconds for Panel A, 5 seconds for Panel B, 10 seconds for Panel C, and 20 seconds for Panel D. Everything else is as described in Table 4.7.

However, one might also assume that the cumulative US price response to the economic news is of value for German price movements. In this robustness analysis, I investigate whether the BUND price response to US economic news is driven by the variable $cumul\_err_t$. $cumul\_err_t$ denotes the cumulative US price response to economic news until time t minus the cumulative German price response until time t. Thus, this variable measure the German cumulative 'response error' relative to the US price response.

Table A.6: Transmission of US macro announcements ('cumulative error' correction)

	Model C: full model				Model D: include error correction			
	Non-ann	Announcement days			Non-ann	Announcement days		
	days	before	during	after	days	before	during	after
cumul_err							**0.004**	**0.0003***
E1			-0.014	0.000			-0.009	0.000
GDP			-0.018	-0.001			-0.015	0.000
CPI2			-0.006	0.000			-0.005	0.000
PPI2			-0.004	0.000			-0.003	0.000
RS2			-0.005	0.000			-0.004	0.000
DGO			-0.008*	0.000			-0.008*	0.000
IJC			0.001	0.000			0.001	0.000
r_t^{US}	0.045*	0.088*	0.188*	0.069*	0.045*	0.088*	0.184*	0.069*
r_{t-1}^{US}	0.058*	0.087*	0.138*	0.082*	0.058*	0.087*	0.135*	0.081*
r_{t-2}^{US}	0.047*	0.060*	0.116*	0.059*	0.047*	0.060*	0.113*	0.059*
r_{t-3}^{US}	0.032*	0.037*	0.069*	0.037*	0.032*	0.037*	0.067*	0.037*
r_{t-4}^{US}	0.021*	0.036*	0.045*	0.022*	0.021*	0.036*	0.043*	0.022*
r_{t-5}^{US}	0.013*	0.030*	0.033*	0.012*	0.013*	0.030*	0.031*	0.012*
$\sum_{i=0}^{5} \gamma_i$	0.215*	0.337*	0.588*	0.281*	0.215*	0.337*	0.572*	0.280*
$\sum_{i=0}^{5} \delta_i$	0.028*	0.033*	0.060*	0.033*	0.028*	0.033*	0.061*	0.033*
$\sum_{i=1}^{5} \lambda_i$	-0.502*	-0.455*	-0.776*	-0.431*	-0.502*	-0.455*	-0.769*	-0.431*
adj. R^2		0.174				0.175		
Coefficient tests			**Model C**				**Model D**	
		difference	F-stat	p(F-stat)		difference	F-stat	p(F-stat)
$\sum_{i=0}^{5} \gamma_i^b = \sum_{i=0}^{5} \gamma_i^n$		0.122	6.4	0.012		0.122	6.4	0.012
$\sum_{i=0}^{5} \gamma_i^d = \sum_{i=0}^{5} \gamma_i^a$		0.307	40.1	0.000		0.292	37.3	0.000
$\sum_{i=0}^{5} \gamma_i^a = \sum_{i=0}^{5} \gamma_i^n$		0.067	140.1	0.000		0.066	135.9	0.000

For this table, I repeat the analysis done for Table 4.7. This time, I additionally estimate a Model D. Model D differs from Model C by including $cumul\_err_t$ as an additional regressor. $cumul\_err_t$ denotes the cumulative US price response to economic news until time t minus the cumulative German price response until time t. Everything else is as described in Table 4.7.

The left part of Table A.6 repeats the results for Model C as reported in Table 4.7 to ease comparison. Additionally, I estimate Model D which only differs by the inclusion of $cumul\_err_t$ as an additional explanatory variable. The main findings of my analysis are untouched by this change. In fact, most coefficient estimates are not only qualitatively but also quantitatively very similar for Model C and D. The coefficient estimate for $cumul\_err_t$ is insignificant in the 'during' interval but significant during the 'after' interval (14:31 - 14:59). This might suggest that immediately following the announcement German traders closely follow US price movements and each US bond price movement is immediately incorporated into German prices. Later, after the public news is processed, German traders correct their 'response error' relative to the US response. However, the magnitude of the coefficient is very small and incorporating $cumul\_err_t$ into the model only marginally increases the adj. R^2.

A.4 Lagged US returns based on equidistant intervals

In my main analysis, I relate BUND midquote returns between two trades to US price movements between to BUND trades. In essence, my approach is similar to Finucane (1999) in that I use variable interval length to avoid problems associated with fixed interval length. These problems occur if the interval length is too long compared to the lead-lag length. For example, if the time required for traders in one market to react to information in the opposite market is less than the interval length, one might arrive at the incorrect conclusion that information is reflected simultaneously in the two markets.

However, since equidistant interval length are more popular in the literature, this section tests the robustness of my results using lagged US returns based on equidistant intervals.

The first subsection uses a VAR analysis and the second subsection regresses BUND transaction returns on lagged US returns based on fixed interval length.

A.4.1 VAR analysis

VAR analyses are popular for investigating cross-market information flow (see, e.g., Eun and Shim (1989)). However, given the high efficiency of the futures markets in my study, very short intervals are needed for calculating returns. Grammig, Melvin, and Schlag (2005) argue that 10 seconds represents a good compromise between having a short enough interval length to keep contemporaneous correlation low and having too short intervals that induce too much noise into the estimation. I conduct my analysis with interval length of 5 and 10 seconds since it is particularly important for my analysis to account for all lead-lag effects. I estimate the equation:

$$\begin{aligned} r^{GE}_{std,t} &= c + \sum_{i=1}^{5} \gamma^{GE}_{i} r^{US}_{std,t-i} + \sum_{i=1}^{5} \xi^{GE}_{i} r^{GE}_{std,t-i} + I^{d}_{t} \sum_{i=1}^{8} \beta^{GE}_{i} S_{i} + \epsilon^{GE}_{t} \\ r^{US}_{std,t} &= c + \sum_{i=1}^{5} \gamma^{US}_{i} r^{GE}_{std,t-i} + \sum_{i=1}^{5} \xi^{US}_{i} r^{US}_{std,t-i} + I^{d}_{t} \sum_{i=1}^{8} \beta^{US}_{i} S_{i} + \epsilon^{US}_{t} \end{aligned}$$

where I^{d}_{t} is an indicator variable that takes the value one if t is in the 'during announcement' interval (2:30:00 to 2:30:59). r_{std} denotes that the respective returns have been standardized by their sample standard deviations to make German and US bond returns comparable.[1] Table A.7 reports results for this estimation. For comparison, the above equation is also estimated only with the announcement surprises.

[1]US bond returns are considerably more volatile than German bond returns.

Table A.7: VAR analysis (14:00 - 14:59)

Panel A: 5sec intervals

	r^{GE}_{std}		r^{US}_{std}	
	only news	VAR + news	only news	VAR + news
E1*I^d	-1.956*	-1.344*	-2.245*	-2.536*
GDP*I^d	-1.462*	-1.316*	-1.350*	-1.401*
CPI2*I^d	-0.583*	-0.469*	-0.469*	-0.518*
PPI2*I^d	-0.444*	-0.357*	-0.414*	-0.452*
RS2*I^d	-0.555*	-0.474*	-0.628*	-0.660*
DGO*I^d	-0.588*	-0.562*	-0.482*	-0.485*
IJC*I^d	0.315*	0.264*	0.290*	0.312*
$\sum_{i=0}^{5} r^{GE}_{t-i}$		-0.359*		0.203*
$\sum_{i=0}^{5} r^{US}_{t-i}$		0.468*		-0.245*
adj. R^2	0.007	0.058	0.007	0.021

Panel B: 10sec intervals

	r^{GE}_{std}		r^{US}_{std}	
	only news	VAR + news	only news	VAR + news
E1*I^d	-2.643*	-2.073*	-3.070*	-3.655*
GDP*I^d	-2.024*	-2.057*	-1.909*	-2.020*
CPI2*I^d	-0.812*	-0.715*	-0.639*	-0.747*
PPI2*I^d	-0.597*	-0.533*	-0.532*	-0.605*
RS2*I^d	-0.767*	-0.720*	-0.848*	-0.916*
DGO*I^d	-0.807*	-0.835*	-0.631*	-0.651*
IJC*I^d	0.439*	0.409*	0.387*	0.436*
$\sum_{i=0}^{5} r^{GE}_{t-i}$		-0.189*		0.127*
$\sum_{i=0}^{5} r^{US}_{t-i}$		0.429*		-0.304*
adj. R^2	0.013	0.064	0.015	0.031

This table reports estimation results for a BUND/T-Note VAR system. Returns are based on 5 second intervals (Panel A) and 10 second intervals (Panel B). I estimate the equation:
$r^{GE}_{std,t} = c + \sum_{i=1}^{5} \gamma_i^{GE} r^{US}_{std,t-i} + \sum_{i=1}^{5} \xi_i^{GE} r^{GE}_{std,t-i} + I_t^d \sum_{i=1}^{8} \beta_i^{GE} S_i + \epsilon_t^{GE}$
$r^{US}_{std,t} = c + \sum_{i=1}^{5} \gamma_i^{US} r^{GE}_{std,t-i} + \sum_{i=1}^{5} \xi_i^{US} r^{US}_{std,t-i} + I_t^d \sum_{i=1}^{8} \beta_i^{US} S_i + \epsilon_t^{US}$
where I_t^d is an indicator variable that takes the value one if t is in the 'during announcement' interval (2:30:00 to 2:30:59). r_{std} denotes that the respective returns have been standardized by their sample standard deviations to make German and US bond returns comparable. S_i is the suprise in announcement i. The results are reported in the column 'VAR + news'. The colum 'only news' reports estimation results without the VAR variables ($r^{US}_{std,t-i}$ and $r^{GE}_{std,t-i}$) as regressors.

1. All announcement surprises are still significant in the VAR analysis. However, for BUND returns based on 5 seconds intervals, all (absolute) announcement surprise coefficients are lower in the VAR analysis compared to the case with only news. This is not the case for T-Note returns. This indicates that while Germans partially learn about US news through observing lagged US returns, the opposite (US traders learning about the news from observing lagged German returns) seems not to be the case.

2. not investigated here

3. not investigated here

In the VAR analysis, the surprise coefficients don't lose as much explanatory power for BUND returns as in the trade-by-trade analysis reported in chapter 4. However, since most of the price transmission occurs within 5 seconds, most of the price movement transmission is not accounted for in the VAR analysis. Comparing the adj. R^2 for the r^{GE} and r^{US} regression reassures that price movement transmission occurs mostly from the US to Germany, and much less vice versa.

A.4.2 Trade-by-trade analysis based on equidistant intervals

The goal in this section is to investigate whether the results hold for returns based on equidistant intervals. The analysis in the previous subsection does not account for price movements from the other market that occured within less than the interval length (i.e. 5 and 10 seconds). In this subsection, I combine the advantages of the VAR analysis with the approach used in my main analysis. On the one hand, I use BUND trade-by-trade transaction returns as the dependent variable. On the other hand, I use lagged US returns based on fixed interval lengths as the explanatory variables. This approach incorporates all

US price movements lagged by more than $\ell = 1$ second. Still, the explanatory variables are based on fixed intervals. I conduct my analysis for 5 and 10 second intervals and include US returns in the analysis lagged up to 30 seconds. For example, if a BUND trade occurs at 2:31:13, then this BUND trade is related to US returns from 2:31:08 to 2:31:12 (r_t^{US}), 2:31:03 to 2:31:07 (r_{t-1}^{US}), . . ., and 2:30:43 to 2:30:47 (r_{t-5}^{US}). The estimation equation is the same as in Model C of my main analysis. I report results in Table A.8.

My main results hold for lagged US returns based on fixed intervals of 5 seconds (Panel A) and 10 seconds (Panel B):

1. All announcement surprises are significant in Model B which does not include lagged US returns. Once lagged US returns are included in Model C the coefficients decrease compared to Model B and most coefficients become insignificant.
2. $\sum_{i=0}^{5} \gamma_i^d = \sum_{i=0}^{5} \gamma_i^n$ can be significantly rejected.
3. $\sum_{i=0}^{5} \gamma_i^a = \sum_{i=0}^{5} \gamma_i^n$ can also be significantly rejected.

A.5 Discussion of robustness analysis

My main findings proved to be robust with one exception. If immediately lagged US returns are excluded from the analysis, for example by assuming a transmission lag $\ell \geq 10$ or using fixed BUND intervals of 5 seconds or more, then some of my main results become insignificant. This leads to either one of two conlcusions:

1. Each US bond price movement is incorporated into German bond prices to a large extent within about five seconds. Thus, an approach that excludes US returns lagged by 5 seconds or less excludes crucial information and is therefore misspecified.

Table A.8: Lagged US returns based on equidistant intervals

Panel A: 5sec intervals

	Model B: include US news				Model C: full model			
	Non-ann	Announcement days			Non-ann	Announcement days		
	days	before	during	after	days	before	during	after
E1			-0.043*	0.000			-0.014	0.000
GDP			-0.030*	-0.001			-0.016	-0.001
CPI2			-0.011*	0.000			-0.006	0.000
PPI2			-0.009*	0.000			-0.004	0.000
RS2			-0.011*	0.000			-0.005	0.000
DGO			-0.011*	0.000			-0.008*	0.000
IJC			0.006*	0.000			0.001	0.000
r_t^{US}					0.056*	0.098*	0.143*	0.073*
r_{t-1}^{US}					0.034*	0.045*	0.066*	0.033*
r_{t-2}^{US}					0.016*	0.027*	0.045*	0.016*
r_{t-3}^{US}					0.011*	0.019*	0.028*	0.012*
r_{t-4}^{US}					0.008*	0.006	0.014*	0.007*
r_{t-5}^{US}					0.004*	0.006	0.001	0.006*
$\sum_{i=0}^{5}\gamma_i$					0.128*	0.201*	0.299*	0.146*
$\sum_{i=0}^{5}\delta_i$	0.029*	0.031*	0.014*	0.033*	0.028*	0.033*	0.080*	0.033*
$\sum_{i=1}^{5}\lambda_i$	-0.427*	-0.311*	0.100	-0.300*	-0.495*	-0.464*	-0.897*	-0.427*
adj. R^2		0.121				0.171		

Coefficient tests	Model B			Model C		
	difference	F-stat	p(F-stat)	difference	F-stat	p(F-stat)
$\sum_{i=0}^{5}\gamma_i^b = \sum_{i=0}^{5}\gamma_i^n$	—	—	—	0.073	5.1	0.024
$\sum_{i=0}^{5}\gamma_i^d = \sum_{i=0}^{5}\gamma_i^a$	—	—	—	0.153	22.0	0.000
$\sum_{i=0}^{5}\gamma_i^a = \sum_{i=0}^{5}\gamma_i^n$	—	—	—	0.018	17.7	0.000

Panel B: 10sec intervals

	Model B: include US news				Model C: full model			
	Non-ann	Announcement days			Non-ann	Announcement days		
	days	before	during	after	days	before	during	after
E1			-0.045*	0.000			-0.014	0.000
GDP			-0.031*	-0.001			-0.016	-0.001
CPI2			-0.011*	0.000			-0.005	0.000
PPI2			-0.009*	0.000			-0.004	0.000
RS2			-0.011*	0.000			-0.005	0.000
DGO			-0.012*	0.000			-0.008*	0.000
IJC			0.006*	0.000			0.001	0.000
r_t^{US}					0.044*	0.075*	0.104*	0.052*
r_{t-1}^{US}					0.014*	0.026*	0.042*	0.016*

r^{US}_{t-2}					0.007*	0.007	0.009*	0.007*
$\sum_{i=0}^{5} \gamma_i$					0.065*	0.108*	0.155*	0.074*
$\sum_{i=0}^{5} \delta_i$	0.029*	0.031*	0.019*	0.033*	0.028*	0.033*	0.088*	0.033*
$\sum_{i=1}^{5} \lambda_i$	-0.427*	-0.316*	0.076	-0.301*	-0.497*	-0.469*	-0.973*	-0.437*
adj. R^2	0.125				0.167			
Coefficient tests		**Model B**				**Model C**		
		difference	F-stat	p(F-stat)		difference	F-stat	p(F-stat)
$\sum_{i=0}^{5} \gamma_i^b = \sum_{i=0}^{5} \gamma_i^n$		—	—	—		0.044	6.2	0.013
$\sum_{i=0}^{5} \gamma_i^d = \sum_{i=0}^{5} \gamma_i^a$		—	—	—		0.081	24.0	0.000
$\sum_{i=0}^{5} \gamma_i^a = \sum_{i=0}^{5} \gamma_i^n$		—	—	—		0.010	20.6	0.000

(description for Table A.8)

For this table, I repeat the analysis done for Table 4.7. There is only one difference. This time lagged US returns r_t^{US} are defined based on fixed interval length of 5 seconds (Panel A) and 10 seconds (Panel B). For example, if a BUND trade occurs at 2:31:13, then this BUND trade is related to US returns from 2:31:08 to 2:31:12 (r_t^{US}), 2:31:03 to 2:31:07 (r_{t-1}^{US}), . . ., and 2:30:43 to 2:30:47 (r_{t-5}^{US}). Everything else is as described in Table 4.7.

2. Both US and German bond prices respond similarly to certain public news for which I do not account in my analysis. Therefore, I falsely find that German returns are strongly related to US returns although German returns are really driven by public news for which I do not account.

These two explanations are difficult to separate. However, my results lean towards the first explanation.

First, it is perfectly conceivable, that most of the price movement transmission occurs within 5 seconds or less. The BUND futures market is highly efficient, and my results (see Table 4.4 and A.1) suggest that the response to many macro announcements is likewise completed after 5 seconds.

Second, I can rule out that my findings are driven by the common response of US and German bonds to the public macro announcements since I account for these in my analysis. Further, I find that price transmission is elevated even 30 to 60 minutes after the announcement (Table 8) when the public news has already been fully processed.

Third, it is unlikely that my results are driven by other public news for which I do not account, since trading in the narrow event window that I study is dominated by the macroeconomic announcements.

Bibliography

ABHYANKAR, A., L. S. COPELAND, AND W. WONG (1999): "LIFFE cycles: intraday evidence from the FTSE-100 Stock Index futures market," *European Journal of Finance* 5, pp. 123–139.

ADAMS, GREG, GRANT MCQUEEN, AND ROBERT WOOD (2004): "The Effects of Inflation News on High Frequency Stock Returns," *Journal of Business* 77, pp. 547–574.

AHN, HEE-JOON, JUN CAI, AND YAN-LEUNG CHEUNG (2002): "What Moves German Bund Futures Contracts On The EUREX?," *Journal of Futures Markets* 22, pp. 679–696.

AHN, HEE-JOON, JUN CAI, YASUSHI HAMAO, AND RICHARD Y.K. HO (2002): "The Components of the Bid-Ask Spread in a Limit-Order Market: Evidence from the Tokyo Stock Exchange," *Journal of Empirical Finance* 9, pp. 399–430.

ALBUQUERQUE, RUI, AND CLARA VEGA (2007): "Asymmetric Information in the Stock Market: Economic News and Co-movement," Working Paper.

ANDERSEN, TORBEN G., AND TIM BOLLERSLEV (1998): "Deutsche Mark-Dollar Volatility: Intraday Activity Patterns, Macroeconomic Announcements, and Longer Run Dependencies," *Journal of Finance* 53, pp. 219–265.

ANDERSEN, TORBEN G., TIM BOLLERSLEV, FRANCIS X. DIEBOLD, AND CLARA VEGA (2003): "Micro Effects of Macro Announcements: Real-Time Price Discovery in Foreign Exchange," *American Economic Review* 93, pp. 38–62.

Andersen, Torben G., Tim Bollerslev, Francis X. Diebold, and Clara Vega (2007): "Real-Time Price Discovery in Stock, Bond and Foreign Exchange Markets," *Journal of International Economics*, forthcoming.

Andersson, Magnus, Lars Jul Hansen, and Szabolcs Sebestyén (2006): "Which news moves the euro area bond market?," European Central Bank Working Paper Series, no 631.

Arnott, Robert D., Jason C. Hsu, and Philip Moore (2005): "Fundamental Indexation," *Financial Analysts Journal* 61, pp. 83–99.

Bae, Kee-Hong, G. Andrew Karolyi, and René M. Stulz (2003): "A New Approach to Measuring Financial Contagion," *Review of Financial Studies* 16, pp. 717–763.

Balduzzi, Pierluigi, Edwin J. Elton, and T. Clifton Green (2001): "Economic News and Bond Prices: Evidence from the U.S. Treasury Market," *Journal of Financial and Quantitative Analysis* 36, pp. 523–543.

Barnhart, Scott W. (1989): "The effects of macroeconomic announcements on commodity prices," *American Journal of Agricultural Economics* 71, pp. 389–403.

Basistha, Arabinda, and Alexander Kurov (2008): "Macroeconomic Cycles and the Stock Market's Reaction to Monetary Policy," *Journal of Banking and Finance*, forthcoming.

Becker, Kent G., Joseph E. Finnerty, and Joseph Friedman (1995): "Economic news and equity market linkages between the U.S. and U.K.," *Journal of Banking and Finance* 19, pp. 1191–1210.

Becker, Kent G., Joseph E. Finnerty, and Kenneth J. Kopecky (1995): "Domestic macroeconomic news and foreign interest rates," *Journal of International Money and Finance* 14, pp. 763–783.

BODIE, ZVI, AND VICTOR I. ROSANSKY (1980): "Risk And Return In Commodity Futures," *Financial Analysts Journal* 36, pp. 27–39.

BOLLERSLEV, TIM, JUN CAI, AND FRANK M. SONG (2000): "Intraday Periodicity, Long-Memory Volatility, and Macroeconomic Announcement Effects in the U.S. Treasury Bond Market," *Journal of Empirical Finance* 7, pp. 37–55.

BOOTH, G. GEOFFREY, RAYMOND W. SO, AND YIUMAN TSE (1999): "Price discovery in the German equity index derivatives markets," *Journal of Futures Markets* 19, pp. 619–643.

BOND, GARY E. (1984): "The Effects of Supply and Interest Rate Shocks in Commodity Futures Markets," *American Journal of Agricultural Economics* 66, pp. 294–301.

BOYD, JOHN H., JIAN HU, AND RAVI JAGANNATHAN (2005): "The Stock Market's Reaction to Unemployment News: Why Bad News Is Usually Good for Stocks," *The Journal of Finance*, 60, 649–672.

CAI, JUN., YAN-LEUNG CHEUNG, AND MICHAEL C. S. WONG (2001): "What moves the gold market?," *Journal of Futures Markets*, 21, 257–278.

CHAMBERS, ROBERT G. (1985): "Credit Constraints, Interest Rates, and Agricultural Prices," *American Journal of Agricultural Economics* 67, pp. 390–395.

CHAN, KALOK (1993): "Imperfect Information and Cross-Autocorrelation Among Stock Prices," *Journal of Finance* 48, pp. 1211–1230.

CHRISTIE-DAVID, ROHAN, MUKESH CHAUDRY, AND TIMOTHY W. KOCH (2000): "Do macroeconomics news releases affect gold and silver prices?," *Journal of Economics and Business*, 52, 405–421.

CONNOLLY, ROBERT A., AND F. ALBERT WANG (2003): "International equity market comovements: Economic fundamentals or contagion?," *Pacific-Basin Finance Journal* 11, pp. 23–43.

DAHLQUIST, MAGNUS, AND CAMPBELL R. HARVEY (2001): "Global Tactical Asset Allocation," *Journal of Global Capital Markets*, 1-9.

D'SOUZA, CHRIS, AND CHARLES GAA (2004): "The Effect of Economic News on Bond Market Liquidity," Bank of Canada Working Paper 2004-16.

EDERINGTON, L. H., AND J. H. LEE (1995): "The Short-Run Dynamics of the Price Adjustment to New Information," *Journal of Financial and Quantitative Analysis* 30, 117–134.

ENTORF, HORST, AND C. STEINER (2007): "Makrokonomische Nachrichten und die Reaktion des 15-Sekunden-DAX: Eine Ereignisstudie zur Wirkung der ZEW-Konjunkturprognose," *Jahrbcher fr Nationalkonomie und Statistik* 227, pp. 2–26.

ERB, CLAUDE B., AND CAMPBELL R. HARVEY (2006): "The Strategic and Tactical Value of Commodity Futures," *Financial Analysts Journal* 62, 69–97.

EUN, CHEOL S., AND SANGDAL SHIM (1989): "International Transmission of Stock Market Movements," *Journal of Financial and Quantitative Analysis* 24, pp. 241–256.

FINUCANE, THOMAS J. (1999): "A new measure of the direction and timing of information flow between markets," *Journal of Financial Markets* 2, pp. 135–151.

FLANNERY, MARK J., AND ARIS A. PROTOPAPADAKIS (2002): "Macroeconomic Factors *Do* Influence Aggregate Stock Returns," *Review of Financial* 15, 751–782.

FLEMING, MICHAEL J., AND ELI M. REMOLONA (1997): "What moves the bond market?," *Federal Reserve Bank of New York Economic Policy Review* 3, 31–50.

FLEMING, MICHAEL J., AND ELI M. REMOLONA (1999): "Price Formation and Liquidity in the U.S. Treasury Market: The Response to Public Information," *Journal of Finance* 54, 1901–1915.

FRANKE, GÜNTHER, AND DIETER HESS (2000): "The Impact of Scheduled News Announcements on T-Bond and Bund Futures Trading," in: Hans-Jürgen Vosgerau (ed.),

Institutional Arrangements for Global Economic Integration, MacMillan, 2000, 337–366.

FRANKEL, JEFFREY A. (2006): "The Effect of Monetary Policy on Real Commodity Prices ," NBER Working Paper No. W12713.

FRINO, ALEX, AND AMELIA HILL (2001): "Intraday futures market behaviour around major scheduled macroeconomic announcements: Australian evidence," *Journal of Banking and Finance* 25, pp. 1319–1337.

FUHRER, JEFFREY C., GEORGE R. MOORE AND SCOTT D. SCHUH (1995): "Estimating the linear-quadratic inventory model Maximum likelihood versus generalized method of moments," *Journal of Monetary Economics* 35, 115–157.

FUNKE, NORBERT, AND AKIMI MATSUDA (2006): "Macroeconomic news and stock returns in the United States and Germany," *German Economic Review* 7, 189–210.

GLOSTEN, L., AND L. HARRIS (1988): "Estimating the components of the bid-ask spread," *Journal of Financial Economics* 21, pp. 123–142.

GLOSTEN, LAWRENCE R., AND PAUL R. MILGROM (1985): "Bid, ask and transaction prices in a specialist market with heterogeneously informed traders," *Journal of Financial Economics* 14, pp. 71–100.

GORTON, GARY, AND K. GEERT ROUWENHORST (2006): "Facts and Fantasies about Commodity Futures," *Financial Analysts Journal* 62, pp. 47–68.

GRAMMIG, JOACHIM, MICHAEL MELVIN, AND CHRISTIAN SCHLAG (2005): "Internationally cross-listed stock prices during overlapping trading hours: price discovery and exchange rate effects," *Journal of Emnpirical Finance* 12, 139–164.

GREEN, T. CLIFTON (2004): "Economic News and the Impact of Trading on Bond Prices," *Journal of Finance* 59, pp. 1201–1233.

Greene, Jason T., and Scott B. Smart (1999): "Liquidity provision and noise trading: Evidence from the Investment Dartboard column," *Journal of Finance* 54, pp. 1885–1899.

Harris, Milton, and Artur Raviv (1993): "Differences of Opinion Make a Horse Race," *Review of Financial Studies* 6, pp. 473–506.

Hasbrouck, Joel (1991): "Measuring the Information Content of Stock Trades," *Journal of Finance* 46, pp. 179–207.

Hautsch, Nikolaus, and Dieter Hess (2002): "The processing of non-anticipated information in financial markets: Analyzing the impact of surprises in the employment report," *European Finance Review* 6, pp. 133–161.

Hautsch, Nikolaus, and Dieter Hess (2007): "Bayesian Learning in Financial Markets: Testing for the Relevance of Information Precision in Price Discovery," *Journal of Financial and Quantitative Analysis* 42, pp. 189–208.

Hautsch, Nikolaus, Dieter Hess, and Christoph Müller (2008): "Price Adjustment to News with Uncertain Precision," Working Paper.

He, Hua, and Jiang Wang (1995): "Differential Information and Dynamic Behavior of Stock Trading Volume," *Review of Financial Studies* 8, pp. 919–972.

Hendershott, Terrence, Charles M. Jones, and Albert J. Menkveld (2008): "Does Algorithmic Trading Improve Liquidity," Working Paper.

Hess, Dieter, and Magdalena Malinowska (2008): "Liquidity Provision in Periods of High Information Flow," Working Paper.

Hess, Dieter, and Alexandra Niessen (2008): "How to attract Investors' Attention? The sequential introduction of two similar economic indicators," Working Paper.

Holden, Craig W., and Avanidhar Subrahmanyam (1992): "Long-lived private information and imperfect competition," *Journal of Finance* 47, pp. 247–270.

Holt, Charles C., Franco Modigliani, John F. Muth, and Herbert A. Simon (1960): "Planning production, inventories, and work force," Prentice-Hall, Englewood Cliffs, NJ.

Karolyi, G. Andrew, and Ren M. Stulz (1996): "Why Do Markets Move Together? An Investigation of U.S.-Japan Stock Return Comovements," *Journal of Finance* 51, pp. 951–986.

Kat, Harry M., and Roel C.A. Oomen (2007): "What Every Investor Should Know About Commodities, Part I," *Journal of Investment Management* 5, pp. 1–25.

Kim, Oliver, and Rober E. Verrecchia (1994): "Market liquidity and volume around earnings announcements," *Journal of Accounting and Economics* 17, pp. 41–67.

King, Mervin A., and Sushil Wadhwani (1990): "Transmission of Volatility between Stock Markets," *Review of Financial Studies* 3, pp. 5–33.

Kunkel, André (2003): "Zur Prognosefhigkeit des ifo Geschftsklimas und seiner Komponenten sowie die berprfung der Dreimal-Regel," ifo discussion papers no. 80.

Lee, Charles M. C., and Mark J. Ready (1991): "Inferring Trade Direction from Intraday Data," *Journal of Finance* 46, pp. 733–746.

Madhavan, Ananth, Mathew Richardson, and Mark Roomans (1997): "Why do security prices change? A transaction-level analysis of NYSE Stocks," *Review of Financial Studies* 10, pp. 1035–1064.

Malinowska, Magdalena (2008): "Price and Volume Response to Public Information," Working Paper.

McQueen, Grant, and V. Vance Roley (1993): "Stock Prices, News, and Business Conditions," *Review of Financial Studies* 6, pp. 683–707.

NEWEY, WHITNEY, AND KENNETH WEST (1987): "A simple, positive semi-definite, heteroskedasticity and autocorrelation consistent covariance matrix," *Econometrica* 55, pp. 703–708.

PEARCE, DOUGLAS K., AND V. VANCE ROLEY (1985): "Stock Prices and Economic News," *Journal of Business* 58, pp. 49–67.

SCHOLES, MYRON S., AND JOSEPH WILLIAMS (1977): "Estimating betas from nonsynchronous data," *Journal of Financial Economics* 5, pp. 309–327.

SHALEN, CATHERINE T. (1993): "Volume, Volatility, and the Dispersion of Beliefs," *Review of Financial Studies* 6, pp. 405–434.

STOLL, HANS R. (1989): "Inferring the components of the bid-ask spread: Theory and empirical tests," *Journal of Finance* 44, pp. 115–134.

TAYLOR, JOHN B. (1993): "Discretion versus Policy Rules in Practice," *Carnegie-Rochester Conference Series on Public Policy* 39, pp. 195–214.

TSE, YIUMAN (1999): "Market microstructure of FTSE 100 index futures: An intraday empirical analysis," *Journal of Futures Markets* 19, pp. 31–58.

UNDERWOOD, SHANE E. (2007): "The Cross-Market Information Content of Stock and Bond Order Flow," Working Paper.

WONGSWAN, JON (2006): "Transmission of Information across International Equity Markets," *Review of Financial Studies* 19, pp. 1157–1189.

ZEBEDEE, ALLAN A. (2001): "A Closer Look at Co-Movements Among Stock Returns," Working Paper.